To order additional copies of this book:

Price:

Library Hardbound Edition: $14.95
Paperbound:
    $4.95 each
    $4.00 each for 10 or more copies
    For organizations: $3.50 each for 10 or more copies, prepaid
    For bookstores: $3.00 each for 10 or more copies, prepaid

    Add $1.00 for the first book and 30 cents each for each additional book to cover postage and handling. Payment should accompany order. Make checks payable to:

Movement for a New Society

Movement for a New Society
4722 Baltimore Avenue
Philadelphia, PA 19143

Tell the American People

Perspectives on the Iranian Revolution

Edited with introduction and chronology
by David H. Albert

Movement for a New Society

Tell the American People: Perspectives on the Iranian Revolution
Copyright © 1980 by Movement for a New Society
All rights reserved. For information, write:
  Movement for a New Society
  4722 Baltimore Avenue
  Philadelphia, PA 19143
Library of Congress #: 80-83577
ISBN: 0-86571-001-5 Hardbound
      0-96571-003-1 Paperbound

Cover Design: Sylvia Maes, after poster by Momayez, "First Anniversary of the
  Islamic Revolution of Iran": Exhibit at Tehran Museum of Contemporary Art,
  Bahman, 1358 (1980).
Layout: Nina Huizinga
Photography: All photos by Randy Goodman, except "Behesht Zahara Cemetery"
  by Javad Rustami, which first appeared in *First Anniversary of the Islamic
  Revolution of Iran*, published by the Embassy of the Islamic Revolution of Iran,
  3005 Massachusetts Avenue NW, Washington, D.C. 20008.

Previously published and copyrighted materials are reprinted with permission as
listed below:

Eqbal Ahmad, "Iran and the West: A Century of Subjugation", from *Christianity
  and Crisis*, March 3, 1980. Copyright © 1980 by *Christianity and Crisis, Inc.*,
  537 West 121st Street, New York, N.Y. 10027.

Michael T. Klare, "Arms and the Shah: The Rise and Fall of the Surrogate Strategy", from *The Progressive*, August, 1979. Copyright © by *The Progressive, Inc.*,
  408 West Gorham Street, Madison, WI 53703.

John Mohawk, "Impressions of South Tehran", from *Akwesasne Notes: A Journal
  of Native and Natural Peoples*, Early Spring, 1980, Mohawk Nation, via Roosevel-
  town, N.Y. 13683.

William Worthy, "Iran Diary", from *The Boston Phoenix*, March 4, 1980. Copyright
  by *The Boston Phoenix, Inc.*, 100 Massachusetts Avenue, Boston, MA 02115.

Ali Shariati, "Approaches to the Understanding of Iran" and "The Ideal Society—
  The Umma", from *On the Sociology of Islam*, translated by Hamid Algar. Copyright © by Mizan Press, P.O. Box 4065, Berkeley, CA 94704.

Mary Hooglund, "One Village in the Revolution", From *MERIP Reports*, No. 87,
  May, 1980. Copyright © 1980 by Middle East Research and Information Project,
  P.O. Box 3122, Washington, DC 20010.

First Edition—5,000 copies—June, 1980
New revised and enlarged edition—5,000 copies—October, 1980

Hardcover by Hallowell & West, Andalusia, PA
Typesetting by Celo Press, Burnsville, NC

2 3 4 5 6 7 8 9

"V" represents victory for the Iranian people.

TABLE OF CONTENTS

FOREWORD *by Bishop C. Dale White*

Perspectives on the Iranian Revolution

Voices of the Revolution

Foreword

Bishop C. Dale White

We went to see the Ayatollah Khomeini on Christmas Day. We were seven clergy who travelled half-way around the world to bring Christmas greetings from Christian leaders at the height of the hostage crisis. We said to the Imam:

"We pray that both the bells of Christian churches and the call from the minarets will join us in summoning our peoples to pray for restoration of justice in the dealings of nations, for expressions of mercy in dealing with people, and for securing of peace for all humanity."

The Imam's manner was gentle, but his words in reply were sharp with anguish. He spoke of horrible brutalities, primitive, sub-human torture by the Pahlavi regime of young people who fought for independence, the rows upon rows of new graves at Behesht-Zahara and elsewhere across the nation. He said:

"Are you not aware of the crimes that have been committed here? Are you not aware that they have plundered the wealth of this country? And that they have left behind a hungry nation? Do you not know that they subjected this nation to oppression and torture over a period of fifty years and robbed her whole wealth to pay the big powers?

"The crimes committed here foul the name and holiness of Jesus Christ in the eyes of the Iranian people. Christian clergymen have a responsibility to rescue Jesus from his entanglements in which your presidents have brought him. Jesus looks to Christian clergymen and scholars."

Returning to New York, I went to see Mansour Farhang, at that time Ambassador to the U.N. from Iran. In one of a series of conversations, this time with a delegation from the United Methodist General Conference, I said,

"Ambassador Farhang, Americans who have studied these issues know, now, that the Iranian people suffered terribly from a cruel dictatorship for 26 years; a government put in power by a

---

Bishop White is Chairman, United States Council of Bishops Taskforce on Iran, and New Jersey Area Bishop, United Methodist Church.

CIA-engineered coup and supported in power by U.S. arms. Informed Americans know about the devastation of much of Iran's agriculture. But they say at least the Shah modernized Iran. He forced a crash program of industrialization which provided jobs for millions and increased the GNP of Iran dramatically."

Ambassador Farhang replied:

"Those who look at the bottom-line figures of economic growth in Iran are like proud parents who keep weighing their baby on the scales and exclaiming at his rapid growth. They so love their baby that they do not notice that one hand is growing out of all proportion to the other; the head is huge and grotesque. They say, 'My, how the baby is growing!' They cannot see that they have produced a monster.

"Those who talk of rapid development in Iran overlook the fact that 5% of the population became rich, while most of the people were reduced to absolute poverty; that our economy is dependent on the whims of the transnational corporations, unbalanced, burdened with armaments, riddled with corruption, while our capital has been hemorrhaging to the West at an alarming rate."

The American people are grossly misinformed about Iran. They know about fascist brutalities and discrimination against Christians by right-wing Moslem fundamentalists. They do not know of the teachings of the great liberation philosopher, Dr. Ali Shariati, whose picture appears everywhere in Tehran. They know about President Bani-Sadr's struggles against the Ayatollah Beheshti and the Parliament. They do not know that the President has published fourteen books, is an accomplished lay theologian as well as economist, and enjoys immense popular support in Iran. Americans know that the students violated international law in taking hostages; they do not know the truth which Dr. Richard Falk elaborates, that international law discriminates in a brutal way against poor peoples who live under oppressive governments.

This volume helps to set the record straight. It helps us to penetrate beneath the distressing headlines to glimpse the agony and the ecstasy, the spring-time of a new hope, of a people who have laid a great burden down, and who are engaged in a struggle, if necessary to the death, for the right to define their own destiny. Freedom and justice are their passion and their dream. They need our prayers.

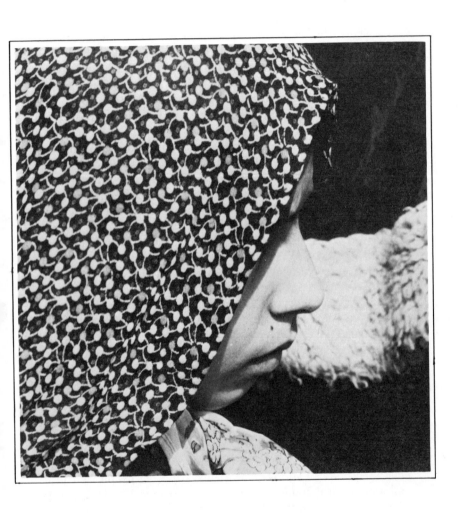

Perspectives on the

Iranian Revolution

"We do not know from where to start, and about whom to talk. About the mothers who have given their dear ones, children with no fathers, about husbands and wives who have lost their beloved, about the days of rebellion and the roar of the revolution, about the cries and chants on our lips, about the clenched fists, about battle and martyrdom, about graves freshly dug, about our clothes soaking in blood, about the mighty Allah O Akbar— "God is Great"— on the rooftops, about the hatred and pride of the mothers, about the vengeance of the fathers. And about the suffering, poverty, deprivation, inequality, oppression, imprisonment and torture or about the renaissance of Islam, about love, hope, faith, perserverance, resistance, rebellion, the honor of martyrdom, the message of the martyrs, or the endless wait for the return of the Imam. We will start from right here, Behesht Zahara, from the graves of those who left us only to stay alive and thus tell us the meaning of life.

Alas you were not here to see."

Message of the Islamic Students Following the Path of the Imam to the Delegation of American People at Behesht Zahara, cemetery of the Martyrs of the Revolution, February 7, 1980.

Student wearing modified chador

Introduction:

The Text and Subtexts of the Iranian Revolution

David H. Albert

وَبَشِّرِالَّذِينَ آمَنُوْاوَعَمِلُواالصَّالِحَاتِ أَنَّ لَهُمْ جَنَّاتٍ تَجْرِي

But give glad tidings to those who believe and work righteousness, that their portion is the Gardens, beneath which rivers flow.

Koran 2:24

Here lies a tale which needs to be told: how a virtually unarmed people overthrew the most vicious and brutally repressive dictatorship in the Middle East—backed by the most powerful military power in the history of the world—and is attempting to build a new society.

The text is still unfinished, and rightfully so. Imagine, if you will, writing the text of the United States less than eighteen months after the last British troops left the soil of thirteen struggling colonies in 1783. And imagine the confusion of the historians, both inside and outside the former colonies, watching a new ideology shaping new social and political forms. In the case of the United States, six years would go by before a president was inaugurated and eight years before a Constitution would be established.

The text contains within it four subtexts: the rising of an unarmed and oppressed people; the characteristics of the dictatorship and its brutality; the nature and interests of the military power of which the dictatorship was a client; and finally, the values and conflicts out of which a new social order is being created. It is only by bringing the four subtexts to the light and by understanding their relation to each other that we can ever hope to fully understand the text and incorporate its lessons into our lives.

1

"Al-nas"—The People

The modern history of Iran is intimately tied up with the history of Western technology, specifically the petrochemical requirements of modern industrial processes and the quest for ever-more consumer goods. The Iranian people have been buffeted by international rivalries and intrigues based on these requirements—first between the Russians and the British, then between the Allies and Axis powers during World War II, and then finally through the establishment of a CIA-backed monarchy in the person of the former Shah in the context of the rivalries of the Cold War. These rivalries and intrigues have taken place without any real consideration of the traditions, interest or aspirations of the Iranian people.

The stakes were and remain high. In 1978, Iran was the fourth largest oil producer in the world, the second largest in the Middle East. During the last year of the Shah's reign, Iran supplied more than 5 per cent of U.S. oil, 18 per cent of Japan's and West Germany's, more than 50 per cent of Israel's, and virtually all of South Africa's. Since the overthrow of the popularly elected government of Mossadegh, led by Kermit Roosevelt of the CIA in 1953, the U.S. government supplied Iran with $1.2 billion worth of military aid and training, and sold the former Shah more than $20 billion in arms, $8.7 billion of which was actually delivered. As in the cases of Chile, Haiti, Brazil, Philippines, Thailand and elsewhere, U.S. foreign policy has favored support of integrated military and quasi-military governments rather than democratic or national ones. And as in the case of these other regimes, the internal economy of Iran was restructured to meet the needs of foreign production and demands.

But there are major differences and these differences have had major implications for the people of Iran. For one thing, as Iranian President Bani-Sadr noted several years before the Revolution, conditions in Iran have not been as favorable to the penetration of the multinational corporations as to the direct manipulation of the U.S. government. Only 0.6 per cent of the labor force was employed in the production of oil. Less than 10 per cent of the population accounted for more than 40 per cent of national consumption. A combination of massive repression, exclusion of popular classes from consumption, a socially and politically weak ruling class without even a semblance of popular social or cultural support, an absence of an industrial base and of specialists have all made Iran *less* attractive for foreign investment even under the former Shah than might otherwise have been the case. Furthermore, the geo-political instability of the Middle East and the weakness of markets serviceable from the Iranian plateau in the north (Turkey, Iraq, Afghanistan, the Soviet Union), or the Persian Gulf in the south (Yemen, Oman, Pakistan, India, East Africa) have all made Iran geographically undesirable for investment. Thus other than for petro-chemicals, conditions have not been favorable for production in Iran for sale in other nations. And though in these days of "oil shortages" and billion-dollar profits for the big oil companies, it seems hard to believe, U.S.-based oil companies were initially very reluctant to enter Iran. They did so in 1954, only after the Eisenhower administration granted them exemption from anti-trust prosecution by the Justice Department which could have deprived them of price-fixing capabilities forever.

Hence, while "modernization"—the relative build-up of an industrial base and infrastructure through the multinationals' exploitation of a cheap labor pool—did take place, the central reality of recent economic change in Iran was based on the sky-rocketting price rises in the world oil market following the 1973 Arab-Israeli war. Subjected to the subtle penetrations of the multinationals, Iran was also subject to the much more direct exploitation of its natural resources, which were paid for largely in the form of arms purchased by the former Shah.

Inside the country, a small "state comprador class" (people who "buy" and invest for the state), tied to the Shah and oil interests, looked elsewhere for other products which could follow this pattern. Such products would require little internal labor relative to capital and would have substantial value in export. In 1961, before the "White Revolution"—the former Shah's massive restructuring of agrarian Iran—79 per cent of agricultural production went for food. By 1971, this percentage had been reduced to 50 per cent as priority was given to production of export crops such as cotton, sugar cane, and sugar beets. The strange anomaly was thus created of the Iranian government subsidizing imports of foreign wheat while national wheat production remained unsubsidized.

What has all this meant for the people of Iran? It has meant the number of villages reduced from 40,000 to 10,000 since 1963, and the swelling of the cities. The shanty towns on the edge of cities burgeoned; people living in refuse heaps or packing crates left over from the shipment of U.S. military ordinance became a common sight. In the last fifteen years, Iran's urban population has risen from 25 per cent to 48 per cent of the total population. Tehran, one of the world's most polluted cities, has doubled in population in the last ten years to almost 5,000,000.

Once food self-sufficient as late as the late 1950's, Iran had come to depend on massive foreign imports, much of which never got down to the people who needed it. The state comprador class controlled the distribution and price of imported food. The state bureaucracy mushroomed. Jobs went begging for lack of skilled personnel, yet unemployment soared. The people remained untrained, 60 per cent illiterate and, for the most part, ignored. For many, hunger became a fact of life even as the Gross National Product reached new heights. John Mohawk in his article gives a vivid impression of what this way of life looks like to an American seeing it for the first time.

But it is easy to overstate the importance of either global economics or the international political situation in looking for the decisive factors behind the Iranian Revolution. These factors may explain misery, oppression, and degradation, but they do not explain the creation of hope, faith, patience, or fortitude, the stuff of which revolutions are made.

Furthermore, to do justice to the people who made the Iranian Revolution, we would do well to examine what they themselves say about their own struggle. Dr. Ali Shariati, sociologist, teacher, martyr, and probably the most important ideologue behind the Iranian Revolution, has this to say in an essay appearing in this volume: "Islam is the first school of social thought that recognizes the masses as the basis, the fundamental and conscious factor in determining history and society . . . . The only fundamental factor in social change development is the people (al-nas), without any particular form of racial or class privilege, or any other distinguishing characteristics."

These are the people, organized in cells, meeting in the basements of mosques at midnight, carrying tape cassettes containing instructions, bearing the scars of oppression, the visions of a different social order, and a belief in the holiness of martyrdom, who carried the Revolution forward unarmed against the tanks of the Shah. This was no new experience, though: as both Eqbal Ahmad and Lynne Shivers point out in this volume, twentieth century Iranian history is little but a history of these visions pushing forward to be realized, only to be crushed by the pretensions of despots and the crass materialism of a world military-industrial system. Generation after generation, the students, the poor, the idealistic went to the mosques, went to the mountains in the north, went to the torture chambers, and prisons and exile in the desert or in foreign lands, went back to the petty preoccupations and tribulations of daily life, never satisfied, in one unending *hajj* (pilgrimage) to their home, a revolutionary Islam in an independent Iran.

4

A Man Without a People

For the Shah, however, there was no *hajj*. If he were a man of greater stature, a human being displaying a greater degree of self-awareness, he might well have been a tragic figure. For here is a man essentially without a people, without a reason for being or acting which grows out of a sense of his own culture or tradition.

Or rather it might be said that the Shah fit perfectly into the brutal traditions of his own family. His father was a Russian-trained Cossack officer who, in seizing control of Iran in 1921, overturned Iran's hard-won constitutional framework in keeping with the needs of British imperialism. Having crowned himself king in 1926, Reza Shah began trying political dissidents, established control over a heavily censored press, and initiated ruthless military repression of all opposition. When it became clear that Germany was in the ascendancy, Reza Shah turned away from British influence and allowed Iran to become the center of Nazi intelligence operations in the Middle East. The Allies, quick to protect their oil interests, invaded Iran in 1941 and forced Reza Shah to abdicate, placing his retiring son Mohammed Reza on the throne.

If placed on the throne as a figurehead to protect the Allies' oil interests in 1941, the Shah was to return after being forced to flee in 1953 as the active agent of the U.S. government. It was a role he always seemed quite content to accept. Without a place or even acceptance among his own people, the Shah sought to fashion a destiny based on a much more private set of values. He amassed a personal fortune estimated in value from two to twenty-five billion dollars, and created a series of palaces complete with crystal bathtubs, solid gold water spigots, and an aviary of exotic talking birds who could pay him homage in at least three different languages. Without an indigenous role in the history of his country, he attempted to create a role based on myth. In October, 1971, hundreds of notables from all over the globe, led by Spiro Agnew, journeyed to air-conditioned tents pitched in the desert by the ruins of Persopolis, feasted on food and drink flown in from Paris, and paid their respects to the army colonel's son, the *"Shahanshah"* ("King of Kings") on the 2500th anniversary of the Persian Empire, all at a cost of $60,000,000.

But his standards were always to remain Western standards. There was always something cruelly lacking in being a living monument to an Oriental empire which had been eclipsed by history. And so, as Michael Klare notes in his essay, when given the opportunity by the pull-out of British forces from the Persian Gulf through the '60s and the carte blanche given to him by Nixon and Kissinger in 1972, the Shah decided to turn Iran into a world class military power, the fifth most powerful in the world by 1985.

The source list of the Shah's military purchases from 1973 to 1978 reads like a directory of American military contractors. The Shah equipped his military with the world's largest armed hydrofoil fleet; six hundred helicopters, the world's third largest such force, used primarily against demonstrations; and an electronic aerial defense system rivalling that of NATO. CIA Director Admiral Stansfield Turner testified that the sale of seven Boeing E-3A *AWACS* (Airborne Warning and Control System) radar patrol planes would gravely compromise U.S. security if such a sophisticated system fell into the wrong hands. The sale went forward, only to be cancelled by the interim government of Shapur Bakhtiar in January, 1979. Other sales included F-14 *Tomcat* Swing-wing jet fighters and a *Spruance*-class destroyer—both, according to Eric Rouleau of the Paris daily *Le Monde*, are more sophisticated than versions currently used by the U.S. By 1978, the Shah's imports into Iran topped $18 billion, the bulk in military hardware and luxury consumer goods for a tiny leisure class.

The delivery of military playthings unsuited to the Shah's own defense needs may have played an important role in keeping the Army loyal to him, and soothed the Shah's ego. But the role of subjugating a population hostile to him was left to the SAVAK, the Shah's deadly efficient political police.

Created in 1957 with, according to a former World Bank advisor to Iran, the personal assistance of a retired Captain of the Chicago police force and the active co-operation of the Central Intelligence Agency, the SAVAK grew to 5,000 full-time "professionals" and enlisted tens of thousands of informers. If the Shah could not win his people's love, he was determined to keep them in a constant state of terror. A trail of death hangs over the cultural and literary world of Iran over the past twenty years, bringing it almost to the point of extinction. Students disappeared from classes, never to be heard from again. Estimates of the numbers of political prisoners kept by the SAVAK between 1957 and 1979 range from 25,000 to 125,000. No one will ever know for certain; too many of the prisoners were never to return. It is almost impossible to find a family in a major city in Iran today which did not have a family member or acquaintance killed, tortured, or imprisoned by the SAVAK. Children were raped and sometimes murdered before the eyes of their parents; broken bottles were forced up the anus of prisoners suspended by their wrists from a beam, prisoners were roasted on electrically-heated bed frames, whipped with electrical cables, burned on the genitals with cigarettes and branding irons. The SAVAK was not very discreet; as William Worthy notes in this volume in his interview with a high-ranking SAVAK official, the purpose of these tortures was not to extract information, but to terrorize the population. For the "interrogation" techniques to become effective, they had to become common knowledge among the people themselves. Each new instrument of brutality required "advertising"; information about these activities and photographs of the results made their way not only to the Iranian people, but also to the *Sunday Times of London, Le Monde,* the United Nations Commission on Human Rights, Amnesty International, the International League for Human Rights, the International Commission of Jurists, and again, with full documentation and photographs, directly to the United States Congress and to at least three Presidents of the United States: Nixon, Ford, and Carter. To complete the circle, statements of "concern" would return to the Shah, confirming once and for all the success of the policy of intimidation.

United States' Interests

United States policy toward Iran since World War II has been very carefully calculated on the economic and political levels, but there has never been even the slightest attempt to separate out the interests of the American people from the repressive policies of the Shah. The Shah's policies, including his reliance on terror and torture, were carried out with the active knowledge, planning, consent, and active participation of the agencies of the U.S. government at all levels. The U.S. training mission to Iran began in 1943 and continued until 1976, when it was merged into the U.S. Military Assistance Advisory Group. One hundred seventy-nine high-ranking Iranian police officers came to the U.S. for training under the Agency for International Development's Public Safety Program before it was abolished on human rights grounds in 1973. A State Department spokesperson confirmed in 1978 that during that year, 175 SAVAK agents were undergoing training at the CIA's McLean, Virginia facilities. During the '70s, an average of more than 350 SAVAK agents were trained in interrogation and torture techniques in Virginia and Texas, along with intelligence operatives from repressive regimes throughout the Third World. This training was augmented by the presence of more than thirty para-military organizations aided by U.S. civilian and military personnel inside Iran, as well as by British and Israeli training missions.

Active support of the Shah's repressive policies extended to the ambassadorial level. Richard Nixon chose to cement the "surrogate'' strategy of using Iran as the gendarme of the Middle East by appointing former CIA Director Richard Helms as Ambassador to Tehran. where he served from 1973 to 1976. And even as President Carter was espousing the cause of human rights in 1977, he appointed William L. Sullivan as Ambassador. Sullivan, it has been noted, helped direct the secret bombing of Laotian peasants during the conflicts in Southeast Asia, and worked closely with the CIA in the Philippines in propping up the martial law regime of President Marcos during its early years. During the autumn of 1978, the U.S., along with *Mossad*—Israel's intelligence organization which aided the Shah in exchange for Iran's supplying Israel with more than 50 per cent of its petroleum needs—supplied tons of new riot-control equipment. And even after the Shah left Iran and during a purported domestic oil shortage, the U.S. sent the Bakhtiar government 200,000 barrels of diesel fuel and gasoline, most probably utilized by the repressive machinery of the military.

For the ruling elite in the United States, the Vietnam debacle pales in significance when compared with the overthrow of the Shah. Henry Kissinger has called the loss of Iran the ''greatest single blow to U.S. foreign policy interests since World War II.'' U.S. interests in Iran were not speculative, nor did Iran represent a lowly domino standing in the way of world Communist domination. Iran was the linchpin of U.S. control of the Persian Gulf and its hedge against a Middle Eastern oil cutoff, its center of operations for surveillance of the southern part of the Soviet Union, a balance to Arab interests in the Israeli-Palestinian conflict, a third party supplier of oil to South Africa, the largest buyer of U.S. military goods and external subsidizer of U.S. military research and development, and a testing ground for U.S. military and para-military operations for use elsewhere around the globe. In short, the overthrow of the Shah spelled the end of a major epoch of bipartisan U.S. foreign policy dating back to the Truman administration.

A New Society?

For some of the reasons stated above, the prognosis for a successful deepening of the Islamic Revolution in Iran is not good. The economy begins from a position of decided weakness, exacerbated by a ''brain drain'' of Iran's technical elite which has gone on for more than twenty years. The former Shah's administrative apparatus, built up year after year through gross governmental mismanagement, will not be replaced overnight. Inflation is rampant and food is dear, though the breaking of economic ties with the West will place the farmlands of Iran back into domestic production.

External threats abound. It was no accident that the U.S. government chose to admit the former Shah into New York in October,

1979, despite repeated warnings from intelligence sources, embassy staffs, and the relatively moderate Provisional Government of Mehdi Bazargan that such action would significantly increase hostilities between the two nations. Past history suggests that U.S. economic and military interests have little stake in seeking peaceful accommodation with an independent Iran and shall be willing to go to great lengths to shatter that independence. The economic and political clout still maintained by the former Shah, particularly as it has been manifested through the agencies of David Rockefeller and Henry Kissinger, should be duly noted in this regard. Furthermore, while hostility from the West may force Iran into closer economic cooperation with the Soviet Union, the Soviet invasion of Afghanistan certainly does not bode well for Iran's attempt to go it alone in international affairs.

Internally there are major questions too. The taking of and refusal to release the American hostages at an early juncture, in violation of international law, not only shows the continued volatility of the Iranian body politic, but also a lack of sophistication, intentional or unintentional, in dealing with the realities of international governmental affairs. Richard Falk explores in this volume the hard questions the hostage situation poses for international law; notwithstanding where justice may ultimately lie, the people of Iran will not easily win in this way the allies they sorely need.

There is, however, an indisputable logic to events going on in Iran today. Ayatollah Khomeini has attempted to curb the self-righteous excesses of "revolutionary justice" exhibited during the first four months of the Islamic Republic. Quietly, away from the glaring eye of the media, 15,000 students have enlisted in the Imam's *jihad* (crusade) for reconstruction and gone out to the villages to build roads, dig irrigation ditches and wells, and rebuild a land shattered by more than two decades of neglect and exploitation.

And the people are in the process of rebuilding themselves. What may look to the uninitiated eye like chaos is in fact the first flowering in twenty-six years of political debate that a once-proud people have had about the future of their country. The freedom to express ideas has brought forth an avalanche of words, slogans, and programs competing for space in a country in which oral traditions are still strong. After opposition to the Shah, support for Imam Khomeini, and resistance to outside interference in Iran's internal affairs—all of which crystallized in the student occupation of the U.S. Embassy—Iranians are divided in their interests. A Western-oriented middle class exists alongside an illiterate peasant majority.

Worker-controlled factories hum side-by-side with a byzantine bureaucratic governmental set-up. Rug dealers and potters and tanners and farmers and importers of plastic dinnerware all hawk their wares in the bazaars. The sounds of the coppersmith and of the poet mingle, sometimes uneasily.

Richard Falk in his article attempts to look at what the future might hold in store for Iran's ethnic and religious minorities. Pamela Haines paints a compelling first-hand picture of the conditions, hopes and aspirations of women in revolutionary Iran.

But again we get a less than complete perspective on the Iranian Revolution unless we allow its acknowledged leaders to speak for themselves. It becomes immediately clear from examining the thought of these figures that the Revolution will stand or fall to the degree that the society can incorporate a revolutionary Islamic ideology as a vital force for change and for social, economic and political justice. Leslie Withers in her article examines the interface of religion and revolution in Iran today from the vantage point of an American coming to terms with it for the first time.

The cry of *Allah O Akbar* is heard from the rooftops. It is a cry of suffering and revolt, praise and lamentation, despair and hope. The Koran teaches the absolute unity and power of God, of *tauhid*, the existence of the world, as Dr. Shariati puts it, "as a single form, a single living and conscious organism, possessing will, intelligence, feeling and purpose." It is here that the ideology of revolutionary Islam is in fundamental, uncompromising, and irreconcilable opposition to Marxism, the only other ideology to have any significant following inside Iran. Revolutionary Islam rejects any world view which regards the universe as a shifting assemblage characterized by heterogeneity, disunity, and contradictions, or that sees these contradictions, as both Shariati and the late Ayatollah Motahheri suggest, as the "motor" of history. Oppression, be it social, political or economic, is not the result of some impersonal, immutable, dialectical force, inherent in materialist social conflict, but a falling away from God which is Truth.

Revolutionary Islam's interpretation of *tauhid* goes even further. *Tauhid* signifies the unity of humankind with nature, of human with human, of God with the world, and of God with humanity. There is no contradiction in existence: no contradiction between the human world and the natural, between spirit and body, between this world and the next, between matter and meaning. *Tauhid* depicts all of these as constituting a total, harmonious, living and self-aware system; such an understanding must inform all aspects of social life. The Islamic Republic of Iran's first President Abolhassan Bani-Sadr, a highly trained economist, describes in this volume how the principle of *tauhid* applies in the economic sphere, particularly in the Islamic conception of ownership, and thus offers the basis for a decentralized economic system which is a true alternative to both the capitalism and Marxism. Finally, Ayatollah Khomeini exhorts Iranians to remember that the experience of the last several decades suggests that a *tauhid* society can only be built on indigenous values, and that it is Iranians themselves who, intoxicated by the materialism of the West and blinded by their own self-alienation, deserted the pursuit of a unified, integrated and humane society based on Islamic principles.

The Fifth Subtext

The text seems to have contained only four subtexts. The fifth subtext remains unnamed, unspoken, unevaluated: the role of the American people.

The majority of Iranians, perhaps as a reflection of their own historical experience, assume a clear distinction between the policies of the United States government and the will and aspirations of the American people. They reason quite clearly, if naively: "How could the American people, who pride themselves on their democratic institutions and traditions, support a government—the U.S. government—that has done such terrible things to us for so very long?" They reason further that since this is impossible, it must be that their cries of pain have never been heard. If the American people only had the information, knew about their plight, they would, as any self-respecting human beings would be expected to, rise up and work in the defense of a once-free people. In its baldest form, this is the reasoning behind the taking of the U.S. Embassy in November, 1979.

What truth can we extract from this great simplicity? To what extent have we, the American people, become hostages of our own lifestyles and thought patterns so that we are willing to purchase our standard of living with the sufferings of others? What price are we willing to accept for the tortured utterances of our sisters and brothers abroad, in South Korea, in Argentina, in the Philippines, in Chile? How easily can we be bought off by a government which preaches peace and arms the nations of the world for the ultimate destruction of humankind, which pursues economic "growth" while our air and water become unfit for human consumption and mothers can't feed their babies their own milk, which holds up the standards of social justice while the poor, the sick, the feeble have lost even the capacity to ask for what is theirs by birthright?

Our leaders no longer have to hide their crimes in shame from our view. We paid good hard cash for the latest in torture exotica; we built with our own hands the tiger cages used in Vietnam, the cattle prods for Uruguay, the "Apollo" helmets, used to magnify the screams of agony in the tortured subject's own ears, for Iran. They bear the inscriptions "made in the United States of America". We have trained the torturers in our torture schools, in Texas and in McLean, Virginia, and honored the teachers with "honorary degrees". We have taken home our paychecks, some larger, some smaller that others, bought our color television sets, and looked on with dismay at people in strange costumes thousands of miles away as they denounced us as murderers. And we feel angry, bewildered, betrayed, impotent. We worry about inflation.

We are the inheritors of a past over which we have had no control, but we are also the midwives of an uncertain future. What is this creature which we shall bring to birth? This is *our* subtext, and it is yet to be written. If this book adds only a little to our understanding of the past, and of the roles that we can play, both individually and collectively, in building a just and humane future for all people, then it will not have been in vain.

Introduction to the Second Edition

As this second edition goes to press, American hostages are still being held in Iran. We hope they are released and reunited with their families and friends soon.

Also as of this writing, the U.S. government has not acknowledged its responsibility in setting up and maintaining the murderous regime of the former Shah, or of training its secret police torturers. Regardless of the outcome of the hostage situation, we as Americans owe it to ourselves and to the integrity of history to ensure that such an acknowledgment is made, if only to prevent such violations of basic human rights by our government from recurring.

Much has happened since the first edition of this book was published. A U.S. military incursion into Iran, purportedly to rescue the hostages, ended in failure. Unconfirmed reports continue to surface about agents being trained in the U.S. and infiltrated into Iran. A military coup in Iran on July 10th was aborted. Columnist Jack Anderson revealed top-secret Administration consideration of a massive military mission in Iran to take place before the U.S. Presidential elections. It is worthy of note that despite appeals from major religious denominations, organizations and leaders around the country, not a single Congressional hearing has been held on past U.S. policy toward Iran since the overthrow of the Shah. One wonders exactly what our representatives are trying to hide.

Ten Americans, including former U.S. Attorney General Ramsey Clark, joined representatives of sixty nations at an international conference to explore U.S. intervention in Iran. The former Shah died in Egypt, his funeral attended by a lonely Richard Nixon.

The general situation in Iran remains uneasy. The new Islamic *Majlis* (Parliament) has convened and a Prime Minister has been named. But the economy, though benefitting from its new reliance on domestic agriculture, continues to be plagued by a lack of spare parts and a general disorder which comes of attempting to free itself from more than a century of imperialist domination. Economic sanctions have forced Iran reluctantly into closer cooperative ties with the Soviet Union and the Eastern European nations. War broke out between Iran and Iraq.

The Islamic Republic's record on human rights thus far is also contradictory. The military has been successfully restrained—a remarkable achievement. Considering the severe international political threats the Revolution continues to face, the degree of democratic debate, freedom of the press, and the establishment of free elections is truly extraordinary. Nonetheless, the resort to summary (if public) trials and executions, while in no way comparable to the excesses sanctioned under the former Shah's regime, is repugnant to all those who believe that revolutionary values must be grounded in the sanctity of human life.

In the long run, most of this will fade from public memory. But as it fades, and as the fate of the hostages, of U.S. military and human rights policy, of the ability of the Islamic Republic to cope with the complex problems of development and international affairs are decided, those committed to human liberation should not lose sight of the enduring historical lesson to be learned from the Iranian Revolution. And that is this: no longer can any liberation movement anywhere truly claim that revolutionary violence is the only path open to them to effect change. For the Iranian Revolution shows without question that it is still possible late in the twentieth century for an unarmed but mobilized population to overthrow a conscienceless, technologically sophisticated, dictatorial regime through recourse to the tactics and strategies of nonviolent action. It is in the spirit of this lesson, one which fills us with hope for the future, that we are glad to publish this second edition of *Tell the American People*.

Acknowledgments

We wish to acknowledge the following, without whom this book would not have been possible: the Committee for an American-Iranian Crisis Resolution, coordinated by Norman Forer of Lawrence, Kansas. Founded in 1976 as the American Committee for Iranian Human Rights, the Committee has continued to promote activities which seek to inform Americans about the hopes and aspirations of the Iranian people and increase understanding through people-to-people initiatives. The Committee arranged for the clergy visit to the hostages held at the U.S. Embassy during Christmas, 1979, and Easter, 1980, and for the visit of 49 Americans to engage in an ''intensive dialogue'' with the students holding the Embassy in February, 1980. Five of the authors and the photojournalist whose work appears here—Randy Goodman, John Mohawk, William Worthy, and Pamela Haines, Leslie Withers, and Lynne Shivers of Movement for a New Society—were all members of that delegation; the Network Service Collective of Movement for a New Society made publication and distribution of this book possible; Robert McClellan of the Network Service Collective provided insightful feedback on the text. A Dabirian of the Islamic Economics Society in New York provided timely aid in the translation of the essay by Bani-Sadr. Jim Best, Nancy Wood, and Ernest Morgan of Celo Press in Burnsville, N.C. helped expedite the typesetting for this book. Alice Maes set up the financial record keeping system and worked on advanced publicity and Nina Huizinga did the entire layout for the book. Finally, we rely on the readers of this book, without whose careful consideration this book can never fulfill its purpose.

Twentieth Century Iranian History: A Chronology

David H. Albert

This brief chronology should serve two purposes. Firstly, it should provide a sense of the sweep of twentieth century history in Iran and make it easier to follow the course of events referred to in the text itself. But perhaps more importantly, the chronology may offer, between the lines, lessons to be learned not to be found anywhere else in this book.

For example, if we look at the events of 1977 from the point of view of the hopes of moderates in Iran, events during the first half of the year seem to offer 1) evidence of possible liberalization of policy inside Iran, and 2) evidence of the direct relationship between the will of President Carter and the practices of the Shah. At the beginning of 1977, Carter presses his human rights advocacy. In April, the first military trial open to the press in more than five years occurs in Iran. In June, three moderate leaders circulate 10,000 copies of an "open letter to the Shah" in Tehran, calling for an end to "despotism in the guise of monarchy." Also in June, the International League for Human Rights protests mass arrests and torture, and sends messages to Congress and Carter claiming that the State Department is witholding information. In August, the Shah names a new liberal prime minister and frees 572 political prisoners. But in November, Carter hosts the Shah at the White House, as 8,500 Iranian protesters gather outside to protest the visit. Later in November, a holiday celebration held at the home of one of the "open letter" signers is broken up by Army Rangers and SAVAK agents, with more than 300 people injured. In December, Carter returns to Iran, just as events have gotten more tense and the human rights situation worsened, and offers strong public support for the Shah. By the end of 1977, moderates in Iran are convinced 1.) that liberalization under the Shah is impossible, and 2.) that there is indeed a direct connection between Carter and the repressive policies of the Shah. The revolution was to begin in earnest eight days later.

1906—After long struggle, including 14,000 people occupying British Legation, Iran's constitution established.

1908—Mohammed Ali Shah suspends constitution.

1909—Mohammed Ali overthrown, replaced by eleven-year-old son Ahmad Shah. Parliament restored. England and Russia divide Iran into two spheres of influence—Russian in north, British in south.

1917—Russian Revolution results in end of long history of direct Russian imperialist influence in Iran.

1921—Colonel Reza Pahlavi, Russian-trained Cossack officer, stages military coup. Crowns himself Shah in 1926.

1926—First military tribunals set up, with British aid, to try political dissidents, in violation of the constitution.

1930's—Reza Shah attempts to lessen Soviet and British influence by fostering relationship with Germany.

1941—Soviets, British occupy Iran, forcing Reza Shah to abdicate; son, Mohammed Reza, becomes figurehead ruler.

1943—U.S. sends first military mission to Iran. Tudeh Party (Marxist, pro-Societ) established.

1945-46—British and Soviet troops withdraw.

1951—Mohammed Mossadegh leads National Front, an Islamic social-democratic movement, into power; foreign-controlled oil fields nationalized. England sets up economic blockade.

1952—Iranian economy weakened; Tudeh Party gaining in strength; Eisenhower fears Communist takeover.

August, 1953—Shah attempts to dismiss Prime Minister Mossadegh at insistence of U.S. Mossadegh refuses to step down; Shah flees. Pro-Shah generals and CIA, directed by Allen Dulles, and personally led by CIA operatives Kermit Roosevelt and H. Norman Schwartzkopf carry out coup. Shah returns three days later. Political opposition to Shah banned.

1954—Eisenhower sends direct aid to Iran. Agreement reached giving Shah nominal control of oil fields, but granting management/development rights to Anglo-American consortium. U.S. companies, fearing political instability, reluctantly lured into Iran in exchange for exemption from anti-trust prosecution by U.S. Justice Department.

1955—Martial law lifted in Tehran for first time since 1951.

1957—SAVAK (Secret Police) formed, trained by British, U.S. and, later, Israeli intelligence. More than 400 agents per year attend training sessions in McLean, Virginia, and Texas at height of operations.

1961—Shah severs diplomatic relations with Arab League and strengthens relations with Israel. Iran nears bankruptcy. Pahlavi Foundation set up as funnel for Shah's personal wealth leaving the country. Iran Freedom Party formed by Dr. Mehdi Bazargan.

1962—National Front getting stronger. Shah visits U.S. to ask for more aid from Congress. Kennedy urges Shah to institute economic reforms, but assures Shah that continued support is contingent upon *American* interests.

November, 1962—Islamic clergy march in Tehran against Shah's dictatorial rule.

1963—"White Revolution" launched by Shah, calling for land reform, literacy, women's rights. Land never redistributed to peasantry, but number of villages in Iran declines from 40,000 in 1963 to 10,000 in 1978. Foreign agribusiness ventures made possible for such companies as Dow Chemical, Bank of America, John Deere, and Royal Dutch Shell. From being almost food self-sufficient in 1969, Iran becomes heavily dependent upon foreign imports by the time of the Shah's overthrow. Estimated 63% of population still illiterate in 1979.

March, 1963—Ayatollah Khomeini speaks out against White Revolution. Shah's commandos attack a gathering at Madressah Faizeyeh theological college.

June 5, 1963—"The 15th of Khordad": thousands of unarmed people murdered in streets and bazaars of Tehran. Massacres continue in Qom, Shiraz, and elsewhere. Khomeini arrested, then exiled to Turkey, later Iraq.

August, 1963—U.S. military advisors given diplomatic immunity.

1964—Dr. Ali Shariati returns to Iran from Paris and is immediately arrested; later teaches at University of Mashad, is dismissed; eventually becomes foremost exponent of a revolutionary Islamic tradition in Iran.

1965-67—Shah orders air strikes against Qashqai tribes in

Southern Iran. Iran buys first two squadrons of F-4 fighter-bombers. SAVAK tortures intensify.

1968—Britain finalizes plans to pull military forces out of Persian Gulf area.

January, 1969—Military court sentences 14 artists and writers to prison where they are tortured. Iranian embassy in Rome occupied by students in protest, as worldwide Iranian student protests intensify. SAVAK begins operations inside U.S.

1970—Amnesty International reports massive jailing of political prisoners. Paris daily *Le Monde* begins to publish reports of arbitrary arrest and torture inside Iran.

1971—Two main guerilla movements become active in Iran and remain so until splintering into a larger number of factions, 1976-77. Fedayeen—an anti-Soviet Marxist-Leninist group; Mujahhadin—radical Islamic nationalist group, though portions later reveal Marxist tendencies.

October, 1971—Vice President Spiro Agnew heads guest list in air-conditioned tents at Persepolis celebrating 2,500th anniversary of Persian Empire. Food and water flown in from Paris. Cost—more than $60,000,000.

May, 1972—Richard Nixon flies to Tehran from Moscow. Students stage silent protest at Tehran University. Surrogate strategy goes into effect—Iran to defend the Middle East for U.S. interests. Iranian military purchases rise from $519 million in 1972 to $5.8 billion in 1977. Shah purchases seven Boeing E-3A *AWACS* radar patrol planes, Grumman F-14 *Tomcat* swing-wing jet fighter, McDonnell-Douglas *Harpoon* anti-ship missiles, Lockheed P-3C *Orion* ocean surveillance planes, *Spruance*-class heavy destroyers, Lockheed C-130 *Hercules* troop-transport planes, McDonnell-Douglas F-4E *Phantom* deep-strike fighter-bombers, and *Tang*-class submarines. (*Tang* submarines are incapable of operation in Iran's shallow waters.)

1973—Arab-Israeli War. Iran does not participate in oil sales boycott, but announces huge price rises. Richard Helms, former head of the U.S. CIA, becomes ambassador to Iran.

1974—Iranian oil revenues rise to $18 billion. French government contracts to build two nuclear plants for $4 billion. (Islamic government later stops construction.)

May, 1974—Amnesty International director notes, ''No

country in the world has a worse record on human rights than Iran.''

1975—Shah declares Iran one-party state. Religious protests in Qom.

1976—International Commission of Jurists in Geneva hears reports by prisoners subjected to SAVAK tortures.

1977—Carter presses human rights advocacy. Names William L. Sullivan new Ambassador to Iran. Sullivan, closely connected with the CIA, helped direct the secret bombing of Laotian peasants during conflicts in Southeast Asia, and worked closely with President Marcos in the Philippines in ''maintaining security'' during the early years of his martial law regime. Sullivan repeatedly meets with Shah and General Azhari to discuss government's strategy for suppression of opposition.

April, 1977—First military trial of dissidents open to press in more than five years.

June, 1977—Dr. Ali Shariati, having been tortured by the SAVAK while imprisoned for eighteen months, and forced to leave Iran, dies under suspicious circumstances in London.

June 12, 1977—10,000 copies of ''open letter to Shah'' signed by Shapur Bakhtiar, Karim Sanjabi, and Darioush Forouhar, moderate leaders of the National Front, call for end of ''despotism in the guise of monarchy,'' free elections.

June 23, 1977—International League for Human Rights protests mass arrests and torture; sends message to Carter and Congress claiming State Department is withholding information.

August, 1977—Shah names Jamshid Amouzegar, a liberal, Prime Minister, frees 572 political prisoners.

October 29, 1977—Ayatollah Khomeini's son dies under suspicious circumstances in Iraq.

November 15, 1977—Carter hosts Shah at White House. 8500 Iranian demonstrators gather outside in protest. Police use mace, tear-gas to disperse crowd. Carter and Shah seen weeping from tear-gas on U.S. television.

November 22, 1977—The ''Karaj Road Incident'': army rangers and SAVAK commandos break up Tehran holiday gathering at home of Darioush Forouhar, moderate middle class leader, injuring 300.

December, 1977—Carter visits Iran; toasts Shah on New Year's Eve: "Your view of human rights and mine are the same."

December 31, 1977—U.S. Department of Defense quarterly report to Congress notes 7,674 Americans in Iran on military contracts, including work with more than thirty para-military organizations. Corporations with military contracts include Bell International, Hughes Aircraft, Computer Sciences Corp., Harsco, TRW, Rockwell International, GTE, Lockheed, and Harris Corp.

January 7, 1978—Ayatollah Khomeini attacked in Tehran newspaper.

January 8, 1978—Islamic clergy stage massive protest in Qom. Police open fire on unarmed demonstrators, killing dozens. Beginning of forty-day cycles of mourning, demonstrations, killings by police and army, then mourning again. Cycles will continue until return of Khomeini, who is now focus of opposition.

February 17, 1978—Religious leaders call for business shutdowns to mourn Qom deaths. Demonstration in Tabriz interrupted by Iranian army tanks; scores killed. Demonstrations in other cities.

Spring, 1978—Demonstrations continue. Army and police continue heavy repression. SAVAK steps up activity. Police kill two Shi'ite clergy at home of Ayatollah Shariat-Madari as he looks on. People outraged at violation of sanctity of religious leader's home.

August 20, 1978—400 people die in movie theatre fire in Abadan. SAVAK suspected.

August 27, 1978—Sharif-Emami becomes prime minister, tries to pacify opposition.

September 4, 1978—Millions of demonstrators march in every major Iranian city.

September 7, 1978—Martial law declared in Tehran and eleven other cities.

September 8, 1978—"17th of Shahrivar—Black Friday": Religious leaders and National Front ask people to stay home. Hundreds of thousands of demonstrators in streets of Tehran. Troops open fire on unarmed demonstrators in Jaleh Square, killing more than 3,000, including 700 women.

September 9, 1978—Carter telephones Shah, reaffirms support.

October 6, 1978—Khomeini expelled from Iraq, goes to Paris;

renews personal contact with Abolhassan Bani-Sadr and Sadegh Ghotbzadeh.

October 31, 1978—Oil workers totally shut down oil industry. Carter meets with Crown Prince Reza, a student at Williams College (the alma mater of both former CIA Director and former Ambassador to Iran Richard Helms and Spiro Agnew's daughter), and declares that "our friendship and our alliance with Iran is one of the most important bases on which our entire policy depends."

November 1, 1978—Hundreds of thousands march in Tehran to commemorate 16th anniversary of Khomeini's exile.

November 5, 1978—Strikes spread through country. Prime Minister Sharif-Emami resigns.

November 6, 1978—Shah appoints military government led by General Azhari. State Department forms working group on Iran, supports Shah's move.

November 8, 1978—State Department confirms that U.S. is supplying Iran with new riot control equipment—tear gas, shields, helmets, batons.

November 14, 1978—Oil workers return to work in response to government threats; begin work slowdown in Ahwaz.

November 19, 1978—Responding to Soviet Premier Brezhnev's warning that U.S. must not interfere militarily in Iranian affairs, Secretary of State Vance affirms that "the U.S. does not intend to interfere in the affairs of any other country," and claims that "reports to the contrary are totally without foundation"

November 28, 1978—Government bans on all processions in any form during holy month of Muharram, vowing to "mercilessly" quell any protests.

November 29, 1978—Wildcat strikes disrupt economy.

December 1-3, 1978—Iranians defy ban on demonstrations. Army kills more than 700.

December 5, 1978—Oil strike renewed.

December 6, 1978—National Front leader Karim Sanjabi is released from prison.

December 10, 1978—Millions of Iranians demonstrate in all major cities.

December 15, 1978—Ayatollah Khomeini calls for national day of mourning and general strike; asks armed forces not to fire on demonstrators.

December 18, 1978—Army insubordination takes place during demonstrations in Tabriz.

December 26, 1978—Oil exports cease.

December 27, 1978—Fuel rationing begins in Iran. State Department spokesperson says that Shah "has an important role to play in moving through a transitional period to a more stable political system."

December 29, 1978—U.S. orders naval task force, including aircraft carrier Constellation with 80-90 fighter planes to leave Philippines and proceed to South China Sea, for possible future action in Persian Gulf. Shah asks National Front Leader Shapur Bakhtiar to form a civilian government.

December 31, 1978—General Azhari resigns. U.S. Embassy advises all Americans to leave Iran.

January 1, 1979—Ayatoallah Khomeini declares willingness to work with U.S. after departure of Shah "if the United States stops interfering in our affairs and respects our nation."

January 3, 1979—White House dispatches Air Force General Robert E. Huyser to Iran with two purposes: to neutralize Iranian military support of Shah and transfer it to Bakhtiar, and to develop detailed plans with senior military leaders for an American-backed coup attempt should the Bakhtiar government fall. Bakhtiar states that his new government would not sell oil to South Africa or Israel, or police the Persian Gulf, but drops demand that Shah leave country.

January 5, 1979—National Front attacks Bakhtiar for attempting to form government under the Shah. Khomeini directs some oil workers to return to work, producing enough for domestic consumption.

January 8, 1979—Ambassador Sullivan receives instructions from Carter advising Shah to leave the country.

January 9, 1979—U.S. sends three more warships into Indian ocean.

January 11, 1979—Secretary of State Vance says that "The decisions on Iran's future must be made by Iranians themselves. No outside government should seek to interfere." Khomeini condemns government of Bakhtiar, notes possibility of good relations with U.S. if it would stop supporting Shah.

January 13, 1979—Khomeini, from Paris, announces creation in Iran of a Provisional Revolutionary Council to replace present "illegal" government. Council would set up provisional government to oversee elections to an assembly which would write constitution.

January 16, 1979—Shah secretly flies out of Iran for "vacation" in Egypt. Between $2-4 billion transferred to royal family's accounts outside of Iran during last two years.

January 18, 1979—Soldiers open fire on anti-Bakhtiar demonstrations in Ahwaz; Khomeini urges continued demonstrations but asks people to preserve public order and win support of armed forces.

January 25, 1979—Carter agrees to Bakhtiar's request for emergency shipment of 200,000 barrels of diesel fuel and gasoline from U.S. to Iran.

January 30, 1979—Iranian government announces Khomeini free to return to Iran.

February 1, 1979—Khomeini returns to Iran, welcomed by millions of Iranians.

February 5, 1979—Khomeini appoints Mehdi Bazargan as prime minister.

February 10, 1979—State Department official inside the White House calls Ambassador Sullivan at U.S. Embassy in Tehran to ask whether coup attempt can be made operational. Sullivan says no, noting that much of the Iranian military has deserted. Official asks for second opinion from General Philip Gast, head of American military operations in Iran. Sullivan says Gast is under siege at Iranian military headquarters in Tehran and cannot be reached.

February 11, 1979—Bakhtiar resigns after army withdraws support; troops withdraw from Tehran.

February 14, 1979—Iranians storm U.S. Embassy. All personnel subsequently released.

February 15, 1979—Four of Shah's generals and SAVAK chief Nematollah Nassiri executed.

March 2, 1979—Pentagon officials admit that secret technical and maintenance manuals for F-14 jet fighters and for the Phoenix missile may have been compromised in Iran.

March 7, 1979—People's Revolutionary Councils set up in many cities to facilitate communications between people and government.

March 8-12, 1979—Several thousand women in Tehran protest against Khomeini's interpretation of required Islamic dress for women; they end demonstrations when they suspect anti-revolutionary forces are using them to split the revolution.

March 31, 1979—Voting begins on national referendum to establish Islamic republic.

April 18-20, 1979—Ayatollah Taleghani airs political differences with Khomeini; then reconciles.

May 1, 1979—Ayatollah Morteza Motahheri, important Revolutionary Council member and ideologue, assassinated by guerillas.

June 9, 1979—Iranian government nationalizes banks.

July 6, 1979—Bazargan announces nationalization of most of Iran's large-scale industries.

July 10, 1979—Khomeini declares amnesty for all people "who committed offenses under past regimes" except those involved in murder or torture. Fewer than 600 people executed by special tribunals (compared with upwards of 20,000 killed by SAVAK under the Shah.)

August 28, 1979—Ayatollah Taleghani and Kurdish rebels agree on ceasefire accords. Minority uprisings reported in U.S. press all through summer.

September 10, 1979—Taleghani dies in sleep; mourned for three days.

September/October, 1979—Henry Kissinger and David Rockefeller reportedly push for former Shah's admission to U.S.

October 19, 1979—U.S. informs Iranian government that it will admit former Shah to U.S. temporarily for medical purposes.

October 20, 1979—Bazargan warns U.S. Charge d'Affairs H. Bruce Laingen that admission of former Shah to U.S. would result in problems for Americans in Tehran.

October 22, 1979—Former Shah flies to New York.

October 26—November 1, 1979—Bazargan government makes four separate complaints concerning former Shah's entry to U.S.

November 4, 1979—Moslem students storm U.S. Embassy, seizing 90 hostages, 63 of them American, and documents concerning U.S. intelligence operations in Iran. (All black and female hostages released two weeks later.)

November 6, 1979—Barzagan government resigns.

November 11, 1979—Abolhassan Bani-Sadr appointed to direct foreign policy, calls for return of Shah and his wealth to people of Iran.

November 12, 1979—Carter orders freeze of Iranian assets in U.S. and suspension of U.S. imports from Iran.

November 28, 1979—Bani-Sadr dismissed as acting Foreign Minister, replaced by Sadegh Ghotbzadeh.

November 29, 1979—Mexican government announces it will not allow Shah to return.

December 1, 1979—Senate Foreign Relations Committee Chairman Frank Church suggests Shah be provided refuge in South Africa.

December 4, 1979—New Islamic constitution adopted.

December 7, 1979—Former Shah charges U.S. aided in his overthrow by sending General Huyser to Iran in January to neutralize Iranian Army and protect American interests, contrary to Secretary of State Vance's statement to Brezhnev.

December 15, 1979—International Court of Justice orders Iran to release hostages. Former Shah arrives in Panama.

December 18, 1979—Carter seeks new naval and air facilities in Somalia, Oman, and Kenya.

December, 1979—January, 1980—Soviet troops sent to Afghanistan, replacing pro-Soviet regime of President Hafizullah Amin with pro-Soviet President Babrak Karmal.

January 25, 1980—Bani-Sadr overwhelmingly elected first President of Iran, taking 75 % of vote. Seems to favor early release of hostages.

January 30, 1980—Canadians assist escape of six Americans from Tehran, upsetting negotiations on hostages.

February 6-15, 1980—Committee for an American-Iranian Crisis Resolution delegation of 49 Americans engage in "intensive dialogue" with the students holding the Embassy and government spokespeople in Iran.

February 11, 1980—First Anniversary of the revolution.

March 1, 1980—United Nations commission investigating crimes of former Shah arrives in Iran, asking to see hostages. Revolutionary Council balks, asking whether hostages are "witnesses." Commission returns to New York several days later.

March 14, 1980—First election for National Assembly. Islamic Republican Party, with strong fundamentalist leanings, wins plurality.

March 23, 1980—Shah flies to Egypt.

April 7, 1980—Carter institutes trade embargo against Iran and breaks off diplomatic relations; not strongly supported by Western European allies or Japan.

April 13, 1980—Carter threatens military action for first time.

April 20, 1980—*New York Times* reporters confirm White House involvement in assessing possibilities of American-backed military coup attempt of February 10, 1979, and Ambassador Sullivan's direct involvement, from the Embassy itself, in assessing such possibilities.

April 22, 1980—Common Market nations, under U.S. pressure, agree to apply full economic sanctions against Iran on May 17th unless decisive progress is made to free hostages. Interviews with officials indicate that move is hoped to head off military action by U.S.

April 23, 1980—Iran announces new trade accords with Soviet Union, Romania, and East Germany.

April 24-25, 1980—U.S. military incursion into Iran, purportedly an attempt to rescue hostages, fails. Eight American servicemen die.

April 28, 1980—U.S. Secretary of State Cyrus Vance resigns in disagreement over rescue mission in Iran.

May 9, 1980—Second round of elections for new Iranian Parliament.

May 18, 1980—Common Market nations refuse to apply meaningful sanctions against Iran.

May 24, 1980—International Court of Justice orders Iran to release hostages.

May 28, 1980—Iranian Parliament opens.

June 2-5, 1980—Sixty countries represented at Conference on U.S. Intervention in Iran held in Tehran, attended by ten Americans, including former U.S. Attorney General Ramsey Clark; Harvard Nobel Prize winning biologist George Wald, and Women's International League for Peace and Freedom International President Kay Camp.

July 10, 1980—Coup attempt, led by Iranian Air Force officers said to be backers of former Prime Minister Bakhtiar, foiled.

July 27, 1980—Former Shah dies in Egypt; funeral attended by Richard Nixon. Praised by Ronald Reagan as a "loyal and valued friend" whose passing "reminds us of the value of remaining true to our friends."

August 9, 1980—Mohammad Ali Rajaie nominated as Prime Minister, approved shortly thereafter.

August 15, 1980—Columnist Jack Anderson reveals Carter Administration consideration of major U.S. military intervention in Iran before the Presidential elections.

September 17, 1980—Iranian *Majlis* agrees to set up a special committee for consideration of next steps in solving the hostage issue.

September 22, 1980—After several months of border skirmishes, large-scale military conflict breaks out between Iraq and Iran. Oil refineries bombed in both nations.

Iran and the West:
A Century of Subjugation

Eqbal Ahmad

As this article is being prepared for publication, a period of more than three months has passed since American hostages were taken in Iran. By the time it is read, developments now occurring may have brought about the release of the hostages. The things I have to say will not be greatly affected by such an event. They are things that have needed saying during all this time and that have in fact been said in one form or another, but that have not had a real hearing. In my judgment, they will remain relevant after the immediate crisis has passed.

This has been a crisis with no real or substantive context. In all this time, basic facts about Iran have remained forgotten. The historic sorrows and anguish of the Iranian people have largely gone unmentioned. Their history, even the history of your own relationship with them, has been neglected. And that is why we have not understood how to solve the problem. One is that the crisis between Iran and the United States is rooted in the historical experience of the Iranians as a people, and particularly in the historical experience of the Iranian people with the United States Government and corporations. I shall go into some detail on that subject. My second proposition is that the crisis has not been resolved as quickly as it might because there exist extraordinary divergences and unities between Iran and the United States.

Let's begin with the second. A point of unity between Iran and the United States is that, on the question of the hostages, the Iranian people seem quite united in feeling that they must not give up the hostages until they can bring the Shah to justice and redeem the assets that he has stolen from Iran. There is an equal degree of unity in the United States that you do not wish to negotiate with the Iranians on the question of the Shah or the assets that the Shah has

This essay first appeared in *Christianity and Crisis*, March 3, 1980, and is reprinted by permission. Copyright 1980, Christianity and Crisis, Inc.

stolen while the hostages are being held in violation of international law.

Beyond this antagonistic similarity there are differences. One very major difference is that since the fall of the Shah Iran has had no effective government: The apparatus of the state has fallen apart. There is a center of legitimacy and authority in Ayatollah Khomeini, who sits 60 miles down in the city of Qum; there are eight or nine centers of ambition that converge on Ayatollah Khomeini. Iran today is a country in which national minorities, poor people, middle class people, peasants, workers, students, Kurds, Azarbeidjianis, Turkomen, Baluchis—i.e., all whose rights were suppressed for 60 years—have found a moment in which they can express themselves and make their demands. This is a revolutionary situation marked by an unprecedented mobilization of the Iranian masses who are expressing long suppressed demands in a political milieu which has an almost non-existent government, one center of authority and multiple centers of ambition.

Contrast that with the United States: As I see it, and as many Iranians see it, the United States doesn't have one but three governments at the same time. For foreigners, it is very difficult to figure out which one is actually ruling at a given time, who is really making crucial decisions such as that of admitting the Shah to America.

The first government is, obviously, the elected constitutional government of the United States which, until the last day of the Shah's fall, supported that tyrant. The Iranians felt the U.S. was responsible even in 1978 for fully supporting the Shah's killing of up to 35-40,000 people in Iran; unarmed, nonviolent protesters gunned down in cold blood while President Carter openly supported the Shah in word and deed.

But after the fall of the Shah on February 12, 1979, it was this same government that judged that admitting the Shah of Iran into the U.S. would further inflame the aroused Iranian public and therefore should be avoided. They stuck to that decision for nine months, until October 22, 1979. During these nine months we know that the Carter government was subject to pressures from the other governments—what we might call the shadow and the invisible governments of the United States.

A Clear Warning

Sometime in July, those pressures were so strong that the State Department asked Bruce Laingen, the U.S. *charge d'affaires* in Tehran, what he thought would happen if the Shah were admitted to the United States on medical grounds. On August 2 Bruce Laingen replied, saying that if the Shah were admitted to the United States, even for medical reasons, it would inflame the Iranian population, and have unforeseen consequences; most probably the government of Dr. Mehdi Bazargan would fall, and it might even lead to the takeover of our embassy. So Laingen had reported. I have read that document and examined its authenticity. When asked, the State Department did not deny its authenticity.

Then, sometime in August, the State Department and the White House are reported to have charged the CIA to make a special report on what would happen if the Shah came. The CIA and defense Intelligence confirmed Bruce Laingen's judgment that it would anger the population in Iran and could produce unforeseen consequences in the Persian Gulf, an area of prime concern to the United States. Despite that, the Shah of Iran was admitted to the United States of America on October 22, 1979.

Now I draw your attention to the second government. Some reports have appeared about the shadow government. Calling it a lobby is an understatement. Some nine months earlier I.F. Stone had warned in *The New York Review of Books* (Feb. 22, 1979) that a Shah lobby was likely to emerge, consisting of his "formidable friends. ''Revolutionary Iran, he predicted, would fight the Pahlavi lobby and the U.S. would again be embroiled with Iran. ''What if Iran demands the Shah's return for trial on charges of plundering the country...for untold tortures and deaths at the hands of the SAVAK?'' Stone asked with alarm. This was the sage's warning of nearly a year ago: ''We should have learned by now, but haven't, to keep out of Iran's domestic politics, and we may get a parallel lesson soon in keeping Iran's politics out of ours.''

The Shah lobby may yet prove more powerful than the China lobby of the 1950's. Already it is performing an analogous function: One helped produce the cold war and legitimize the warfar · economy; the other is trying to restore the cold war, rid America ot what they call the Viet Nam Syndrome (i.e., a non-interventionist public opinion), accelerate the arms race, augment global militarism, multiply ''covert'' interventions.

We know that sometime in August or so, the lobby consisting of the leading banks, the arms industry, the oil trusts and construction cartels, and of such individual eminences as Mr. Kissinger, Mr. Connally and the Rockefeller family, was joined by J.J. McCloy, the doyen of America's foreign policy establishment. It is important to note here a fact unreported by the U.S. media—that well before the Shah was admitted here, U.S. corporations and agencies conducted a sustained economic war against Iran. (See Eric Rouleau's article in the Manchester *Guardian*, Dec. 2, 1979. Rouleau is a senior reporter for *Le Monde* of Paris and is the West's most respected journalistic expert on the Middle East.)

I also assume that the third government of the United States must have tipped the balance in favor of the shadow government. This third government I am referring to is the invisible government, the government of intelligence operatives: part of the CIA, defense intelligence, national security agencies and so on.

What happened when the Shah came to New York? Most people have forgotten, and the media do not remind us. For 13 long days the Iranians did everything that everybody has said they ought to have done; peacefully, nonviolently and legally they protested the admission of the Shah and demanded that he be returned to Iran, or at least expelled from the U.S. Their protests included two demonstrations that Khomeini called in Iran, one of which brought out some three and a half million people. These protests also included Iranian students' holding the Statue of Liberty for three days; other demonstrations coast to coast; the closure of Washington, D.C. of the Iranian Embassy for a day.

No one responded to these peaceful protests or to diplomatic representations. Then the hostages were taken, and America reacted with righteous outrage.

The simple point I am making is that, in a world in which people are finding it easier to organize, they are willing ultimately to take the last step when everything else fails. Neither in the developed countries nor in the underdeveloped countries have we created the mechanism, the will and the capacity to respond to the peaceful, legitimate, rightful demands of people when they are properly, politically and nonviolently made. As long as we do not develop that, I don't think we have the right to one-sidedly invoke such things as international law.

The Iranian taking of hostages is disliked by every third world *government*, as the vote in the United Nations indicates. But I tell you, they are liked by the *people* of the third world for one bad reason: They feel some pride that at least this one time the weak, the poor, the oppressed have openly violated international law, which they see as a law of the powerful for use against the weak. We of the third world ask: When the CIA went to destabilize the constitutionally elected government of Allende in Chile through people who were actually carrying diplomatic passports and diplomatic immunity, or when they destabilized the constitutional government of Mohammed Mossadegh, was that in accordance with international law? What's big about this Iran affair is that it's a weak, poor, underdeveloped country that has now violated the law.

The Power of Memory

These are not insignificant matters, and yet we are still at the periphery. It remains to ask: Why did the Iranians act as they did, and why are they still behaving the way they are behaving? What could they fear from an ailing former monarch coming to a New York hospital?

The most important reason probably is their historical experience. The battle that you saw being fought in Iran against the Shah in 1978-79 was the seventh or the eighth time in 100 years that that same battle has been fought between the Iranian national movement on the one hand and the Iranian monarchy on the other with foreign corporations and governments allied to it.

The first time a national coalition emerged in Iran was in 1872. It was the movement against the Reuter's Concession. The ruling monarch of Iran had given Baron Julius du Reuter, who later founded the news agency, a 50-year monopoly on all the mining and communication resources of Iran. A coalition consisting of religious, middle-class intelligentsia leaders, and Bazaaris emerged to protest and got the concessions canceled. They won the battle against a foreign corporation's control of Iran; but they did not win the war. Their victory ended neither the exploitative foreign interests in Iran nor the royal family's connections with them.

So the movement returned in 1895, against the Tobacco Concessions granted to a Major Talbot. This uprising lasted for 18 months. It too succeeded; the concessions to Major Talbot were canceled. Yet, that was followed by the expansion of British interests and interventionary role in Iran. The nationalists next came back in 1905, four years after the D'Arcy Concessions which opened Iran's oil resources to the West. This time, they said, we must break down the power of the monarch, as well as the power of the foreign corporations; without attacking both we shall never win. That was the constitutionalist movement which produced Iran's first modern constitution in 1906. A constitutional government was formed and it ruled until 1911 when Czarist Russia and Britain intervened again to overthrow the constitutional government.

Seven years later, in 1919, the nationalist forces returned once more, when Lord Curzon wished to impose the Anglo-Persian Treaty which would have turned Iran into a virtual colony of Britain. They fought against the treaty and defeated it. But again a battle was won, a war was lost. For two years later, in 1921, the British produced a coup d' etat, led by a sergeant-turned-colonel named Mohammed Reza Khan. In 1923, the dictator Reza Khan declared himself monarch and established the Pahlevi dynasty. He was the father of the present ex-Shah.

Reza Khan's rule saw the beginning of centralization of power in Iran; the creation of a massive police force, a centralized bureaucracy, and a modern standing army. This man was called the great modernizer by the Western press. In fact, Oriental despotism came to Iran, as to many other third world countries, in the form of Westernization and modernization under the aegis of foreign domination.

The nationalists came back against Reza Khan in 1940-41. It was an easy fight this time; the British cooperated with the nationalists because Reza Khan was suspected of cozying up to Adolph Hitler. This time Reza Khan was exiled to South Africa. But, instead of giving the nationalists their power, the British maintained a regency while the son grew up under colonial tutelage. And that's how we got the present Shah.

The nationalist movement reasserted itself in 1950 and, after some struggle, forced new elections under the 1906 constitution, elected the government of Dr. Mossadegh, cut down the absolute powers of the Shah and nationalized the oil resources of Iran. Then, in 1953, the CIA carried out the coup against Mossadegh, and Allen Dulles, then the director of the CIA, personally flew back with the Shah of Iran from Rome to Tehran.

For the Iranian people, a nightmare began that lasted some 26 years. Between 1953 and 1973, about 125,000 Iranians are believed to have died under torture or by execution. And during the uprising in 1978, an estimated 30-40,000 were killed. (Iranians believe it was 150,000 or more, but God only knows.) Iran's best poets died under torture. Iran's finest writers lived in prisons. Iran's wealth was looted, transferred and spent in the West.

Ground for Fear

It the people of the United States understood this history, they would be less ready to dismiss the Iranian revolutionaries as emotional fanatics. A people who won six battles in a century at heavy cost to themselves, each time to lose the war to foreign intervention, were not going to believe in 1979 that the Shah of Iran had been flown from Mexico to a hospital in New York City only to be treated by two Canadian doctors. The United States, after all, is not Mexico. It is the country which in 1953 had restored the Shah to power, trained and equipped his dreaded secret police, built his armies, chosen him to be its gendarme in the Persian Gulf, sold him $19 billion worth of weapons and supported his repressions until the last murderous days of his reign. Remember also that this is the Shah who has powerful friends in the United States, who has not yet abdicated his throne. In principle, he is still on vacation—as he was in 1953.

I have gone into this much detail to help Americans realize that abroad you are often dealing with very ancient peoples, and they are burdened as much by history as by poverty and oppression. By contrast, you are a young people, a newly settled people. Yours has been a history of success, of victories and expansion. The Indians, the blacks, the Chicanos, the Filipinos, the Vietnamese, the Laotians and the Cambodians, among others, can tell you that you have been at the giving end of pain.

Furthermore, powerful interests in America suppress your history, the memories of whatever experience you have had with oppression and resistance. For example, on May Day, a historic event of enormous social significance is commemorated in every country of the world except the United States, where the Chicago Haymarket killings happened. Thus, also the Viet Nam War and the anti-war movements are now being subjected to cold-war revisionism, hegemonious historiography.

The result of all this is that the political culture of America lacks a sense of the tragic, the capacity to understand the anguish of a Ho Chi Minh, the sorrows of a Khomeini or the dogged determination of displaced Palestinians. In order to understand a people and their political reflexes, it is important always to inquire about their historical experience, for the past shapes our present, informs our future. The Iranians know that they have suffered greatly from foreign intervention, and the war does not end when they win a battle. Now, if you ask yourself why did the U.S. admit the Shah, what were the forces at work here, you will probably discover a number of things.

First, you will discover that in the process of 30 or 35 years of sustaining a corrupt, repressive regime, you also corrupt yourself. A culture of corruption is established. Between the ex-Shah and the elite of this country, there exists a relationship that, if it were to become known to the world, would produce anywhere from six to twelve Watergates. It gave the Shah's extended ''family''—which had enough time to spirit away documents—a great deal of power. But that is only one part of the story.

The second thing to remember is that the lowest estimate of the

Shah's wealth, stolen from Iran, is now $2.5 billion; the highest estimate is about $25 billion. Let's take the lowest—that puts the Shah at par with the declared assets of the Rockefeller family. That is a great deal of money, and therefore a lot of power. Reza Shah is not a helpless man, a politically dead duck running around for cancer treatment. He and his associates have both material resources and much information implicating the corporate and political biggies of America and Western Europe; hence, he still wields great power.

The Uselessness of Doctrine

Then there is a third interest, which is probably the most powerful. After information, after money, there is something else—militarism, which on a global scale, involves the marriage of power with money.

At the end of the 60's the biggest single problem that the American foreign policy establishment faced was that in the United States there was no longer any public consensus for the doctrine of limited wars—i.e., for the doctrine of intervention. Without intervention, you can't have global militarism. Without global militarism, you can't have the military-industrial complex. The doctrine of limited wars was basic to American interventions of the post-World War II period. Between 1948 and 1970, the year of the Cambodian intervention, the United States intervened on an average of once every 14 months in a third world country against a government or a movement of which it did not approve—from Guatemala, Nicaragua and the Dominican Republic to Lebanon, the Congo, Indonesia and Iran. All these interventions were based on the doctrine of limited wars.

These wars were obviously limited only in their consequences for the intervening power, not in their consequences for those who had been invaded. As in Guatemala or the Dominican Republic, the U.S. intervention against Dr. Mossadegh's government was limited. It cost no American lives, and it gained American companies a full 40 per cent share of Iranian oil where they previously had none. (The five American majors to join the Iranian oil consortium after the CIA coup were Exxon, Gulf, Mobil, Texaco, and Standard of California.)

But the costs were enormous to the Iranian people, who were held hostage to the Shah and his foreign benefactors for two and a half decades. Today, the Iranian revolutionaries, who are deeply religious and somewhat confessionary in character, demand an accounting of the costs and a few sincere gestures of expiation from

America. Unfortunately, the hostages, the symbols and representatives of American power in Iran, have become the instruments of inducing America to come to terms with its Iranian past.

"Limited" wars have also been called "invisible" wars. Invisible to whom? Obviously to you, the American public. When Senator Mike Mansfield held hearings on Laos in 1969 it was revealed that between 1956 and 1968 the U.S. Government had dropped on Laos the equivalent of all the TNT used in World War II. A secret army no less than 50,000 strong, aided by a secret air force, had been in existence. Yet, the American taxpayers who were footing the bill for the men and guns, the bombings and killings, did not know about it for years. During the Nixon Administration, the pattern was repeated with the secret bombings of Cambodia, and the CIA and naval intelligence services' violent, historically momentous war—and it was nothing less than that—on the constitutional government of Salvador Allende.

These wars were not invisible to the people attacked. The Laotians and Cambodians saw the planes, died from the bombs, were burned by the napalm. The Chileans knew who stood behind the destruction of their dreams of achieving justice with democracy. These wars were limited only in terms of their impact on the aggressor, they were invisible only to the American people.

Then the United States experienced the full results of Viet Nam, and the doctrine of limited wars came apart. While advocating an augmentation of U.S. "limited war" capability, Henry Kissinger had written in 1958 that, "Every war in which we have engaged in the Western Hemisphere was a limited war." And he called them "*productive*."

No one will ever make that statement about Viet Nam. What was supposed to be a "limited war"—in terms of its consequences for the interventionist power—cost more than a quarter million American casualties, an estimated $200 billion, an economic recession and a divided nation. And the "invisible war" became manifest to the entire world. The "forgotten" war—so well remembered by its victims—imposed itself upon the consciousness of the American people. With their consciences aroused, nuns and priests went to jail; the Rev. William Coffin went on trial with Dr. Spock and Mark Raskin; young blue-eyed blond-haired kids from Yale, Princeton, Harvard—the cream of the crop—burned their draft cards and went singing into prison. The American consensus for a forward foreign policy came to an end.

An exponent of limited wars—wars not of conquest nor of defense as he would say but of conservation—Kissinger understood the meaning of Viet Nam. In 1968, shortly before coming to power, he had written: "Whatever the outcome of the war in Viet Nam, it is clear that is has greatly diminished the American willingness to become involved in this form of warfare elsewhere. *Its utility* as a precedent has therefore been importantly undermined."

A Chance for Change

At this point, the American policy toward the third world came to a crossroads. The interventionist, ideologically conservative policies of the past had come into question; U.S. support for third world dictators such as Diem, Trujillo and Batista had proved unproductive; its economy required and public opinion favored a policy of reconciliation, restitution and development in the third world including Viet Nam, Cuba, Iran, Pakistan, Chile and Cuba. In other words, the U.S. had the choice between taking a new road more in tune with the needs of the time or treading the old beaten path.

Unfortunately for all of us, those who wielded real power chose to walk the old way but in different shoes. Their decision was to continue the interventionist, militarist policy but have someone else bear the burden. The cruder manifestations of this new-old approach were the destablization, in cooperation with Brazil, of President Allende's government, the callous reneging on the Paris Peace Agreement's provisions for the reconstruction of Viet Nam, and the encouragement given to the South African invasion of Angola. At first, they called the new policy Vietnamization, then the Nixon Doctrine.

President Carter was essentially a prisoner of the choices made by Kissinger and Nixon, and now he is having to gather the bitter harvest he inherited. In the process of doing so, he is falling into deeper quagmire. Carter's style is, of course, different from Nixon's. His rhetoric of human rights is also distinguishable from Nixon's "structure of peace." But President Carter in effect embraced the Nixon Doctrine. And the militarily bloated Shah, like the juntas in Brazil and Indonesia or Marcos in the Philippines, had come with the Kissinger-Nixon baggage.

The fall of the Shah marked the total collapse of the Nixon Doctrine in the region of primary American strategic concentration. With the collapse of the Shah went one of the last pillars of Kissinger's structure of peace. With no shoes of his own to stand in, President Carter appears to have decided now to look for the worn-out shoes of John Foster Dulles' brand. In the process, the United

States will probably end up with the Kissinger-Nixon shoe on one foot and the Dulles boot on the other. Let me explain.

The much heralded but rarely explained global design of Henry Kissinger contained three fundamental features. These were (a) *detente* as a policy of antagonistic collaboration between the U.S. and the U.S.S.R.; (b) Sino-American *entente* as a major American card in the Washington-Moscow poker game; and (c) the Nixon Doctrine which was a "low-profile, low-cost" strategy designed to overcome domestic constraints against United States interventions in the third world while attempting to exploit the expanding wealth of resource-rich allies and clients like Iran and Indonesia. For my purposes here, it is most relevant to examine the Nixon Doctrine, the consequences of its collapse and the Carter Administration's continued adherence to it.

The doctrine entailed (a) the promotion of regional constellations of pro-American power in strategically important areas of the world; (b) the reorganization of U.S. armed forces, as Admiral Zumwalt put it, into "high-technology capital-intensive services... to support the indigenous armies of threatened allies"; and (c) a lowering of the existing threshold on the use of nuclear weapons. As Kissinger explained the doctrine, "The United States is no longer in a position to operate programs globally. Regional groupings by the United States will have to take over the major responsibility for their immediate areas...." Its aim was to minimize the deployment of American "boys" by making maximum use of surrogates and mercenaries and of advanced military technology. Its tactical premises were rehearsed in the program of "Vietnamization" and the invasion of Cambodia. Its global application witnessed the promotion of countries like Brazil, Iran, Israel, Greece, Turkey, Portugal, Indonesia and South Africa as regional powers.

The centerpiece of the Nixon Doctrine emerged in the area bounded by the Mediterranean and Indian Oceans. There, Kissinger and Nixon assiduously constructed a new constellation of pro-American power consisting of Turkey, Greece, Israel, Iran, Portugal, Zaire, South Africa; some weaker client states such as Ethiopia, Morocco, Jordan and Pakistan belonged in it as secondary surrogates.

Iran on the eastern flank of the oil belt, Israel on the west, were assigned the role of chief marshals. Thus, in its first five years, the Nixon Administration provided Israel with some 20 times more military aid than the total of all U.S. administrations in the previous 22 years of Israel's existence. And Nixon began the untrammelled sales of weapons to the Shah, so that Iran's arms expenditure soared from some $10 million in 1950 to $5 billion in fiscal 1974. Thus, the self-styled King of Kings, Light of the Aryans, displaced West Germany, by a large margin, as the biggest buyer of American arms, and Israel became the largest benefactor in history of a U.S. military aid program.

Farther toward the Indian Ocean and the South Atlantic, Kissinger's Southern Strategy stretched out to include colonial Portugal, with which Washington entered in 1970 the defense agreement of the Azores, Zaire and, hopefully, South Africa with which Kissinger had envisaged more intimate ties, as the leaked National Security Memorandum 39 and NATO's negotiations over Simonstown naval base revealed.

This "design" had an impressive conceptual coherence. It was a logical, geopolitical scheme based on classical balance-of-power precepts. But beneath the much publicized brilliance of Kissinger's construction, there were pitfalls which a managerial mind could not perceive. A conservative bureaucratic mind, however brilliant, is necessarily closed to the future.

The Basic Flaw

This policy suffered from the same fundamental defect which contributed to U.S. failures in Southeast Asia, and to the early demise of the Baghdad Pact in the Middle East: It ran counter to the ongoing force of history, underestimated the power of emerging social forces, sought stability in an era of change and looked for client nations in a century of national liberation. Its future was linked to the dying status quo of injustice; its logic led dialectically to symbiosis with tyranny. Fascist Portugal, militarist Greece, monarchical Iran and Ethiopia and expansionist Israel: In the second half of the 20th century, these were falling dominoes.

By mid-1974, Nixon's structure of peace had nearly collapsed in the area of its greatest concentration. The Arab-Israeli War of October 1973 proved Israel's power to be too derivative to be absolutely dependable. Far from acting as a Middle Eastern Sparta in the service of North Atlantic Rome, Israel had to be rescued by the largest arms airlift of American history.

More importantly, the October War and the Arab oil boycott revealed an obvious flaw in Kissinger's design—that its linkage with America's Arab allies was extremely weak. Even Saudi Arabia, Washington's closest friend, was imperfectly integrated in the "regional grouping." Thus, the primary objects of this policy were inhibited—because of their problem with Israel—from participating in it. Kissinger's response to this discovery was typically managerial—a step-by-step approach which, instead of seeking a comprehensive settlement of the Arab-Israeli conflict, sought to pry Egypt out of its Arab commitment.

By mid-1974, as the pro-U.S. regimes in Portugal, Ethiopia and Greece fell; as, contrary to the assumptions of National Security Memorandum 39, the national liberation movements of Angola, Mozambique and Guinea-Bissau rose to power; and as Turkey, fighting with Greece over Cyprus, became alienated from Washington, the backbone of Kissinger's structured peace—already weakened by the Arab-Israeli War—broke. The Shah stood nearly alone, perhaps feeling immortal, buying more arms than he could carry, imposing more burdens than Iran could bear.

When he acceded to power, President Carter inherited this obviously discredited policy. Yet—such is the power of vested interests in America and so rooted in the past are its political minds —that the new Administration was unable or unwilling to move away even from the wreckage of its predecessor.

I leave the reader to figure out why. Could it be that it is the interests of the oil lobby and the South African lobby, and not the interests of the American people that shape U.S. policies in this region? Could it be that the corporations, executives and politicians are linked with each other by mutual interests that run counter to popular and national interests?

Whatever the answer, it seems that Carter at first knew better than he actually did. It was thus that after promising an effort toward a comprehensive settlement of the Middle East conflict in Geneva, he moved away from it to continue on Kissinger's favored path. It was thus also that after announcing his commitment to human rights, he chose to spend the first New Year of his Presidency in the company of a notorious tyrant, a monarch whose regime Amnesty International had already described as the world's worst violator of human rights. And there, in the splendor of Tehran's Niavaran Palace, Jimmy Carter toasted the Shah in words which will become memorable for his lack of prescience: "Iran, under the great leadership of the Shah, is an island of stability in one of the most troubled areas of the world. This is a great tribute to you, your Majesty, and to your leadership and to the respect, admiration and love which your people give you."

A year later, the Shah fled Iran, and the collapse of U.S. policy in the region was complete. The choices again were to forge a new policy responsive to the realities of our world, or to try again to pour old wine in new bottles. The current crisis is the product of the second choice.

There was a military dimension to the Nixon Doctrine which, as I said earlier, envisaged a high-technology, capital-intensive force to support "the indigenous armies of threatened allies." Highly mobile, mechanized, managed by computers and manned by all-volunteer soldier-technicians, the New Action Army was designed for rapid deployment, swift assault and fast disengagement. As Admiral Zumwalt said, it was to be an expeditionary force of the last resort; one of several instruments of assuring the "overall framework of order." "Only if the buffer proves insufficient does the great power become involved," Nixon had explained, "and then in terms that make victory more attainable and the enterprise more palatable *to the American public.*"

With minor adjustment of style and rhetoric, President Carter went along with the policy he had inherited. But first Kissinger, then Carter, encountered two problems with the New Action Army. One, they discovered that U.S. public opinion was actively opposed to the deployment of U.S. combat forces in the third world. That lesson was learned most dramatically in Angola in 1975. When the CIA's covert operations against the leftist revolutionary regime in Luanda failed, South Africa invaded Angola in order to unseat the government; the government invited Cuban help and Castro responded. At the time, Kissinger sought to arouse the country to support a strong American response but popular opinion was against it and Congress, returning from a recess, was responsive to the public. And so the Kissingers and Connallys and Northrop and Lockheed bewailed the "loss" of Angola, and blamed it on the American public's infliction with the "Viet Nam Syndrome."

Uses of Provocation

They knew that, in order to sell America even a revised, watered-down interventionist policy, they would have to get rid of the "Viet Nam Syndrome." It was tempting to heat up a bit of the cold war, in a region of perceived national interests to the U.S., to stir up the threatening images of fanatical Moslem mobs wanting to cut off the lifeblood of Western civilization in the strategic straits of Hormuz. I am not suggesting that the Shah was brought here in the specific hope that Iranians would take hostages. But it is evident that people who pushed to bring him here and the Carter Administration which admitted him knew that they were not merely making a humane gesture. They knew that admitting the Shah was a political act which would inflame Iran and create a climate in which there would be a greater legitimacy for an enlargement of U.S. military presence throughout the world, especially in the Middle East and Western Asia.

A second problem the military-industrial complex ran into with the Nixon-Carter Doctrine was that the allies who were supposed to police the region fell apart from internal contradictions, often with a speed too stunning to allow for reaction. If the New Action Army was supposed to support "the indigenous armies of threatened allies," the problem in Ethiopia was that it was the army itself which overthrew Emperor Haile Selassie, and there was no indigenous army for the New Action Army to support.

Similarly, in Iran, the "buffer" fell apart despite U.S. General Huyser's up-to-the-last-minute attempt to keep it together; and only a full-scale American invasion and occupation of Iran could conceivably have kept the Shah on the Peacock Throne for a few more months or years—and that at a cost of perhaps millions of Iranian and thousands of American lives. Yet, it was the alleged "loss" of Ethiopia, Angola and Iran (they have, for complex reasons, kept the rhetoric down on Nicaragua) that gave added impetus to the pressures for a return to the pre-Viet Nam strategy of direct U.S. military presence abroad, an augmented and modernized navy and a new interventionist force—the Rapid Deployment Force.

It is useful to remember that before the hostage crisis began, the defense lobby had already made a successful push toward a Rapid Deployment Force, for the establishment of U.S. military bases in the region (Israel, Egypt, Somalia, Kenya and Oman had already been discussing the matter with the U.S. well before the hostage crisis), for the enlargement of the U.S. naval base in Diego Garcia, for the expansion of the U.S. naval presence in the Persian Gulf and for the creation of a Rapid Deployment Force.

These measures, which President Carter is now legitimizing in an unreal environment created by the confrontation with Iran and the augmentation of Soviet military presence in Afghanistan, had already been discussed and planned when the present Iranian and Afghanistan crises began. It is difficult to argue this in the present climate of cold war revival; but it is our moral and political duty to oppose this manipulation of events in order to militarize the world and the United States.

To take two quick examples, let us ask what good President Carter's plans for military aid to Pakistan can do; and what good the Rapid Deployment Force can do in the Persian Gulf? In Zia ul-Haq of Pakistan, the U.S. is acquiring another Shah without oil. It is hard for me to imagine a regime more unpopular, isolated and shaky than Zia's in Pakistan. The arms he will receive will be used to suppress my own people and jeopardize the security of the nation internally. Carter appears on the verge of making a Cambodia of Pakistan.

And what could the Rapid Deployment Force (RDF) do in the region if it were there today? Let us take three problems the U.S. has there today, and ask if the RDF could help. One, the U.S. has a problem with Israel, for the Israelis are undermining Carter's Camp David initiative for peace in the Middle East by setting up new settlements on the West Bank, etc. Will the RDF be used to push Israel out of the West Bank and Gaza? Obviously not. Two, there are American hostages in Tehran; could the RDF go and rescue them? No one has recommended a military option to free the hostages. In Iran the RDF would have no army to fight, just multitudes to kill—swinging swords in water, said a Pentagon official. Three, Afghanistan; let us note briefly that the Soviet intervention there occurred precisely at the moment when the U.S. had its largest military presence in the Persian Gulf—two aircraft carrier Task Forces with 150 fighter-bomber planes, 590 helicopters and about 40,000 combat troops. Yet, this force served neither as a deterrent nor as a means of rescue.

Given the realities of the world today, there are no military solutions to problems of international relations. As long as we remain focused on the military equation, the solutions will evade us, and we shall remain victims of war, violence and repression. I understand very well that this does not tell Americans what *should* be done; but that may not be a proper role for me. I do think it is right for me to tell Americans that they ought not to act in the world without knowing the effects of their policies on other peoples with differing histories.

Arms and the Shah

Michael T. Klare

Between 1970 and 1978, the Shah of Iran ordered $20 billion worth of arms, ammunition, and other military merchandise from the United States in what one member of Congress has called "the most rapid buildup of military power under peacetime conditions of any nation in the history of the world."

This extraordinary accumulation of war-making capabilities was intended to transform Iran into a major military power and thus fulfill the Shah's ambition of restoring "the Great Persian Empire of the past." American leaders, who cultivated and nourished the Shah's imperial visions, hoped in turn that U.S. arms would make Iran the "guardian" of Western oil supplies in the Persian Gulf area.

U.S. arms sales were also expected to perform other miracles: to wipe out America's trade imbalance; to underwrite the cost of U.S. weapons development; to assure high employment in the aerospace industry, and to accelerate the "modernization" of Iranian society. Never, in fact, have arms transfers played such a central role in U.S. foreign policy as they did in Iran.

But whatever the assumptions of U.S. policymakers, all these arms could not save the Shah once his subjects were determined to overthrow the monarchy. On January 16, 1979, Shah Mohammed Reza Pahlavi, the "King of Kings" and "Light of the Aryans," was forced into permanent exile in the West. While many factors undoubtedly contributed to the downfall of the Shah, the most critical may have been the ill-conceived U.S. arms supply program.

To understand how that program corroded and finally destroyed the Pahlavi Dynasty—and with it, the U.S. policy of converting Iran into the gendarme of the Persian Gulf—we must begin by identifying some of its principal features.

This essay first appeared in *The Progressive*, August, 1979, and is reprinted by permission. Copyright 1979 by The Progressive, Inc.

Volume: Since 1971, Iran has been the world's leading customer for American arms, accounting for 25 per cent of all U.S. arms sales between 1970 and 1978. Since many of the arms were not scheduled for delivery until the early 1980s, however, actual *shipments* to Iran had reached only $10 billion of the $20 billion ordered when the regime fell in January 1979. (The new government of Mehdi Bazargan has, of course, canceled all remaining orders.)

Sophistication: Although Washington originally discouraged sales of high-technology weapons to Iran, in 1972 President Nixon agreed to sell the Shah the most advanced and powerful U.S. munitions. The Shah subsequently ordered a wide array of supersophisticated arms, including the swing-wing F-14 air-superiority fighter, the DD-963 *Spruance*-class missile destroyer, and the Boeing E-3A AWACS radar patrol plane.

Technology transfers: Not only did Iran acquire vast quantities of U.S. arms, but also the technology to *produce* them. Under an ambitious billion-dollar scheme involving many U.S. arms firms, the Shah was determined to create his own modern military-industrial complex by the late 1980s. (These plans, too, were abrogated by the Bazargan regime.)

Military technical assistance: Because the Shah was importing high-technology arms faster than U.S. instructors could train Iranians to maintain and operate them, Iran was forced to hire tens of thousands of foreign technicians—"white-collar mercenaries"—to perform all the necessary back-up functions. By 1978, an estimated 10,000 American support personnel were working on arms-related projects in Iran.

Repression exports: In addition to all the conventional military gear, Washington also supplied vast quantities of police weapons and paramilitary hardware (tear gas, riot sticks, small arms) to Iran. The United States also provided training to Iranian police officials—including officials of SAVAK, the notorious secret police—and advised the military on counterinsurgency operations.

Besides these relatively overt transactions, a number of covert or hidden dimensions to the arms program figured significantly in the U.S.-Iranian relationship. These included bribery and corruption, government mismanagement, and political intrigue, and they combined with the unintended and undesired consequences of the overt transactions to undermine the Shah's position.

Though Iran was considered an important ally of the United States throughout the Cold War period, it was at first no more important than the other garrison states which anchored the U.S. alliance system that extended from Greece to Pakistan and around Asia to Korea. The real turning point in the U.S.-Iranian relationship did not come until December 1967, when then Prime Minister Harold Wilson announced that Britain would terminate its military presence in the Persian Gulf by the end of 1971.

Wilson's announcement caused consternation in Washington: U.S. strategists had always relied on London to serve as the official guardian of Western interests in the vital Gulf region. With London now out of the picture and no apparent successor in sight for the "guardian" role, Washington had to construct its own Persian Gulf strategy.

Wilson's announcement came late in Lyndon Johnson's Presidency, so it was left to the new Administration of Richard Nixon to undertake the necessary policy-formulation effort. Nixon ordered the National Security Council (NSC), then headed by Henry Kissinger, to explore the various policy options open to the United States and recommend a basic policy. Although preoccupied with the Vietnam war, Kissinger apparently gave this project high priority and the resulting document—National Security Council Study Memorandum No., 66 (NSSM-66)—was submitted to the White House on July 12, 1969. After reviewing the recommendations contained in NSSM-66, President Nixon issued a National Security Decision Memorandum, NSDM-92, to govern U.S. policy in the region.

Although NSSM-66 and NSDM-92 were given a high security classification and their contents never made public, we can reconstruct their findings from assorted public sources. First, the NSC would have set forth Washington's basic policy options, which boiled down to three:

Option 1: Stay Out: The United States would continue, as before, to provide military aid to pro-Western governments in the Gulf, but would not assume a direct military role in the area.

Option 2: Move In: U.S. forces would be deployed in the Gulf to perform the "police" functions previously performed by the British.

Option 3: Find a Surrogate: Instead of deploying U.S. forces, Washington would recruit some other power to serve as regional "gendarme" in place of Great Britain.

In attempting to choose among these three options, the NSC would weigh U.S. strategic interests in the area and then calculate the costs of each option. Here again, we can reconstruct the main lines of reasoning.

Although the United States was, at that time, importing less than 3 per cent of its oil supplies from the Gulf, all reliable projections indicated that such imports would have to rise significantly to meet U.S. energy needs in the 1970s and beyond. Furthermore, America's chief allies in Europe and the Far East had already become highly dependent on Middle Eastern oil, which was also used to fuel U.S. Navy forces in the Mediterranean and the Pacific. Any interruption in these supplies would, therefore, constitute a major threat to Western security.

This consideration would almost automatically have ruled out Option 1, Stay Out. In the conventional wisdom of the time, the British withdrawal would create a "power vacuum" in the area which the Russians would inevitably fill—unless someone else were there to stop them.

The real problem thus became, who would protect Western interests in the Gulf? Many U.S. leaders would certainly have selected Option 2, a direct American presence, as the surest way of filling the impending power vacuum. But there were several major obstacles to such a choice: It was 1969, and the United States was deeply embroiled in an unpopular war in Southeast Asia. Not only would a Persian Gulf presence divert forces needed for the war effort in Vietnam, but it would arouse the ire of Congress, which had already become disenchanted with America's role as "the world's policeman."

Moreover, an American presence in the Gulf would be viewed by the more radical Arab states as evidence of a U.S. "imperialist" design, and thus would frustrate U.S. efforts to wrest these countries out of the Soviet orbit. The only prudent course, therefore, was to reject Option 2, Move In.

Only one viable choice was left: Find a Surrogate. This choice accorded nicely with the Administration's newly adopted "Nixon Doctrine." But it still posed an awkward question: Who could be relied upon to serve U.S. interests in the area? Some policymakers may have suggested Israel, but that probably would have pushed the Arab countries into an anti-U.S. alliance, and thus facilitated further Soviet penetration of the region. Other possible choices—France, perhaps, or even India—were too far from the scene or lacked the motivation to take on such a role. The only remaining candidates, therefore, were the countries of the Gulf itself.

However, even the most prosperous and advanced nations of the region lacked the wherewithal to serve as regional gendarme. That meant, inevitably, that Washington would have to serve as the organizer and quartermaster of this delicate maneuver. "What we decided," former Under Secretary of State Joseph J. Sisco later explained, "is that we would try to stimulate and be helpful to the two key countries in this area—namely, Iran and Saudi Arabia—

that, to the degree to which we could stimulate cooperation between these two countries, they could become the major elements of stability as the British were getting out."

Thus, a new doctrine, the Surrogate Strategy, was born. The United States would help Iran and Saudi Arabia to assume a regional peacekeeping role, but would otherwise stay out of the area. In one of the few public references to NSSM-66, Deputy Assistant Secretary of Defense James H. Noyes testified in 1973:

"A major conclusion of that study...was that the United States would not assume the former British role of protector in the Gulf area, but that primary responsibility for peace and stability should henceforth fall on the states of the region....In the spirit of the Nixon Doctrine, we are willing to assist the Gulf states but we look to them to bear the main responsibility for their own defense and to cooperate among themselves to ensure regional peace and stability. We especially look to the leading states of the area, Iran and Saudi Arabia, to cooperate for this purpose.

Implementing the Surrogate Strategy

As suggested by Sisco and Noyes, this policy assumed equal roles for Iran and Saudi Arabia. But as U.S. policymakers began to undertake the difficult job of carrying out the new strategy, it rapidly became apparent that the two countries were hardly capable of assuming an equal share of the burden. Saudi Arabia did not even possess a navy at that time, and its small army of some 30,000 men (most of whom were committed to internal security functions) was hardly capable of performing Gulf-wide peacekeeping missions. Iran, on the other hand, possessed a sizeable navy and air force, and its well-equipped army of 150,000 was considered among the most powerful in the region. In practice, therefore, the Surrogate Strategy inevitably became an Iranian Strategy.

Aside from such military considerations, however, the selection of Iran as America's principal surrogate was essentially predetermined by the attitudes of the rulers involved. The Saudi leadership was largely concerned with dynastic matters and intra-Arab affairs, but the Shah had long affirmed Iran's role as the "guardian" of the Persian Gulf and was not averse to assuming an even grander role.

"Not only do we have national and regional responsibilities," he told Arnaud de Borchgrave of *Newsweek* in 1973, "but also a *world role* as guardian and protector of 60 per cent of the world's oil reserves." (*Emphasis added.*) Even more important, from the American point of view, the Shah seemed ready to *act* on this premise when real threats emerged: In 1973, for instance, he sent Iranian forces to Oman to help crush a leftist uprising in Dhofar Province.

A U.S.-Iranian alliance had another advantage: Washington needed to consult only one individual—the Shah—when critical decisions had to be made. In Saudi Arabia, a whole covey of princes (many of whom were inaccessible to U.S. influence) was involved in decision-making, but in Iran all major foreign policy decisions were made by the Shah himself—and no one dared defy him. In the decade following 1953, when the CIA had organized a coup against Prime Minister Mohammed Mossadegh, the Shah had gradually eliminated all remaining challengers to imperial rule, and had established near-totalitarian control of Iranian society.

Moreover, U.S. analysts believed the Shah's all-powerful position would be unshakable for the indefinite future. With control over Iran's abundant oil wealth, he could buy off the most ambitious bureaucrats and entrepreneurs, while the constant vigilance of SAVAK, the infamous secret police established with CIA help, ensured that all dissidents would be quickly dealt with. The only institution with the power to question the Shah's survival—the army—was kept in line by lucrative perquisites on the one hand and the oversight of SAVAK on the other. "Iranian society is like a pyramid," *U.S. News & World Report* observed in 1973, "with the Shah at the apex and the army a privileged caste."

For U.S. policymakers, forced to grapple with the agonies of Vietnam and growing discontent at home, a U.S.-Iranian alliance must have seemed irresistible. But there was to be a pricetag for this unprecedented partnership—a modern military arsenal. While the Shah was more than willing to serve as the U.S. surrogate in the Persian Gulf, he expected to acquire military capabilities commensurate with his country's new stature. Not content with the obsolete hand-me-downs supplied through the Military Assistance Program, he began to eye America's latest and most sophisticated military hardware. And the first thing he desired was a modern air force, equipped with America's newest fighters, the McDonnell Douglas F-15 *Eagle* and the Grumman F-14 *Tomcat*.

When the Shah first proposed an Iranian purchase of F-14s or F-15s in 1971-72, some Pentagon officials were opposed. Never before had Washington sold such an advanced aircraft to a Third World nation, and there were feelings that such a move could compromise U.S. security by entrusting American defense secrets to foreigners. Such hesitations must have infuriated the Shah, who had come to view Iran's role in increasingly grandiose terms. Eventually, he must have handed Washington an ultimatum: Either sell us what we want, or the whole surrogate arrangement is defunct. Lacking an alternative policy, Washington gave in. In May 1972, President Nixon and Henry Kissinger flew to Tehran and signed a secret agreement with the Shah whereby Iran was permitted to order virtually any weapons systems it wanted.

Within months of the May 1972 showdown, the Shah ordered eighty F-14s at an estimated cost of $2 billion, as well as dozens of other U.S. weapons systems. Iranian spending on U.S. arms soared from $500 million in 1972 to $2.2 billion in 1973 and a staggering $4.3 billion in 1974. In addition to the F-14s, major Iranian purchases included:

— 169 Northrop F-5E/F fighters for $480 million.
— 209 McDonnell-Douglas F-4 *Phantom* fighter-bombers for $1 billion.
— 160 General Dynamics F-16 fighters for $3.2 billion.
— 7 Boeing E-3A AWACS radar surveillance planes for $1.2 billion.
— 202 Bell AH-1J *Cobra* helicopter gunships for $367 million.
— 326 Bell Model-214 troop-carrying helicopters for $496 million.
— 25,000 *TOW* and *Dragon* anti-tank missiles for $150 million.
— 4 DD-963 *Spruance*-class heavy destroyers for $1.5 billion.

To round out the Iranian shopping list, one would have to include billions of dollars worth of such mundane items as transport planes, armored personnel carriers, and artillery pieces. All told, the Shah ordered $20 billion worth of U.S. arms between 1972 and 1978, or about double America's military sales to all countries of the world for the twenty-five years following World War II.

Critics of Iran's extraordinary arms buildup have charged that Washington lost all control over the weapons program after the May 1972 agreement. In a much-publicized report, *U.S. Military Sales to Iran,* a Senate Foreign Relations Committee research team concluded in 1976 that "for at least three years U.S. arms sales to Iran were out of control." Not only had the 1972 agreement been concluded without any prior review of U.S. arms policies, but the President's decision also "effectively exempted sales to Iran from the normal arms sales decision-making process in the State and Defense Departments."

Administration officials insisted, however, that the Nixon-Shah agreement was neither ill-conceived nor hastily contrived. "Our [arms] supply policy is not the result of a series of improvisations," Deputy Assistant Secretary of Defense Noyes testified in 1973, but followed directly from the 1969 decision to encourage Iran to assume "primary responsibility for peace and stability" in the

Gulf. Indeed, once Washington elected to convert Iran into a surrogate police power, it had no option but to honor the Shah's requests for the weapons he felt he needed to perform the job.

There was another dimension to the Administration's strategic design which it could not openly use in its defense, but which constituted an important justification for the Iranian arms program. Modern weapons require constant maintenance, servicing, and inspection by skilled technicians, and Iran simply lacked the trained manpower to perform these services. Consequently, each new purchase of sophisticated gear by the Shah created an additional requirement for backup support which could be provided only by U.S. technicians.

By 1973, an estimated 3,600 U.S. technicians were employed on arms-related projects in Iran, and the number was expected to rise to 25,000 or more by 1980. These "white-collar mercenaries" rapidly became an essential component of the Shah's high-technology war machine—and thus Washington, by threatening to recall these specialists, could exercise a form of "veto power" over Iranian military activities. By continuously expanding the Shah's dependency on American technical skills, the U.S. arms program was meant to ensure that the "surrogate" never operated independently of its assigned role as guardian of Western oil interests.

If the Nixon Administration's original 1972 decision to sell the Shah "anything he wants" was prompted largely by strategic considerations, its continued adherence to the agreement was soon to be assured by another major consideration—the oil-inspired balance-of-payments crisis. Following the fourfold rise in oil prices announced by the OPEC nations early in 1974, America's balance-of-payments accounts went rapidly into the red. With the nation heading into a recession, the White House was under immense pressure to recover as many U.S. "petrodollars" as possible by selling the oil-producers whatever they could be persuaded to buy. And there is no doubt what the Iranian government wanted to buy—arms, arms, and still more arms.

Military sales thus became a critical *economic* as well as military objective. As then Deputy Secretary of Defense William P. Clements told Congress at the time, any slowdown in the export of arms "decreases the potential contribution of sales...to strengthening both free world security and the U.S. balance-of-payments position."

If the rise in oil prices created new incentives for Washington to sell weapons, it also furnished the Shah with a vast increase in funds with which to buy them. While he could talk in reasoned tones about

Iran's role as "guardian" of Western oil supplies, his arms-buying activities were also motivated by his desire to recreate "the Great Persian Empire of the past."

In 1971, the Shah seized three strategic islands belonging to the United Arab Emirates at the entrance to the Gulf, and he began to build a navy capable of operating in the Indian Ocean and beyond. At ceremonies marking the forty-second anniversary of the founding of the Imperial Iranian Navy, he declared, "In building up a modern navy our aim has not been confined to leadership in the Persian Gulf or Iran's territorial waters...because in the world today Iran enjoys a position which gives its duties regional dimension." U.S. leaders did nothing to discourage the Shah's megalomania.

The Shah's appetite for arms was also fed by what can only be called an obsession with weaponry. A licensed pilot who often test-flew the warplanes he intended to buy, the Shah prided himself on his technical knowledge of military systems and made no effort to hide his zeal in buying arms—as demonstrated by this comment in a 1973 interview with Arnaud de Borchgrave:

"We now have 80 *Phantoms* which cost $2.5 million each, and another 100 coming in that will cost $5 million each that will give us a fighter-bomber force of well over 300. We've ordered 700 choppers, including 200 gunships plus ten large *Chinooks* and eighteen ASW (antisubmarine warfare) *Sikorskys*....We're also buying 800 *Chieftain* tanks from Britain which will cost us another $480 million and meanwile we're modernizing 400 M-47 tanks that we have. That will give us a tank force of about 1,700."

The Shah did not have to worry about Congressional budget-cutters or Treasury officials when he went shopping for still more arms. "What the Shah wants, he gets," one American arms salesman observed in 1974. "There are no inter-service rivalries or bureaucratic squabbles, either. He decides what he wants and those under him carry out his orders—or else."

With Washington anxious to recover as many "petrodollars" as possible, and with the Shah eager to modernize Iranian military forces as quickly as possible, Iran soon became the largest single outlet for U.S. arms exports. At this point, a new factor entered the arms picture: greed. As the Senate Foreign Relations Committee noted in 1976, "The 1972 [Nixon] sales decision coupled with the increase in Iranian revenues following the quadrupling of oil prices created a situation not unlike that of bees swarming around a pot of honey. Defense industries, both U.S. and foreign, rushed to Iran to persuade the government to procure their products."

With such large contracts in the offing, and many companies

competing for the same orders, it is hardly surprising that some of them took shortcuts in the marketing process. A certain amount of corruption had always been endemic in Iran, but it never approached the multi-million dollar bribes and "commissions" paid by U.S. firms to secure Iranian arms contracts.

Grumman reportedly paid as much as $28 million in commissions to Iranian government officials while negotiating its $2 billion sale of F-14s, and Northrop shelled out at least $10 million to expedite sales of its F-5E fighter telecommunications equipment. (Both companies were later forced to compensate the Iranian government for some of these funds when the payments became public knowledge in 1976.) Other U.S. firms, including Rockwell International and McDonnell Douglas, have also been accused of paying bribes to Iranian officials or unnamed "agents" in the course of arms negotiations, and it is safe to assume that Iranian officials pocketed much of the $200 million which U.S. arms companies paid to foreign sales agents between 1972 and 1975.

Although the U.S. miliary services lacked purely pecuniary motives for generating arms sales, they had their own reasons for promoting particular sales transactions. Since the U.S. Government regularly billed Iran for a share of the development costs of weapons ordered by the Shah, Iranian orders could result in a significant reduction in the price paid by the services for their own supplies. And since the various services are often forced to compete with one another for Pentagon funds, a major sale to Iran could result in the procurement of one service's product at the expense of the others'.

For this reason, the services often sent their own representatives to Iran to assist allied defense contractors in marketing their products. In the case of the proposed F-14/F-15 sale, for instance, the Navy (sponsor of the F-15) sent teams to Iran in an effort to secure an Iranian purchase.

This is not the kind of atmosphere that would promote restraint, and there is no doubt that high Iranian military officials became immensely wealthy as a result of the American arms programs. One U.S. official, writing in *Armed Forces Journal*, observed:

"Senior military officers obtained vast wealth from commissions....The Shah's brother-in-law and then head of the Air Force, Mohammed Khatemi, became involved in highly publicized contingency deals for Air Force purchases which netted him millions. The Vice Minister of War for Armaments, General Hassan Toufanian, acquired equal visibility for similar commission operations. Lower-level officials took their cuts and money began to pour into safe hiding places in the West."

53

Corruption on this scale could not be concealed, and by 1976 it was common knowledge that high government officials—including members of the royal family—were on the take. Although the Shah belatedly tried to dissociate himself from the spreading infection by arresting a few cronies whose extortions could no longer be hidden, his government had been tarnished and he began to lose the support of the smaller merchants and businessmen who suffered from the pervasive corruption.

The Strategy Goes Awry

By the late 1970s, U.S. arms programs began to backfire in other ways. In the halcyon days of 1973-74, the Shah had consumed his new oil wealth as if the petrodollars would go on accumulating forever. But the OPEC price rise precipitated an economic recession in the West, and sales of Iranian oil began to decline. Unwilling to curtail his massive arms programs and disinclined to listen to the advice of his economists, the Shah went on buying arms as if his wealth was inexhaustible.

Although Iran's oil exports dropped by 12.5 per cent in 1975, the Shah ordered a 26 per cent spending increase—much of it for arms and other military-related projects. The results were predictable: Inflation, already a problem in suddenly affluent Iran, soared out of control. By 1977, it was running at the rate of 30 per cent a year, far outstripping wage increases for most salaried workers. Civil servants, oil workers, rank-and-file soldiers, and most of the middle class experienced a drop in real income at the same time that high-level corruption was becoming common knowledge. Although the Shah briefly cut back on arms spending, his persistence in buying foreign arms at a time of widespread belt-tightening at home provoked much resentment.

The resentment was directed particularly at the Shah's efforts to create a modern military-industrial complex in Iran. By 1976, he had signed contracts with several American and British firms to begin construction of new arms factories in Iran. Westinghouse and Hughes Aircraft were invited to join with the state-owned Iran Electronics Industry in building a missile repair and assembly plant in Shiraz, and Bell Helicopter was commissioned to construct an entire helicopter industry in Isfahan. And this was just the beginning: Before he was forced out of the country in 1979, the Shah had announced plans to establish an indigenous aerospace industry and a tank production facility.

These projects were described by the Shah as the cutting edge of his efforts to introduce modern industrial technology, but many

Iranian intellectuals and economists viewed them as a diversion from less glamorous but more important development programs. The critics argued that the arms projects would create a small enclave of capital-intensive, high-technology production in an otherwise underdeveloped economy, while more broad-based and labor-intensive projects were being allowed to languish because of Iran's budget crunch. Ultimately, the dispute evolved into a wide-ranging debate over the benefits of what the Shah and his supporters called "modernization," which many Iranians viewed as the introduction of foreign-dominated military ventures which contributed little to economic and social progress in Iran.

At this point, the presence of large numbers of foreign technicians also became a serious problem. Weapons began arriving at an ever-increasing pace in the mid-1970s, placing enormous strains on Iran's technical support capabilities. "Mountains of munitions are piling up in Iranian docks and fields," columnist Jack Anderson wrote in 1975. "Planes, helicopters, and other sophisticated weapons are left in crates for weeks, waiting to be assembled."

The Shah responded in characteristic fashion: He hired still more Americans to help straighten out the mess. The number of U.S. technicians working on arms-related programs in Iran jumped from 1,207 in 1975 to 4,473 in 1977—an increase of 270 per cent. Other Americans (along with British, French, and West German specialists) were recruited to help manage Iran's overstrained transportation, communications, and energy systems.

The conspicuous presence of affluent Westerners at a time of declining real income for most Iranians naturally created much bitterness. Moreover, these foreigners—recruited at high salaries and with lucrative expense accounts—began competing with middle-class Iranians for apartments in Tehran's already tight housing market, thus driving up rents and adding to the growing inflation rate. The resulting friction was further compounded by religious animosity as the foreigners began introducing Western behavior patterns—public drinking, revealing clothing, sexually explicit movies—which offended Iran's conservative Moslem population.

Within the military, the Shah's recruitment policies provoked the alienation of nationalistic junior officers, cadets, and technicians who found themselves under the *de facto* supervision of foreigners. Iranian technicians, who lacked the privileges accorded to high-ranking officers, felt their skills and commitment were being short-changed by the Shah in his preference for Americans. These tensions became most pronounced in the Air Force—recipient of the most advanced U.S. technology—where military personnel first demonstrated their disaffection in December 1978 by sabotaging several F-5 fighter planes.

Before these divisions had become fully apparent, however, the Shah ordered Iranian troops into the streets to crush demonstrations by anti-government students, workers, and religious leaders. Thousands of unarmed civilians lost their lives in these confrontations and many more were wounded or taken off to Iran's notorious prisons. Gradually, more and more segments of Iranian society joined in the protests, until it appeared that the entire population was united in its opposition to the Shah.

As the protests gained momentum, American arms sales again became controversial when Iranian troops began using their U.S.-supplied weapons against unarmed civilians. Just as the Shah was ordering martial law throughout Iran, the Carter Administration announced an emergency delivery of riot sticks, tear-gas, helmets, and shields to the Iranian army, providing a highly visible sign of U.S. support for the faltering regime. Once Iranian troops were ordered to occupy Iranian cities, moreover, the distinction rapidly broke down between arms supplied for conventional defensive purposes and those provided for internal security.

As Iranian pilots fired into the streets of Tehran from their U.S.-supplied helicopters, and as Army units patrolled the streets in their American tanks and armored vehicles, the United States became irretrievably identified with the Shah's bloody efforts to retain power. It is hardly surprising, therefore, that the anti-Shah demonstrations eventually took on an anti-American cast as well.

Long before the Shah's final departure, it had become painfully obvious that the extraordinary U.S.-Iranian arms relationship would never be restored to its original stature. With oil production down to zero and the economy devastated by months of turmoil, there was no money left to pay for imported arms. (Most of the millions acquired by Iranian officials through shady arms transactions had, of course, long been sequestered in numbered bank accounts in Switzerland and Panama.) and even the Shah's hand-picked successor, Dr. Shapour Bakhtiar, announced on January 3 that Iran would no longer serve as "the gendarme of the Persian Gulf." The final ascendancy of the "revolutionary government" of Medhi Barzagan on February 11 merely signed the *coup de grace* to the Surrogate Strategy.

Looking back, it is easy to see how the U.S. arms program exacerbated and in some cases created the problems that led to the monarchy's collapse. As early as 1976, some U.S. analysts had warned that excessive arms sales were contributing to the regime's difficulties. The Senate Foreign Relations Committee report of 1976 provided many indicators of the deteriorating situation. But Washington's hands had become tied by its unwavering commitment to the Surrogate Strategy.

Having contracted with the Shah to assume responsibility for policing the Gulf on behalf of the West, the United States could take no action that would alienate the Shah or undermine his authority at home without threatening the survival of the Strategy itself. Whereas the Shah had once been dependent on the United States for aid and political support, now, in a sense, America had become dependent on *him* for preservation of its strategic interests. And the more arms we provided him, the greater our stake in Iran and in the survival of the Shah.

Ultimately, Washington fell victim to its own misguided policies. Perhaps no more symptomatic epitaph for the Surrogate Doctrine will be found than President Carter's extraordinary 1978 New Year's toast to the King of Kings: "Iran under the great leadership of the Shah is an island of stability in one of the most troubled areas of the world. This is a great tribute to you, Your Majesty, and to your leadership, and to the respect, admiration and love which your people give to you."

Inside the Iranian Revolution

Lynne Shivers

Evening, December 2, 1978, eve of the holy month of Muharram, in an isolated section of Tehran: people are up on their flat rooftops, calling out, "Allah o Akbar! Allah o Akbar!" ("God is great.") In the distance, sounds of machine guns can be heard. The cries become louder and more strident: "Allah o Akbar! ALLAH O AKBAR!" Machine guns answer them again, continuing throughout the night.

The same event occurs again the following night, this time throughout the city, and the next night and the next and the next. "ALLAH O AKBAR!" deh-deh-deh-deh-deh-deh-deh . . . "ALLAH O AKBAR! ALLAH O AKBAR!" deh-deh-deh-deh-deh-deh . . . .

In another part of the city, a lonely and sick and prematurely old man paces the halls of his palace, pensively, knowing that the days of his reign are nearing their end . . . .

~ ~ ~ ~ ~

Our images of the Iranian Revolution are very sketchy, based on a few television news broadcasts or reports at the time. We as Americans have little understanding of how events developed, much less why events led from one to another. Yet, understanding the forces of the revolution can lead us to a greater understanding of Iran as a whole. This, in turn, might help us think and act more thoughtfully about America's role in Iran and in world affairs in general.

Social change on a national scale involves many elements. This article will attempt to identify the ones which made the Iranian Revolution possible. It is divided into four sections: the legacy of resistance; the underground resistance from 1963-1978; the open resistance which we often refer to incorrectly as "the Revolution" (since it was visible, but the Revolution actually began in 1963); and finally, some reflections on the Revolution itself.

58

A LEGACY OF RESISTANCE

A History of Embassy Takeovers?

The occupation of embassies is a clear violation of international law, and for good reason. The presence of embassies and their immunity to domestic upheaval is crucial to the practice of diplomacy, especially between nations which are no longer on friendly terms.

At the same time, however, it must be noted that foreign embassies in the poorer nations of the world have long been centers of intrigue and the active "command posts", as well as the symbols of foreign domination. It was not lost on Iranians that when President Nixon wanted to show increased support for the former Shah, and during a period in which SAVAK tortures were stepped up, former CIA Director Richard Helms headed the American Embassy in Tehran. When President Carter wished to signal the continuation of that support, he appointed William L. Sullivan as ambassador, a man with a long history of connections with repressive regimes and activities in Southeast Asia and the Pacific. What may come as a surprise, however, is that the occupation of embassies has been a commonplace and successful tactic of the Iranian revolutionary tradition during this century.

In July, 1906, during the bloody struggles for a constitution which was denied the Iranian people by Shah Muzaffara'd-Din, a few bankers and merchants took refuge in the British Legation when told that they would be immune there from the repression of the Shah's henchmen. Within three days, their numbers increased from just a few to 858; three days later, there were 5000, all camped on the Legation grounds. Seeing that the occupation gave them new political power, the occupiers demanded the dismissal of the Grand Vizier (the Shah's foremost official), a constitution, a representative national assembly, and guarantees of the Shah's good faith. By August 1st, the crowd had grown to more than 14,000. On August 5, 1906, the Shah, under pressure from the British, signed a document agreeing to all the demands, a document which even today is considered by Iranians as the "Magna Carta of Persia".

In January, 1969, a military tribunal sentenced fourteen of Iran's best-known writers and artists to prison. To protest the sentences, Iranian students in Italy occupied the Iranian Embassy in Rome. This action triggered off worldwide Iranian student protests against the excesses of the Shah, the first such open protests since the Shah was returned to power by the CIA in 1953.

On February 14, 1979, three days after the fall of the Bakhtiar government, armed Iranians occupied the U.S. Embassy in Tehran for several hours, ostensibly to prevent U.S. coordination of an attempted military coup. Information which has come out since then tends to justify their suspicion. *The New York Times*, on April 20, 1980, reported that U.S. Air Force General Robert E. Huyser went to Iran on January 3, 1979, and later, after the departure of the Shah, met with senior Iranian military leaders in order to develop detailed plans for a coup in the event of the fall of the Bakhtiar government. Although the desertion of thousands of Iranian troops made the success of the coup impossible, the *Times* noted that one official working in the embassy that night (February 10, 1979) said that Ambassador Sullivan received a call from the situation room at the White House in which a State Department official asked if it was still possible to make the coup plans operational. Mr. Sullivan is quoted as saying that it was not.

Not satisfied, the caller asked for a second opinion from General Philip C. Gast, the chief of American military operations in Iran. Mr. Sullivan reportedly advised Washington that General Gast and twenty-two other American officials were under siege at the Iranian military headquarters and could not be reached. It may just be that the siege of the Iranian military headquarters on February 10th, and the subsequent takeover of the U.S. Embassy on February 14th, was a decisive factor in saving the Iranian Revolution from an early abortion.

Finally, it should be noted that before the occupation of the American Embassy in Tehran in November, 1979, no fewer than six separate complaints were made by the relatively moderate government of Medhi Bazargan to the United States about the admission of the Shah to New York, noting that the reaction of the Iran people would result in difficulties for Americans still in Tehran. Thousands of Iranian Students protested in major American cities—some even occupied the Statue of Liberty—all, we must note, to no good effect. Given the realities of Iranian political history, the resulting occupation of the U.S. Embassy should not have been a particularly unexpected response.

Other Early Acts of Resistance

In the early twentieth century, two acts of noncooperation took place which people in Iran now remember as relevant to the present revolution. An exporting license was granted to the British Tobacco Company; the exportation of tobacco under British license would prevent profits from remaining in the country. In protest, a large percentage of the smoking population stopped smoking for four months. The effects on the industry were so devastating that the license was revoked.

During the reign of Reza Pahlavi (the current Shah's father), soldiers were ordered to remove women's *chadors* (veils) with bayonets. In an Islamic society where Islamic law encourages women to dress modestly, this would amount to symbolic rape. In order to noncooperate with this order, since they were unwilling to walk in public without wearing *chadors*, large numbers of women stayed at home for as long as ten months or walked together only with other women as a demonstration of solidarity. Regardless of how we as Westerners might feel about the wearing of the *chador,* it is important to note that Iranian women had to struggle for the right to wear it at all.

UNDERGROUND RESISTANCE: 1963-1978
The Shah's SAVAK

Mohammed Reza Pahlavi returned to power through CIA intervention against the nationalist Mossadegh government in 1953; the SAVAK (secret police) was created in 1957. Eventually there were 5000 officials and 60,000 people hired to gather information. The SAVAK was originally created supposedly to fight communism. However, its main goal became to bolster the Shah's government by creating a climate of sufficient fear so that all resistance would be eliminated. SAVAK agents were in most university classrooms; in a class of forty students, two or three would be agents. They posed as faculty members as well. Discussion stopped whenever it moved toward politics. People eventually were arrested for gathering in groups larger than three people, for carrying the Koran, for passing out leaflets, or for complaining about the price of meat. Friends disappeared. Or they returned from prison with the scars of torture.

Outside of Iran, we have the impression that SAVAK agents were everywhere. This is not quite accurate. What was everywhere was the fear of the SAVAK. As resistance grew, more people disappeared or were tortured. A state of terror developed nationwide.

It is difficult for people outside of Iran to understand how such a massive network of SAVAK agents could have been created. The government hired people who had no ideology or political analysis simply to gather information. They were asked, "Would you like to work for the government?" It was made to look like a patriotic duty; students were described as disreputable people so that agents would not object to "gathering information" about them. Agents became torturers at the command of superiors, as a public duty, with the advice and training of Americans, and probably, for some, in fear of their own safety.

Sparks of Resistance

In 1963, the Shah started a massive "Westernization" plan whose liberal-sounding goals served mainly to increase the power of the already privileged. It also deeply alienated the people-at-large whose traditions, culture, and religious values were being attacked. The "White Revolution"—the agricultural reform—for example, ended up in concentrating land in large holdings where it could be used for the production of export crops. This forced hundreds of thousands of peasants off the land into marginal urban existence.

Ayatollah Khomeini was only one of many prominent people who criticized the Shah. But his condemnation was pivotal because he had consistently criticized since 1923 when an earlier Shah had attempted to reduce the clergy's authority. In 1941, Khomeini published a book called *Discovery of Secrets,* an attack on the Pahlavi dynasty in which Khomeini called for an end to foreign domination in Iran. His opposition was stepped up from 1952 to 1960. As a result, people began to identify Khomeini as a consistent critic of the Shah. After he spoke against the White Revolution in 1963, the first anti-Shah demonstration took place in Qom, followed shortly after in other cities. The army's response was brutal; thousands were killed. Many prominent religious leaders were imprisoned or tortured, and Khomeini was forced into exile, first to Turkey, then to Iraq. From that point until January, 1978, the resistance was entirely underground.

Underground Resistance

During this period, it was mainly students who carried on the resisitance. It was virtually impossible to work in groups of more than a few, if that, since the SAVAK was too powerful. One after another, resistance groups were infiltrated and destroyed. Sometimes the SAVAK themselves formed "resistance groups" in order to attract and identify the true resistance. Therefore, most people in the resistance did not know each other; most work was done singly. Some mosques were used as meeting places: after 2 AM, the door was locked and a few students would meet with an ayatollah to discuss problems and issues. One such ayatollah was Ayatollah Taleghani at the Hedayat Mosque in Tehran. Later, some of these mosques were destroyed in retaliation. It was safer to deliver messages to other resistance people at night; some people were arrested, but fewer at night than during the day. Resistance participants woke in the morning to find explicit instructions on a paper slipped under the door. The courage and determination of members of such groups is awesome; but they had still not found the key to unlock the door to participation of the masses.

Preparation and Training

Training for what was to become the mass resistance later had political, ideological, and military aspects. The most important preparation came through people learning more about the Islamic culture and values as well as cutting dependence with the West and Western values. Political discussions were sometimes able to be held in mosques with students as well as with older people. Underground films of earlier historical Iranian resistance were shown as well as films of other revolutions, especially Algeria and Cuba. The 1905-06 Constitutional resistance referred to earlier occurred at the time of the abortive Russian 1905 revolution, and the latter had many aspects of nonviolent struggle. Thus, Maxim Gorgy's books about the 1905 Russian revolution were also widely read.

It was customary for a central committee of ayatollahs to recommend religious readings which would reach all students in the national public school system. Between 1975 and 1977, these recommended readings had significance to the developing resistance which students would understand.

One of the most imaginative forms of training was detailed to us during our February, 1980, visit to Iran: "We went mountain climbing, and people who expressed interest in the resistance were invited to come along. We ushered them into a room where there were different bundles and backpacks, each with a different weight. We knew that people who picked the lighter loads were not ready for the struggle, since they were giving heavier loads to others in the movement. People who voluntarily picked the heavier loads would be ready for sacrifice in the resistance. In this way, we were able to identify potential resistance members, spiritually and materially."

This description of training was followed by a short sermon which deserves to be quoted here, since it gives much of the flavor of the resistance: "Be ready for sacrifice; cut dependence to family, wealth, enjoyments. Otherwise, since you will be vulnerable in these areas of dependence, and since the government will use your weakness against the movement, you will inflict blows against it. It is most important to sacrifice wealth. All dependencies must be destroyed."

But the most important aspect of the preliminary and preparatory action was Imam Khomeini's speeches and messages from exile. Many people claim that there was no special training or preparation; once people became aware, they were an inspiration for each other. Khomeini's special function was to unify people and to provide analysis.

Ali Shariati

During the underground period of resistance, academic figures and intellectuals provided much of the necessary consciousness-raising and public education needed to build the movement. The most important of these figures was Dr. Ali Shariati, a sociologist trained in Iran and France. While in France, he was drawn to and influenced by existentialists like Camus as well as Marxist writers. When Shariati returned to Iran in 1964, he was arrested at the border and served a brief prison term. He taught in colleges and high schools, then at Mashad University, explaining the problems of Moslem societies in the light of Islamic principles. When he moved to Tehran, he taught at the Hossein-e-Ershad Institute. There he attracted thousands of students for summer school programs as well as people from different backgrounds.

It is impossible to overemphasize Shariati's value to the resistance movement at this time. He excited people by his breadth of vision and his analysis that their own cultural and religious literature could be the source of fresh and vital ideas. In 1973, Shariati was arrested and served eighteen months of a harsh prison term. Upon his release in March, 1975, he remained under close surveillance and was unable to publish or teach. As a result, he moved to England where he died in mysterious circumstances in 1977.

Students's Analysis

Important centers of resistance included the science faculties at the University of Tehran, and the universities at Tabriz and Shiraz (Pahlavi University), and religious centers in Qom, Mashad, and Isfahan. When students during the underground period began developing their political analysis, many were, at first, Marxists. But as they read Marx and Marxist analysis, many found it difficult to apply it to their own situation. One reason that students were distrustful of Marxism was the traditional Iranian mistrust of Russia. Russia even before the 1917 revolution had had designs on Iranian soil; there was no love lost between the two nations. Secondly, Marxist analysis denied the existence or importance of spiritual values. Yet it seemed to the students that if any one element of revolutionary consciousness was more important than any other, it was Islamic religious and cultural values that people discovered in their own tradition. Thus, students turned more toward Shariati, Mehdi Bazargan, and other Iranian intellectuals who were providing new revolutionary interpretations of familiar texts.

But they also searched through other countries' revolutionary literature. Many works from foreign writers, such as Sartre, were translated, but these appealed only to a few Iranian intellectuals. The most important among these, however, was Shariati's translation of Franz Fanon's *The Wretched of the Earth*. Its chapters on national consciousness and national culture must have been especially appealing. But it is important to keep in mind that the most important readings by far were Iranian books and religious writings that people discovered to be fresh and vital. Students read the works of banned Iranian poets and intellectuals, a vast number of whom were tortured and put to death by the SAVAK. These works included the writings of Jalal al-Ahmad, Samad Behrangi, and Sadegh Chubak and Reza Baraheni, whose works were passed hand-to-hand in well-worn, very limited editions.

Communications and Symbolic Gestures

During the underground period, communications were especially important, and women played an important role here. People would Xerox and tape messages and orders and women would circulate them around universities and mosques.

When a ban was imposed against demonstrations and gatherings at the universities, students at the University of Tehran found symbolic ways to resist. There was no ban on silent meetings! For an extended period of time—perhaps for months—students would gather on the steps of the library of the science building at noon and stand in silence. This was an eloquent act of defiance and a powerful symbol of the demand for freedom of speech. The ban on meetings larger than three people was too difficult to enforce and was eventually rescinded.

When Richard Nixon visited Iran in May, 1972, to offer major new military support to the Shah, Fidel Castro was on a well-publicized tour of Eastern Europe at the same time. A photo of Castro playing basketball with the Polish national team had appeared in Tehran newspapers. As the Nixon-Shah official motorcade passed by the University, hundreds of students stood silently, rigidly, outside the university gates, bouncing basketballs on the pavement. Everyone in Tehran caught the significance.

No doubt there were many other symbolic gestures as well.

Resistance to the SAVAK

As SAVAK imprisonment and tortures increased, family members were sometimes forced to witness torture of family members.

65

Members of the resistance, as they left prison, memorized faces of their torturers. At one time photographs and descriptions of SAVAK agents were even published so that agents might be identified; thus, resistance groups could protect themselves from infiltration. Prisoners' refusal to give any information moved other resistance members and strengthened their resolve. Stories circulated that people tortured said only, "Allah o Akbar!" during interrogation and torture sessions.

Armed Guerrila Groups

Two armed guerrilla organizations were active in the 1960's and 1970's during the underground resistance period. The *Fedayeen* (Iranian People's Fedayeen Guerrillas) had a secular and Marxist-Leninist ideology. It was formed from three groups created in 1964. By 1967, the *Fedayeen* was infiltrated by the SAVAK. Nevertheless, it was able to develop small discussion groups on the thinking of Che Guevara, Debray, and other revolutionary figures. These groups merged into the *Fedayeen* in 1970. A year later, the group attacked a police post in Siakal in northern Iran, and the SAVAK killed or captured most of the *Fedayeen* members. New cells were formed and the group carried out military attacks on banks, offices of multi-national corporations, and police headquarters, as well as assassinations. Its members came mainly from the Tudeh Party (the pro-Soviet Iranian Communist Party) and the Marxist wing of the old National Front.

The *Mujahhadin* (Organization of the People's Fighters) was formed mainly from the Liberation Movement of Iran, created by Mehdi Bazargan and Ayatollah Taleghani in 1961. The membership of the *Mujahhadin* came mainly from the religious wing of the National Front; it started military operations in 1971 which included bombings and assassinations. The *Muhahaddin* were mainly Islamic, although with strong socialistic leanings.

Guerilla activity reached its peak in 1975-76. The ideologies of the *Fedayeen* and *Mujahhadin* changed over the years. By 1977, there were four main armed guerrilla groups, split mainly over the issue of whether or not Islamic thinking could be the basis for a revolution. The guerrilla movements suffered from SAVAK infiltration and small membership; analysts estimate that their membership even at its peak did not go beyond 300 people. The Shah's government, however, used the existence of these groups to raise fears of Communist presence and to paint all resistance as Soviet-inspired. Thus, the Shah was able to justify greater SAVAK and police repression toward all resistance attempts. In general, the guerrilla movement offered one major contribution to the underground resistance period: its members were models for the whole Iranian society willing to struggle and die for fundamental changes in Iran.

Iranians Abroad

Open resistance to the Shah's regime occurred outside Iran eleven months before it started inside Iran. On February 10, 1977, six students chained themselves inside the Statue of Liberty to protest the treatment of political prisoners in Iran. On July 7, Iranian students demonstrated at the University of Southern California when Empress Farah was given an honorary degree. On July 12, the Empress visited the White House, and that event was marked by about one thousand masked demonstrators protesting political prisoners and human rights violations in Iran. On November 12, 1977, the Shah visited the White House, and tear gas was used to disperse a crowd of more than 8,000 Iranian students demonstrating against his government. President Carter and the Shah were pictured on national television crying involuntary tears from the gas.

OPEN RESISTANCE

Religious Leadership

Students took the initiative for consciousness-raising, communications, and resistance during the underground period. But from this point on, the religious figures were the leadership along with their powerful national network of mosques and communications. Understanding this structure gives important context for the year to follow. Shi'ite Islam is the majority religion in Iran, though it is a minority in the Islamic world as a whole, where most are Sunnis. The Shi'ite structure includes an "Imam," leader; five Great Ayatollahs, who have large followings; roughly 10,000 ayatollahs who are in charge of mosques; roughly 20,000 hojatoleslam who give sermons; and roughly 50,000 seghatoleslam and students, who study. One should note that religious leaders would vary in their power and degree of radical analysis.

Throughout this period, Khomeini and his messages from exile provided the focus of the resistance. Khomeini's students, having had personal ties to the Imam and now prominent religious leaders, infused the spirit of revolt. Tapes of instruction were sent back, copied, and played in mosques throughout the country. On these tapes, Khomeini provided explicit directives, calling for strikes, boycotts, and noncooperation and that members of the armed forces should be viewed as brothers. Abolhassan Sadegh, a government official with the Ministry of National Guidance with special responsibility for communications with foreign media, has noted with a touch of irony that, "Tape cassettes are stronger than fighter planes."

Important religious leaders at home received Khomeini's tapes and distributed them; without these leaders, the revolution would have failed. Some of the most important figures were Ayatollahs Kazem Shariat-Madari, Taleghani, Montazeri, Motahheri, and Khamanei. Information about these men is still scarce in the U.S., but the 49 Americans who visited Iran in February, 1980, met Ayatollah Khamanei, and we learned something about his background. He was a close friend of Ali Shariati and a student of Khomeini. He was sent to prison six or seven times; each sentence was for six months to a year because of his work with the underground resistance. Before 1977, Khamanei had been sent to exile to the desert town of Iranshah in south Iran near the Pakistan border. He was forced to do hard manual labor in the desert heat, carrying buckets of sand to make bricks for building houses. Khamanei was the first person to document proof of tortures going on in Kometei Prison in Tehran. In mid-1977, he was released from internal exile, and he went to Mashad in northern Iran where he was Khomeini's representative. After the Shah left, Khamanei was appointed to the Revolutionary Council and later became the assistant Minister of Defense. He is also the ayatollah who gives the sermon at the Friday prayer services in Tehran.

Of course, there were other important leaders outside the religious network: Bani-Sadr, Bazargan, Habibi (professor at the University of Tehran and one of the spokesmen for the Revolutionary Council), and others. But the religious leaders were pivotal since they were the link between Khomeini, the already active student body, shopkeepers and workers, and the illiterate poor.

Constituencies

By now, we can clearly identify a number of groups which were ready to commit themselves to a revolution: the students, the small underground movement, the clergy, and the new rootless urban proletariat thrown off the land. The last important group, and clearly vital, was the bazaar merchant community. Bazaars still control over two-thirds of the wholesale domestic trade and 30% of the import trade in Iran. Most bazaar merchants are conservative and practicing Moslems; as clergy became more and more anti-Shah, bazaar merchants did not need much convincing. When demonstrators were killed, the bazaar offered financial support to their families; later, the bazaar supported striking workers. By autumn, 1978, the merchants calling for the Shah's overthrow were an important revolutionary constituency.

Events Leading to Open Revolt

In June, 1977, three respected moderate political figures—Dr. Karim Sanjabi, Dr. Shapur Bakhtiar, and Darioush Forouhar—sent the Shah an open letter. It was a plea to establish individual freedoms, permit democratic institutions such as freedom of the press and freedom of association, release political prisoners, and establish a popularly elected government. The letter was ignored by the Shah, but 10,000 copies were quickly circulated. A few other similarly mild protests were initiated in mid-1977: a telegram, two manifestos, and a letter to the Supreme Court, all of which set the scene for events to follow.

In October, 1977, Khomeini's son Mostafa was killed in Iraq under questionable circumstances. On November 22, the "Karaj Road" incident (as it came to be known) took place. A dinner party being hosted by Darioush Forouhar, a signer of the aforementioned letter, was disrupted by what appeared to be thugs and 300 people were injured. Upon closer investigation, it was learned that the SAVAK and army rangers were responsible for the injuries and damage. Furthermore, the affair was engineered in person by a high leader of the Tehran State Gendarmerie. This event was crucial in drawing even larger segments of the Western-oriented urban middle classes into open hostility to the Shah. New Year's Eve in Tehran found President and Mrs. Carter toasting the Shah's health and long life. Just a week later on January 7, the national newspaper published in Tehran, *Ettelaat,* published an article critical of Khomeini, accusing him of being "connected with a foreign power." These were the sparks which ignited the fire smoldering for so many years.

Open Revolt

On January 8, in Qom, people demonstrated against the slanderous attack on Khomeini; people were killed and injured as the police and army responded brutally. This is the event that most people use as the date of open resistance and revolution. The Islamic tradition of public mourning forty days after a death meant that from this date, the momentum of popular resistance steadily built. If people were killed in a demonstration, others could expect another demonstration forty days later. As the resistance continued and deaths occurred more frequently, these forty-day periods overlapped. The pace of the resistance accelerated.

After the January Qom demonstration, others followed: February 17 in Tabriz, with deaths reported, and again in early March. On April 22, eighty people were arrested in Tehran for distributing anti-government leaflets. In early May many cities saw demonstrations: Tehran, Qom, Tabriz, Kazerun, Mashad, and Isfahan. A group of important demonstrations occurred in July. On the 18th, there was a peaceful demonstration in Qom to protest the government killing of a theology student. In late July, thirteen cities saw people injured and killed in demonstrations.

It was around this time that the movement developed its own language, symbols, and gestures. "Marghbar Shah!" ("Down with the Shah!"), "Down with American imperialism!", "Khomeini-e-Imam" ("Our Leader is Khomeini"), "Allah o Akbar!" ("God is Great") filled the streets. People carried the Iranian and Islamic flags and huge photographs of Khomeini, Shariati, and of people killed in previous demonstrations. People frequently gave the "V sign" for victory, and they held their hands clenched above their heads in a symbol of strength and solidarity with others. After so many Iranians had been killed by SAVAK torture or on the streets, Khomeini sent back this message: "The blood of martyrs will become fields of tulips which will cover the countryside." Little wonder, then, that tulips and their pictures are today seen everywhere in Iran. The tulip in Iran today signifies not only the suffering the people experienced but the hope for a new society as well. [Editor's note: The cover design of this book is based on a poster announcing a contemporary art exhibit shown in Tehran in early February, 1980.] As people continued to be killed, people put flowers at the places in the streets where people died. People also dipped their hands in the dead person's blood and would mark the place where the person died with a bloody handprint on a wall nearby. For a culture which reveres martyrdom, this gesture became very important. Black *chadors* became the symbol for women of resistance and solidarity.

Abadan and "Black Friday"

In most revolutions, there are key incidents that either strengthen the resistance or smother it. The Abadan Fire and "Black Friday" were just such crucial events. The Cinema Rex movie theater in Abadan was set on fire at night on August 20, and 800 people were locked inside the burning building for forty minutes. 410 people died. A number of rumors and "explanations" circulated later from the government: fire equipment was slow to arrive, the fire was started by gun powder or jet fuel or plastic bombs thrown by "terrorists," people confessed, and so on. For a variety of substantial reasons, none of these explanations seemed valid. People's belief in the brutality of the Shah was reinforced by their strong belief that the Abadan fire was set by government officials. In the U.S., Iranian students demonstrated as a protest against distorted media coverage of the Abadan event.

Black Friday, the 17th of Shahrivar in the Iranian calendar, was a major turning point in the revolution. On September 4 and 7, marches were held in Tehran and other cities to mourn the dead in Abadan and elsewhere. By the evening of September 7, martial law was declared and curfew was imposed from 9 PM to 5 AM in Tehran and eleven other major cities. Attempts to encourage soldiers to defect or noncooperate with orders began to frighten military officials. Many people did not learn about the imposition of martial law. Only a few ayatollahs made a call for people to demonstrate on September 8. Communication on the evening of September 7 was poor; there was a lot of confusion in Tehran that night.

So when 15,000 people gathered at Jaleh Square at 8 AM, they gathered without encouragement from many religious leaders. However, by 8:30 AM, Ayatollah Nouri, whose mosque is located on Jaleh Square, arrived. He asked people to sit down, and they did. But with the launching of tear gas, the crowd rose and advanced toward the line of soldiers at the other side of the square. Several bursts of machine guns were heard. People panicked and scattered, but then regrouped, and some moved slowly toward the line of soldiers. A few moments later, the soldiers opened fire; some fired in the air to disperse the crowd, others aimed to kill. Many people fell. Everyone figured that if women surrounded men, the army would be less likely to fire. They were wrong. Of the 3000 people killed on Black Friday, at least 700 were women. One soldier was ordered by his officer to fire into the crowd at Jaleh Square. He refused, killed his commanding officer and then turned the gun on himself.

But not all the victims of Black Friday were killed at Jaleh Square. Throughout the day in Tehran there were running battles between grieving people and frightened and angry soldiers throughout the city, all spontaneous, all hostile and sudden. On September 11, Iranians in the U.S. demonstrated against distorted press coverage of Black Friday, this time at Camp David. After Black Friday the pendulum of the Revolution was in full swing.

Acceleration

Within a week, a Moslem leader and several journalists had been arrested; Ayatollah Shariat-Madari announced a campaign of noncooperation. Cemeteries—Behesht Zahara and Jan-Abad Guristan—became free zones. The people's spirit of resistance was so strong that the SAVAK and the army dared not enter and arrest people. Ayatollah Khomeini moved from Iraq to France in early October and demonstrations in Iran continued. On October 7, workers in state-run hospitals in Tehran struck for "higher pay", joining other striking public employees. A few days later, two major newspapers ceased publication to protest the imposition of censorship. From then on walls on the street became the medium of exchanging news of the Revolution. A general strike was called in Mashad, and there were major anti-government demonstrations across Iran in late October.

On October 31, the oil workers struck, demanding the release of political prisoners. Within a week, this strike alone cost the government $60 million a day. On November 5, Prime Minister Jafan Sharif-Emami resigned and martial law was imposed nationwide. By mid-November, oil workers temporarily returned to work after the government began to carry out its threat to arrest strike leaders. November 6 marked a one-day nationwide general strike as work stoppages and demonstrations took place in Iran.

As already noted, in Iranian society the bazaar is a central place since a lot of business is conducted there and news travels quickly. Almost 15,000 people had been machine-gunned to death by the Shah's army in the Tehran bazaar in 1963. On November 14, 1978, demonstrators clashed with soldiers and the bazaar was closed for a week. Four days later, thousands of oil workers staged a slow-down on the job. Three days later, 200 workers at the Shahryar power station in Tehran staged a walk-out. During this accelerating phase, the Shah's representative would regularly give propaganda radio speeches each night. And, each night, technical workers would cause a "power failure" at 8:30 when the program was scheduled. When the speech was over at 9:00, power would be restored.

The Holy Month of Muharram

In early December, the pace of events accelerated again. Instead of major traumatic events happening every few days, they happened every day without ceasing. On December 2, demonstrators in Tehran defied the curfew. The next day, troops fired on demonstrators in Tehran again. If troops used tear gas in demonstrations, people would set small fires to lessen its effects by burning tires in the middle of streets. On December 4, thousands of oil workers renewed their strike. A week later, a peaceful march with hundreds of thousands took place in Tehran. In Frankfurt, West Germany, on the same day, Iranian, Turkish, and West German demonstrators marched to protest the Shah's rule. And on the same day, demonstrators were injured and killed in Isfahan. On December 14, there were demonstrations in fifteen cities. People carried sheets stained with bloody handprints to remind people of the high value of martyrdom and the sacrifice others were giving. Khomeini called for a day of mourning and a general strike to support the striking oil workers; this general strike took place on December 16. Demonstrations took place around the country during the next week. People carried large poster boards of the Shah's face, either held upside down or with a big X marked across it. On December 28, the oil workers' strike shut down the oil industry completely. The next day, the general strike deepened: the central bank and oil refineries were shut down; demonstrations and shootings continued in Tehran. On December 29, Iranians and Americans blocked traffic in San Francisco to protest the Shah's rule. On December 30, the Shah named Shapur Bakhtiar to form a civilian government as demonstrations took place and continued well into January.

Khomeini's Return

On January 6, major newspapers started printing again, and Ayatollah Taleghani publically opposed the new government. A week later, the *New York Times* reported 100,000 people peacefully marched, celebrating the re-opening of Tehran University. On the same day, Khomeini also denounced Bakhtiar and announced the formation of a Revolutionary Council.

On January 16, 1979, the Shah finally left the country, and thousands celebrated in the streets. People cut pictures of the Shah from paper currency and waved them about, proudly. People carried leafy branches, their symbolic answer to soldiers' rifles, and put flowers in the barrels of soldiers' rifles.

For the next two weeks, demonstrations continued as Khomeini called on people to continue resistance to the Bakhtiar government. Hundreds were killed as troops fired on crowds, even though Khomeini called on people to try to win over troops. At other times, Khomeini urged people to see soldiers as their brothers; soldiers who deserted were carried on people's shoulders in the mass marches.

On February 1, Khomeini returned to Iran after seventeen

years in exile. He went immediately to Behesht Zahara Cemetery to honor the thousands of martyrs. On February 6, Khomeini appointed Mehdi Bazargan as Prime Minister, thus establishing a parallel government. On February 11, Bakhtiar resigned; millions of people rejoiced when the army withdrew troops from Tehran. This is the date which Iranians use to mark the anniversary of the Revolution.

REFLECTIONS

Why Didn't We Know?

Why weren't we aware of these events as they happened or shortly after? Many reasons have come to light. There were objective events which made news transference difficult. For one, *The New York Times* was on strike from August 10 (ten days before Abadan) to November 5 (just after the call for a general strike was given). Secondly, the events in Jonestown, Guyana, began to be known on November 19, and the disbelief, anguish, and confusion continued for many Americans until Christmas.

But there were political reasons as well for our ignorance. The Shah's government, throughout the build-up of resistance in early 1978, tried to interpret the Revolution as engineered by "terrorists," "communists," and other labels designed to give credibility to his regime and no credibility to the resistance. Only a few people realized the significance of the oil workers' strike and knew that when that occurred, the Revolution was assured. Most significantly, of course, was that the American government had overriding vested interests in Iran and wanted to protect them. Iranians, particularly students in the U.S., had been calling attention to events in Iran before open resistance developed at home. But they were unable, for the most part, to communicate to the general American public the significance of events in Iran. Americans were not prepared to understand what cries of "Death to the Shah!" meant when we heard them in front of the White House.

Finally, the American news media, by ignorance or design, frequently offered inaccurate coverage of the Revolution. Journalists usually had little political analysis of events in Iran and no understanding of the context of the Revolution. Thus they were unable to interpret events, up to Black Friday, with any real significance. Reporters were not able to foresee where events were going. In addition, during at least the last few years of his reign, the Shah presented gifts to a number of prominent American journalists in the hope and expectation that they would file reports favorable to the Shah and his government. According to a prominent Iranian government official, these journalists included David Brinkley, Tom Brokaw, Art Buchwald, John Chancellor, Otis Chandler, Walter Cronkite, Harry Ellis of the *Christian Science Monitor*, Rowland Evans, Peter Jennings, Marvin Kalb, Melvin Laird, William Monroe, Bill Moyers, Crosly Noyes of the *Washington Star*, Richard Valeriani, Bruce van Vorst of *Time Magazine*, Mike Wallace, and Barbara Walters.

What Was It Really Like?

We cannot know the reality of revolution unless we are participants in it. All too often, social historians write about social change as though it were a tidy affair. We seem to take our theories of how change occurs and fit the events of profound massive social change into those models; then we say we have "understood" them. Even a brief visit to Iran a year later dispels that myth immediately. We sat with people watching films of the demonstrations and we heard family members of SAVAK victims tell us first hand what they were forced to witness. We saw Iranian people weep openly and leave the room as they remembered the pain and fear that they lived with as events of the Revolution unfolded. We need to be aware, too, of the effects of that brutalization on the people who survived those experiences which they carry inside them now as painful memories.

SAVAK and Martyrdom

There is a profound relationship between the SAVAK and the central importance of the value of martyrdom in Shi'ite Moslem thinking. Without the SAVAK and the army, the large number of martyrs would not have been created. Without these martyrs, the Revolution very likely would not have occurred. It is as though the dark side of a culture fed the sacrificial side. Brutality and sacrifice met in a powerful and horrifying drama in which thousands of people were willing to sacrifice themselves rather than live under terror and oppression any longer.

Other revolutions have experienced single brutal events like Black Friday. In India, it was Amritsar when in 1919, British soldiers fired into an unarmed crowd, killing 379 people. The event served the strengthen the commitment for an independent India. In South Africa, in 1960, it was at Sharpeville where 72 unarmed Africans were killed by soldiers firing into a crowd. Sharpeville meant the end of organized resistance. The difference between strengthening resolve and crushing it is whether or not there is organization and a culture behind the resistance. There was, both at Amritsar and in Tehran.

A Nonviolent Revolution?

Why ask the question at all? We assume of course that revolutions are, by their very nature, violent. But, it we discover that it is possible for revolutions to occur nonviolently, then we have the opportunity to re-think our basic assumptions about the nature of change. This includes change at all levels of society, from interpersonal to international.

The idea of a "nonviolent revolution" is not so outlandish as it may at first seem. A magazine as respected as the *New Yorker* wrote in its January 29, 1979 issue: "The opposition did not espouse a philosophy of nonviolence (its slogan, 'Death to the Shah,' was hardly pacific); yet the fact is that it carried out one of the very few nonviolent revolutions in history. Its first move was to launch enormous public demonstrations; its second move was to go on strike, most notably in the country's oil fields; and its coup de grace was to physically embrace the soldiers in the streets and put carnations in their gun barrels."

But many of us have a number of difficulties in thinking that it is possible to have a nonviolent revolution at all. We have all sorts of stereotypic images of what "nonviolence" is. We confuse it with pacifism, passivity, purity, holiness, non-action, and not injuring anyone, even to the point of verbal abuse. We may interpret the violence and bloodshed perpetrated by the oppressor as somehow reflecting upon the nonviolent character of the opposition. Secondly, all Westerners carry around in their brains vague historical images of Moslems riding across the Sahara sands, lopping off the heads of "disbelieving infidels". If we allow these images to prevent us from taking in new information about a significant world event, we cannot hope to understand what recently happened in Iran.

We should realistically not expect to find a completely nonviolent revolution in history. Since we are talking about mass societal change, we are per force talking about the active involvement of millions of people. The question is, rather, whether or not it is possible for a revolution to be mainly nonviolent.

Yet, there are glimpses of nonviolent revolutions; certainly most people think of Gandhi and the Indian Independence Movement (but since people grudgingly admit that it was mostly nonviolent, we eschew the word "revolution" even with that struggle). The fact is many revolutions have used a mixed strategy. We point to Guatemala and El Salvador in 1944, and France in 1968 as examples of massive social change events which in the main followed nonviolent strategies.

The Islamic revolution in Iran was, in reality, a nonviolent revolution. Khomeini's speeches issued from November 7 through November 24, 1978—during the time of some of the largest and most impressive acts of resistance against the Shah's government—contained these messages:

—"The goal is (a) the overthrow of the Pahlavi dynasty and the sinister monarchical regime, (b) the establishment of an Islamic republic based on the principles of Islam and the will of the people. The movement should continue in various ways, particularly by strikes in all government departments. The military government of Iran is illegitimate and illegal, and it is the duty of the people to not obey it, and to try to paralyze it by whatever means. I am grateful to all government employees and others who, by staging strikes, have declared support for their brothers and sisters. This is an Islamic duty and binding on all . . . I am grateful to the students . . . who have stood against the Shah with clenched fists . . . ."

(November 7)

—"Every day and every hour of your strike is valuable and damaging . . . ."

(November 15)

—". . . our Imam Hossein . . . showed us how the clenched fists of freedom fighters can crush the tanks and guns of the oppressors, ultimately giving the victory to Truth . . . . If Islam is endangered, we should be willing to sacrifice ourselves and save Islam by our blood . . . . The military government of Iran is illegal, and is condemned by the principles of Islam. It is the duty of all to protest it and to refuse to be a part of it in any way. People should refuse to pay taxes to the government, and all employees of the Iranian oil company should endeavor to stop the flow of oil abroad . . . . The clergy should fulfill their duties to God by disclosing the crimes of the regime more than ever . . . . I call on the clergy, the students, journalists, workers, peasants, merchants, civil servants and all the tribes to work side by side . . . . You . . . should hold mourning sessions without acquiring the permission of SAVAK or the police . . . ."

(November 22)

Strikes, clenched fists, tax refusal, solidarity, civil disobedience: these are traditional and frequently-used tactics in the arsenal of nonviolent resistance. We have seen them at other times in history and in other situations, often in our own country. During the last phase of the Revolution, scenes of members of the resistance killing others were very rare, nor did crowds set fire to government buildings; looting and sacking did not take place. Khomeini could have made very different pronouncements.

As revolutions unfold, we expect to hear cries of "kill the enemy!". Throughout the Iranian Revolution, leaders consistently referred people to the concept of martyrdom: " . . . *save* Islam by *our* blood." Self-sacrifice is the cornerstone of the Iranian Revolution, even to the point of giving one's life. This is no accident. Imam Hossein, an early Islamic historic figure, centuries ago, established martyrdom as a central concept in the thinking of Shi'ite Islam. Many cultures seem to identify martyrdom as a powerful element in a revolution. Thomas Jefferson wrote, "The tree of liberty must be refreshed from time to time with the blood of patriots." The Iranian concept of martyrdom has many similarities to the Gandhian concept of self-sacrifice: rather give your own life than take that of another. Although the image of spilling blood may seem violent and brutal, it nevertheless was a central compelling image of the Iranian Revolution. The mass solidarity.; understanding people in their roles instead of seeing people themselves as evil (seeing soldiers as brothers); the attempt to transform people through a revolution which was social and cultural as well as economic and political; the call for Iranian self-reliance (important hallmarks in the Indian revolution as well): these are marks of a revolution with large elements of nonviolence. Even in the American press, there are no reports whatsoever of Khomeini calling for an armed attack on anyone during the entire course of the revolution.

From the information now available, it is clear that the use of organized violence played no role in the revolutionary leadership's strategy or tactics. Furthermore, it is also clear that the Islamic cultural equivalent of nonviolent self-sacrifice was crucial to the power of the revolutionary struggle. That occasional unplanned and unorganized incidents of violence did occur, or that groups not associated with the Revolution's leadership were armed, should not blind us to the central reality of revolutionary practice in Iran.

Executions

A number of people have questioned the label of "nonviolent revolution" since a number of executions have taken place since the Revolution. In this context, it has become necessary for me to remember that people who carried out the Revolution had just experienced over twenty-six years of repression and brutality. The level of anger, confusion, and bitterness was, and is, staggering. If people experience a generation of massive structural and direct violence, we should appreciate, if reluctantly, that violence will be released wherever it finds an outlet that is socially acceptable to the people in that society.

It may be helpful also to note that when you compare revolutions, you learn quickly that almost all new governments carry out executions, usually many more than the new Iran government has. The major significance in Iran is not that executions have taken place, but that there have been so many fewer than after most revolutions. Instead of hundreds, there are sometimes thousands! It is also important to note that Khomeini called off executions on July 12, 1979, except for those involved in torture or murder. Attempting to limit officially sanctioned executions is clearly a nonviolent initiative.

The resort to executions is based on fear. And while executions may be unjustifiable, the fears of the Iranian people have more than ample justification. The people had struggled for so long and there had been so many victims that people wanted to protect their revolution. Even up to the day of the Bakhtiar government's fall, counter-revolutionary forces backed by the U.S. government were hard at work. Prominent leaders of state-initiated violence under the Shah's government were executed, not only as retribution, but to serve as warning to those who would continue to cooperate with U.S. subversive activity inside Iran. Thus, executions were an irrational outlet for anger and fear, but also an unfortunate but quite rational response to the continued threat and/or reality of U.S. backed subversion and terrorist activity. Placed in this context, Khomeini's restraint is all the more extraordinary.

Carter—The Cause of the Revolution?

Some people have suggested that President Carter really caused the Iranian Revolution through calling for human rights. This is illogical on one hand since it denies completely the sacrifice and struggle of the Iranian people. But from another point of view, there is some validity to the argument. When Carter called for "human rights in Iran," the Iranian people took that to mean Carter was urging the Shah to reduce state-sanctioned brutality. The Iranian people's hopes were raised; perhaps Carter was their ally. But then, when the President visited the Shah in late 1977 and drank a toast to him which appeared on national television; and then when Carter phoned the Shah the day following Black Friday to give him support—the people's hopes were destroyed, and bitterness took the place of hope. This may account for some of the anti-Carter language coming from the people of Iran.

But it is clear from this analysis that the oppressed people of the Third World listen very carefully to the pronouncements of American leaders, and examine events critically to see whether the actions of the U.S. government in supporting their aspirations are as strong as their words. If we expect to prevent still more conflict and bloodshed in Iran, and in the Third World generally, we need to learn to hold our leaders as accountable for their actions as the struggling peoples of the Third World do.

Recommended Readings

I have found five resources especially helpful in writing this article:

1. Robert Graham, *Iran: The Illusion of Power*. St. Martin's Press, New York: 1979. 272 pp., including map and index. Graham was Middle East correspondent for the London *Financial Times* and was based in Tehran, 1975-1977. Most other books on Iran use Graham as a source of information and interpretation. Paperback, $5.95.

2. Fred Halliday, *Iran: Dictatorship and Development*. Penguin Books, New York: 1979. Paperback, 348 pp., including bibliography. Frequently a sourcebook on Iran for other writers. $3.95.

3. G.H. Jansen, *Military Islam*. Harper Colophon Books, New York: 1979. Paperback, 224 pp., index. Documented and readable brief overview and analysis of militant Islam all over the Islamic world, not just Iran. $3.95.

4. Ali-Reza Nobari (editor), *Iran Erupts*. Published by the Iran-America Documentation Group, Stanford Univ., P.O. Box 2346, Stanford, CA 94305. 1978. Paperback, 237 pp.; order by mail only. Important background documentation of the Iranian Revolution with articles by Bani-Sadr, Eric Rouleau, interviews with Khomeini; also covers SAVAK, military programs, U.S. connections, economics, highlights of the revolution. Photos and illustrations. $5.95 plus postage.

5. Ali Shariati, *On the Sociology of Islam* and *Marxism and Other Western Fallacies*. Both edited by Hamid Algar and available from Mizan Press, Box 4056, Berkeley, CA 97404. Each $3.95 plus postage.

Iran: Human Rights and
International Law

Richard Falk

In early 1979 a revolutionary movement toppled the Shah of Iran. It was a startling development for many reasons. Here, we consider only some aspects of its human rights significance. The rationale for the revolution was centered upon the rights of the Iranian people to rise up against the bloody tyranny of Pahlavi rule, whose gross violations of human rights were attested to be among the worst in a world notable for human rights abuse.

After the revolutionary seizure of power under the leadership of Ayatollah Khomeini a new governing process was responsive to the will of the revolutionary forces and operated without benefit of any framework of constraint. The first of the two parts that comprise this essay considers the special question of human rights observance and violation in the atmosphere of revolutionary immediacy.

As of October 1979 a new situation arose as a consequence of the Shah's admission to the United States to receive medical treatment. On November 4, 1979 militant students seized the American Embassy and held hostage there some 50 Americans who were officially connected in various ways with the exercise of diplomatic function. The student leaders, supported by mass demonstrations and Khomeini, demanded the physical return of the Shah to face criminal charges and the return to the Iranian people of wealth allegedly plundered by the Shah and his family. In the second part of this essay we will attempt to examine whether in the setting of the encounter between the United States and Iran, arising as a consequence of the hostage crisis, the existing structure of international law is not one-sided in upholding the immunity claims of the American diplomatic personnel, but failing to uphold either extradition claims directed at the Shah or charges that the American Embassy in Tehran has been used to encroach upon the political and personal human rights of the Iranian people.

This essay is excerpted by permission of the author from the forthcoming book tentatively titled *On Human Rights*.

PRELIMINARY NOTES ON HUMAN RIGHTS IN A REVOLUTIONARY SITUATION

The Iranian Revolution took power largely by nonviolent means: a general strike, mass demonstrations, cassettes bearing the messages of exiled leader Ayatollah Khomeini, Xerox machines to coordinate and report on the movement largely through the mosque network of mullahs. It was also a popular revolution enjoying overwhelming support from the Iranian masses in all parts of the country and among all social classes. It was, of course, a revolution inspired by Shi'ia Islamic religious thought and tradition, indigenous to the Third World, owing virtually nothing to the great Western revolutionary experience emanating from the American, French, and Russian Revolutions.

The success of this revolution offers great hope to oppressed peoples elsewhere. It demonstrates once and for all that the relation of forces in a Third World society has not decisively shifted from the people to the state. Iran is such an important case because the populist possibility seemed so remote until it exploded into success. The Shah's apparatus of state power was immense given the scale of Iranian society, reinforced by a large and ruthless secret police and various categories of armed forces available for use against unarmed opposition. Also, the Shah had built up a network of supporting links with outside governments that included, among others, favorable relations with the United States, the Soviet Union, and China, as well as with regional neighbors including Saudi Arabia, Egypt and Israel. As activists in the Khomeini movement like to put it, "we won although the whole world was against us."

What is important is the confirmation that relative power in a revolutionary situation is more a matter of political will than military and paramilitary capability. The Iranian success resulted from the mobilization of the Iranian people on the basis of leadership and beliefs that had intense mass appeal and deep domestic roots. In that sense, the activation of the Shi'ia perspective by Ayatollah Khomeini, and its ideological expression in the influential work of Ali Shariati, were crucial catalysts. In the end, however, it was the willingness of the Iranian masses to persist in challenging state power, carrying on with their demonstrations despite the Shah's willingness to inflict widespread casualties with heavy machine guns, helicopter gunships, and tanks.

At the last stage of the revolutionary struggle, that is, between the time that the Shah left on January 16, 1978 and resistance by the armed forces collapsed a few weeks later, the old regime was virtually isolated from the Iranian people as no significant social remnant was willing to lend its support, much less to fight for the survival of the Pahlavi order. In February small arms were distributed to the people in great numbers. During the last stage of struggle against the Shah crowds chanted "leaders, leaders give us guns." At issue was achieving total control over the state, including its military bureaucracy. The revolutionary leadership was not prepared to reach a negotiated settlement with the military leadership that left the command structure of the Shah intact. The Allende experience in Chile indicated to Iranian leaders how dangerous it can be for a governing body to seek to implement radical social and economic programs and yet rely on a hostile military and governmental bureaucracy. This insistence on a complete victory over the old order led the Iranian revolutionary movement to shift their tactics at the end in the direction of armed struggle. This terminal violent phase was brief, centering on the weekend of February 11, 1978, but it did alter the character of the revolutionary orientation toward the role of violence in their struggle. The dissident elements in the armed forces and the guerrilla groups (People's Fedayeen and Mujahhadin carried Iran just over the brink of civil war before securing the *de facto* surrender and dissolution of the armed forces loyal to the Shah.

This type of ending also meant, however, that at the moment of victory the stage was set for an orgy of retribution. One of the first tasks for the Khomeini movement was to establish minimum order in an atmosphere of accumulated rage and a situation in which the means to pursue vindicative justice were available to a population long abused by a repressive, bloodthirsty tyranny. In understanding the early weeks of revolutionary governance this crucial background element must be kept in mind.

In addition, although the morale of the armed forces was shattered, its leadership remained at large and unreconciled to the revolutionary outcome. Ibrahim Yazdi, originally designated as Deputy Prime Minister for Revolutionary Affairs, contended that a principal reason for the summary executions was the persisting fear that a more orderly process might expose the country to a desperate coup attempt by the remnant of pro-Shah forces. In the early weeks the Khomeini leadership, aside from its hastily contrived popular militia, had no way to protect itself against a counterrevolutionary thrust, whether mounted from without or within the country, or possibly a mixture of the two.

There are other factors. As with any revolution an artificial unity against a common enemy suppresses cleavage at the moment of victory. The Shah was such a hated enemy that the level of unity temporarily achieved was especially deceptive. With the Pahlavi collapse, however, these cleavages came to the fore. The left was immediately eager to establish its presence and to claim for itself a share of credit for the victory. The armed struggle groups, militant for many years, had given many martyrs to the revolution. They were insistent on being recognized and given a part to play in the emerging post-revolutionary governing process. And the main ethnic minorities, Kurds, Azerbaijanis, Baluchis, Bakhtiaris, Arabs and Turkomans, who together make up just under half of Iran's population, seized the opportunity, possibly abetted by outsiders, to assert their persistent demands for autonomy and an acknowledgment from the new leadership of their rights of national self-determination. This challenge confronted the new leadership with an immediate threat to the territorial integrity of the state. Besides, ethnic separatism in Iran, while genuine, has also been a fertile ground for foreign intervention. It is reasonable to suspect that both the Soviet Union and the United States will exploit these separatist tendencies to weaken the new government in Iran, especially if eager to show its incapacity to maintain order in the country. In reality, the fear of outside intervention was never far from the new leadership, given vivid memories of the American-sponsored coup in 1953 that toppled the Mossadegh government.

It is against this background that we consider prospects for human rights in Iran. It is, of course, a hazardous moment for conjecture. The situation is changing rapidly. Not everything is known about what is happening, nor do we have access to the full rationale. Events will supersede any current diagnosis, and yet the interplay of human rights with a fluid revolutionary situation is itself a focus worthy of attention.

Furthermore, it is important to put what is now known in some perspective, if only to correct fashionable distortions. Because such powerful outside interests were and are aligned with the policies of the old order in Iran an enormous incentive exists to discredit the new order. The most prevalent way to achieve this result is to point up human rights abuses that support a most malicious falsehood, namely, that what has happened in Iran is that one tyranny has been replaced by another.

Such claims are outrageous, and suggest the role for a different assessment. First of all, it is necessary to compare the post-Shah situation with the situation under the Shah. Secondly, human rights in Iran have to be understood within a regional and cultural context where levels of abuse are widespread and severe. Such comparisons in time and space are not meant to excuse violations of human rights in Iran, but merely to expose the motivation of those who suddenly focus disproportionate attention to Iran. Many of these new "voices of conscience" were exquisitely silent during the long years of repression by the Shah and remain so about the routine of systematic abuse in neighboring states with more Westernized geopolitical orientations.

Here, briefly then, is an attempt to take account of context, while exploring the prospects for human rights in the early stages of post-revolutionary Iran.

Repression under the Shah

The evidence of torture, summary execution, denial of minimal rights of the person, and the absence of democratic process were all staple elements of the Shah's rule. Even the most cautious outside observers of the human rights situation in Iran confirmed this impression. Amnesty International issued a report late in 1978 indicating the continuation of systematic torture. Many members of the revolutionary leadership were personally abused by the SAVAK, spending years in jail and being victims of various forms of harrassment.

No rights of discussion or criticism were permitted, not even the intellectual preconditions of democratic process. Students and others periodically disappeared from classes. Signs of opposition, such as demonstrations or meetings, were brutally broken up. Iranians abroad were subject to surveillance and cruel punishment upon their return if political activity was reported.

In every sense, then, the Shah's rule must be perceived as one of severe repression backed up by a willingness to use military power to contain the opposition of a hostile population. Heavy casualties were repeatedly inflicted by using modern weaponry against unarmed demonstrators.

Revolutionary Justice

In the aftermath of the revolution a series of summary executions occurred after brief trials before secret revolutionary tribunals. This process was authorized by the Revolutionary Council, originally without the knowledge or backing of Prime Minister Medhi Bazargan, then head of the Provisional Government. Bazargan denounced the process and threatened to resign, a threat he subsequently carried out after Ayatollah Khomeini endorsed the student seizure of the American Embassy on November 4, 1979.

The approximately 700 executions were mainly directed

against principal agents of repression in the Shah era, leaders of the armed forces or SAVAK associated personally with massive crimes against the Iranian people. Several Iranians were also executed according to the dictates of Koranic law for alleged criminal acts, including homosexual rape and violent crimes. This mode of assessing guilt and imposing punishment obviously violated the rights of the accused to open trials with due process protection. At the same time given the revolutionary turmoil, the fear of private vengeance, and the long record of mass abuse associated with Pahlavi rule, extenuating circumstances existed.

The number of executions were relatively limited, and as of early 1980, executions associated with criminal activity on behalf of the Shah's regime have virtually ceased. Khomeini did not repudiate Bazargan despite the harshness of Bazargan's response (". . . irreligious, inhuman, and a disgrace") to this method of pursuing "revolutionary justice." On March 16, 1979 Khomeini called for an end to closed trials and summary executions, a call only partially heeded.

Formation of an Islamic Republic

The Khomeini movement has been criticized because it assessed popular support for an Islamic Republic by a simple "yes"/"no" question on a referendum. Critics allege that the choice could have been more subtle, asking whether the people preferred a monarchy, a constitutional monarchy, a non-religious republic, or an Islamic Republic. The constitutional referendum provided an insufficient democratic sanction, it is argued, on which to base a mandate for an Islamic Republic.

In response, however, it should be noted that the Khomeini movement made it clear throughout the revolution that an Islamic Republic was its objective. This political outcome was promised to followers of Khomeini, and, in a sense, the extent of popular support for that promise is the only relevant question with regard to the reorganization of the Iranian state. The argument that a range of other options should have been presented to the Iranian people is both an academic insistence given the level of support for an Islamic Republic and probably overstates the political sophistication of the Iranian people, so long victimized by a monochromatic tyranny.

The Role of the Left and Non-Religious Dissent

On numerous occasions before coming to power and shortly thereafter Khomeini has affirmed the rights of Marxists and others to express their views and participate in the political life of an Islamic Republic. Such an affirmation has been qualified to the extent that if the left were to establish links with foreign governments, then its freedom to operate would be curtailed. The historical memory of the disruptive role played by the Tudeh Party in the early 1950's remains fresh, especially its apparent subordination to the will of Moscow and its contribution to the 1953 collapse of Mossadegh's government. As Khomeini put it, every country is entitled to protect itself "against those who would commit treason."

Underneath Khomeini's attitude lies another, given expression by Abolhassan Bani-Sadr; namely, the view that when Marxists in Iran genuinely come to understand the goals of an Islamic Republic then they will renounce Marxism and realize that Shi'ia Islam provides a better framework for the pursuit of social justice. And, indeed, the ideas of Ali Shariati have had great appeal for many progressive Iranians, convincing even some Marxists that Islam correctly understood provided a revolutionary ideology that is indigenous to Iran and enjoys a mass following.

As matters now stand a substantial left will remain a critical presence within any Islamic Republic and will test the democratic character of the governing process both by its oppositional style and by the extent to which its rights of expression and activity are allowed.

Several ambiguities exist. First of all, there is the Fedayeen, that element on the extreme left that is now heavily armed and had engaged in armed struggle against the Shah. Will it renounce armed struggle at this new stage? Will it be suppressed? If so, by what means? Can this extreme left be integrated in any sense within the framework of an Islamic Republic? Secondly, will the populist mainstream of the revolution tolerate an active left? There have already been indications within university settings of interference by religious militant groups with meetings, the distribution of literature, and the carrying of Marxist placards at demonstrations and marches. It remains uncertain whether the government will discourage such interference and protect the democratic rights of the left. So far, Khomeini has zigzagged between tolerance and repression. Thirdly, there are some disturbing allegations that the religious leadership intends to repress the left as soon as it consolidates its own power, and that reassurances of tolerance are merely tactical. The death of Ayatollah Teleghani, the most liberal of religious leaders, is a further blow to the hopes for a government of unity and reconciliation.

The interaction between the left and the emergent governing process in Iran will definitely reveal one dimension of the human rights situation. As suggested, however, this revelation will be two-sided, depending on the political approach of the left (or segments of the left) toward opposition (renunciation of foreign links, of armed struggle), as well as on the attitudes of new political leaders, their religious guides, and the populist tides of the Islamic movement. In the short run, Ayatollah Khomeini's individual guidance is likely to be decisive in setting the tone.

Ethnic Minorities

Iran is a multinational state. The Shah repressed these minorities through military and paramilitary means. With the collapse of the armed forces and the weakening of the central state, these national groups have become insistent to varying degrees on improvements in their economic, political, and cultural situation in Iran. It seems indisputable that these national minorities have been victims of discrimination in the past, receiving a disproportionately low share of investment, social services, and so forth. Also, several of these minorities (e.g., Kurds, Baluchis) are predominantly adherents of Sunni Islam. Some minority nationalities also contend that in exchange for their support of the Khomeini movement they had received assurances that a larger measure of autonomy and self-rule would be granted in an Islamic Republic.

As with the left, it is difficult to assess the situation at this stage. Signs of agitation have been evident throughout the minority territories, and serious fighting had broken out in Kurdish areas. One issue is whether these minorities, or some of them, are secessionist in character, intend to rely on violence to achieve their goals, and maintain contact with outside forces (either transnational links with their own people—especially, Kurds in Iraq, Ajerbaijaniis and Turkomen in the Soviet Union, Baluchis in Pakistan). The separatist orientation, it is feared, may also provide fertile areas for covert operations by hostile foreign intelligence organizations seeking to destabilize an Islamic Republic in Iran.

These national minorities together dominate the peripheral region of Iran, including the oil-producing region of Khuzistan, remote from the political and spatial center of the country. Clearly one test of human rights in an Islamic Republic will be the capacity of the central government to deal fairly and nonviolently with these national minorities and their claims for some measure of self-determination. At the same time, the role of foreign governments, the reliance by minorities or factional groups in their midst on armed struggle, and the extent to which self-determination becomes a euphemism for secession will shape the setting within which these issues arise.

Religious Minorities

In Iran there are a number of religious minorities, including Sunnis, Armenian Christians, Jews, Zoroastrians, Nestorians, and Bahais. For various reasons the problematic relations are likely to concern Sunnis, Jews, and Bahais. With the exception of the Bahais, the Khomeini leadership has promised freedom of worship and an atmosphere of religious toleration.

The Sunni minority is troubled by the tension it perceives likely to result from an Islamic Republic in Iran drawn along strictly Shi'ia lines, especially given the strong hostility expressed by the Shi'ia leaders to the role of Sunni Islam. Furthermore, the concentration of Sunnis among national minority groups hostile to the state may reinforce the perception of Sunnis as subversive elements.

With respect to the 80,000 or so Jews, the root of the problem involves the hostile relationship between an Islamic Republic and Israel. One of the first diplomatic acts of the Khomeini movement was to invite PLO leader Yasir Arafat to Iran and pledge solidarity, symbolized by turning over the former Israeli Embassy to the PLO. The situation is aggravated by the extent to which Israel is perceived as having been a bulwark of support of the Shah, including the role that the Israeli intelligence service, *Mossad,* played in setting up and working with the SAVAK.

Here again a key issue will be whether Iranian Jews are perceived as Zionists with operational emotional and material links to Israel. The government's capacity and will to discourage anti-semitic attitudes within the population is also crucial. Khomeini has given the Jewish community repeated reassurances, including his assertion that it would be a tragedy for Iran if Jews leave. So far, between 5,000 and 18,000 Jews have left Iran since the fall of the Shah, apparently fearing for their safety and well-being in an Islamic Republic. Despite fears, the record of the Khomeini period toward the Jewish community as a whole has been quite positive as of this time.

The circumstances of the 300,000 or so Bahais is of especial concern. Here, alone, Khomeini refuses to provide reassurance. Indeed, he has said that Bahais have no place in an Islamic Republic, that it is a political rather than a religious sect, and that its leading members were closely tied up with Pahlavi rule. In the background is the Shi'ia view of the Bahai religion as heretical, founded by Baha'u'llah, regarded by adherents as a subsequent and superior prophet to Mohammed. Reports of abuse of Bahais and their religious property in various parts of Iran by members of

Revolutionary Committees have been received and have elicited the first formal acts of protest by human rights groups.

Women

The status of women in Iran is another symbolic battleground. It is also a confusing one. Yardsticks for progress cannot be supplied on the basis of Western experience. Since the revolution is Islamic at its core, there are obvious tensions between religious fundamentalism and achieving equality of treatment for women in Iran. The issue, like others in the human rights area, is susceptible to manipulation by those within and without the country seeking to destabilize the new governing process.

Khomeini and other religious leaders have been generally reassuring about the rights of women. After an initial insistence on traditional dress, Khomeini made it plain that the *chador* was optional. Demonstrations by women in Iran were not officially suppressed, and, in fact, those taking part were protected by a peculiar mixture of Fedayeen and some units of the Popular Militia working under the control of the Revolutionary Committees. At the same time, many incidents of harrassment and intimidation of activist women have been reported in the course of the first year of the revolution.

The main short-run issue is whether women who participated so bravely in the struggle against the Shah, will be able to advance their claims for equality, participation, and dignity within a democratic framework. It will involve a difficult struggle, and by no means are women in Iran united as to their priorities or goals. Also, no Islamic society has yet succeeded in producing a satisfactory readjustment of traditional status and roles for women.

Purges and Purity

In the media and government ministries, allegations are being made that new revolutionary authorities have instituted "purges." Here again, the facts are difficult to sort out. The claim on behalf of the revolution is that those who worked loyally for the old order need to be replaced. The claim of the critics is that anyone who is not subordinate to the religious leadership is neither trusted nor wanted. How much ideological conformity is imposed upon radio, television, and newspapers will certainly determine the atmosphere of freedom in the new Iran. The first twelve months have produced an inconsistent record, one in which the mood has shifted back and forth.

Again, the recent heritage has been one of censorship and

control. Iranians were deeply moved back in January 1979 when long lines were observed at Tehran newsstands because finally newspapers and magazines contained real news and diverse interpretations. Later on liberal disenchantment set in when newspapers and magazines critical of government policy were closed down, attacked or censored.

The issue of "purity" is closely related to the general applicability of Islamic law. How strict and literal will be the lines drawn between Koranic text and behavioral compulsion in the new Iranian state? Already there are indications that liquor will be forbidden in public places and that entertainment featuring violence and sex will not be allowed in any form. Especially in provincial law these new imperatives are likely to be supplemented by harsh punishment for violators. Law enforcement on these matters has been uneven and decentralized, with some very harsh regimes evidently operating in parts of the new Iran.

This sketch of human rights prospects for Iran is incomplete and tentative. The unfolding of the Islamic Republic will reveal the degree to which human rights will flourish or not. At present, outsiders should watch, learn, and wait, as well as judge and appraise. The process of post-revolutionary adjustment has been difficult for every polity. There are enemies of the revolution that continue to be active. In Iran's case, outside states have an incentive to provoke the collapse of the Islamic Government and the restoration of Western-oriented leadership, this time directly under military rather than dynastic auspices.

At minimum, let us not confuse the tyranny of the past with the problems of the present and future. Ayatollah Khomeini seems dedicated to evolving a form of governance for the people of Iran that includes a central commitment to social justice for the poor, a closing of gaps between social classes, and an elimination of the kinds of wasteful consumption and production patterns that grew up during the Shah's years. He continues to enjoy an intense popular mandate to achieve this goal. Success will enable Iran to demonstrate that a revolutionary victory need not by spoiled by the tensions raised in the post-revolutionary period of consolidation.

THE HOSTAGE CRISIS AND INTERNATIONAL LAW

All during the crisis over the seizure of the U.S. Embassy in Tehran, there has been much talk of international law and even more about geopolitics. In both areas, however, the discussion has been marked by an astonishing narrowness of focus that deprives the public of adequate insight into the realities of the global order and of the United States' position in the world.

On the legal aspect, the U.S. Government has insisted from the outset that international law supports its basic demand for release of the American hostages. This position has been upheld by a unanimous finding of the International Court of Justice, the highest organ for interpreting international law that exists in the world. For the United States, then, the only inadequacy of international law has been the lack of means to enforce the court's mandate upon a defiant ruler.

Ayatollah Khomeini's refusal to honor the rules of international law relating to diplomatic immunity are among the most serious charges brought against his leadership. Even Hitler, it is alleged, never violated the diplomatic immunity of his enemies. In fact, one has to search the books of diplomatic history to find isolated precedents for the events of recent months in Tehran, and in each such instance the challenge to diplomatic decorum came from what is portrayed as being a barbarian, non-Western source. Indeed, it is not a long step from condemning Khomeini as a law-breaker to the more virulent demands to "nuke Iran" or "hang Khomeini."

And yet one must wonder about this supposed clarity of international law. After all, is it not a serious matter when an embassy is used to subvert the constitutional order of a country, as was done by the United Stated in staging the coup that brought the Shah back to power in 1953? Is it not also serious that embassy personnel evidently helped establish and train the SAVAK, the secret police that committed so many crimes against the people of Iran? The response to these Iranian grievances is also clear: "Everybody knows that embassies are spy-nests." True, vague prohibitions against intervening in the internal affairs of sovereign states exist, but no one takes them seriously. Diplomacy, it is said, is inevitably interventionary. This is the game of politics played on a global scale, for better or worse.

Existing international law also supports the American refusal to extradite the Shah. First of all, it is claimed that the Shah was a recipient of the American prerogative to give asylum, especially on this occasion where a supposed medical necessity existed. On a more technical level, the absence of an extradition treaty between the U.S. and Iran would have made it virtually impossible to return the Shah to Iranian custody, even if Jimmy Carter had wanted to do so. Finally, even if an extradition treaty had existed, it is doubtful that an American court would have found the Shah extraditable. The evidence against him is connected with his repressive rule, but accusations of "political crimes" are not recognized as grounds for extradition. International law as it exists, then supports the U.S. claim about the hostages but gives Iran almost no comfort. The very clarity of international law, given the underlying equities, raises questions about its one-sidedness. Why should the rules protecting diplomatic immunity be so much clearer than the rules protecting a weak country against intervention? Or why should "asylum" be available to a cruel tyrant associated with the massive commission of state crimes, including torture, arbitrary execution, and economic plunder? What kind of international law is it that protects foreign police and torture specialists by conferring upon them the status of "diplomat"?

In part, the drift of international law reflects the history of international relations since the birth of the modern state system in the middle of the 17th century. It is a law of, for and by governments, especially governments that are powerful. In that sense, *all* governments have a shared interest in upholding the absolute rights of their diplomatic representatives. Relations depend on communications, even in periods of stress, and hence the case for diplomatic immunity seems strong. As an organization of governments, the United Nations is the world's strongest lobby for diplomatic immunity.

On other aspects of the situation, interests are not so clearly shared. In an interdependent world, intervention is not altogether avoidable and it represents one of the instruments by which the strong control the weak. To renounce intervention would be, for a superpower, tantamount to renouncing power politics. It can be done quite easily in words, but not in deeds.

Who's Next?

Similarly, regarding the treatment of deposed wandering tyrants, many existing governments grow nervous, as well they might. Many rulers are potential defendants in trials alleging state crime. The idea of granting sanctuary to deposed leaders has some appeal, partly because a ruler who has the option of comfortable exile may choose it as preferable to other options: protracted civil strife or surrender. Even Idi Amin, Emperor Bokassa, Pol Pot and Anastasio Debayle Somoza have found foreign places of refuge; if returned home, each of them would almost surely be executed.

What we find, then, is a pro-governmental bias built into modern international law. This bias is a natural consequence of a system in which nation-states dominate the global scene and some states dominate others. The adequacy or inadequacy of this framework is one of the deeper, unexamined issues posed by the Iran crisis. Khomeini clearly rejects the built-in bias of the system:

> What kind of law is this? It permits the U.S. Government to exploit and colonize peoples all over the world for decades. But it does not allow the extradition of an individual who has staged great massacres. Can you call it law? (*Time*, interview, Jan. 7)

Given the way that international diplomacy operates, nevertheless, how is it reasonable to expect international law to be different than it is? Perhaps the Iran crisis will move us to an act of imagination that will create another set of possibilities. More people may begin to ask: Why should big-power governments alone establish the rules that govern behavior on the planet? Why should not citizens organize to insist on a framework of law that corresponds to a minimal framework of morality?

Part of the moving force for change can come through a conventional diplomatic effort toward reform of international law, making it less one-sided. The governments of some third world nations have exerted some pressure along these lines with respect to international economic relations, ocean rights and duties, and the status of irregular forces (guerrillas, liberation armies) in time of war. Because of the Iranian encounter, it becomes highly appropriate to consider redrafting the Vienna Convention on Diplomatic and Consular Immunity so as to more nearly balance the rights of the host country to political independence with the rights of the foreign country to diplomatic security. We can imagine a commission of inquiry being established under United Nations auspices that would have the legal competence to examine charges against tyrants (deposed or not) and recommend, as feasible, the formation of special tribunals.

But once the hostages are released and things calm down, it seems doubtful that much global reform along the lines proposed above will be undertaken. On the contrary: Efforts are under way in the U.S. to restore the covert operations mission to the CIA repertoire and to establish military forces and doctrine for intervention in foreign countries. The one-sidedness of international law is but a reflection of the one-sidedness of international life in general.

Given this reality, have we not reached the stage where citizens through voluntary associations should organize to regulate the behavior of governments? At least, it would seem constructive to have a mechanism available for inquiring into the commission of state crime. Some precedents already exist. In Europe, the British philosopher Bertrand Russell established in 1966-67 a "tribunal" to investigate charges of war crimes arising out of the American involvement in the Viet Nam War. More recently, a group of international legal and cultural figures joined in an effort to proclaim a legal framework for human rights, issuing the Algiers Declaration of the Rights of Peoples on July 4, 1976. Preliminary steps have been taken by an Italian entity, the Lelio Basso Foundation, to establish a tribunal that would investigate charges against governments and leaders flowing out of violations of the Algiers Declaration. The Delhi Declaration of 1978 condemned nuclear weapons and proposed a treaty for their renunciation as weapons of war. In 1975 a group of economists gathered in Mexico issued the Cocoyac Declaration, which called for a new global economic order going beyond the demands of governments for "a new international economic order."

The events in Iran show us that some clear rules of international law have been broken, but they also suggest that the content and impact of this law are arbitrary and one-sided. Given the historical shifts in the world, including the upsurge of power in the third world, it is not clear why the old law should be kept as is. It is most unlikely, however, that governments will act on their own motion to create more balanced laws surrounding the issues of embassy use and abuse and the question whether persons accused of serious state crime are entitled to asylum rather than to a fair trial under impartial auspices. This is the moment when individuals, churches and voluntary associations of various kinds can assert human concern—that the future of international law is not *only* a matter for governments, that we ought not unconditionally surrender our birthright as moral beings to the monopolizing tendencies of the sovereign state.

Women In Today's Iran

Pamela Haines

The sense of being at a women's event was delightful. The translator was a woman; the technical engineer on the recording system was a woman. The speaker, Mrs. Zahra Rahnavard, was a leader among Islamic women. She had a background in sociology, had written several books on women's issues, and, though not a religious person in the past, had rediscovered the relevance of Islam in the last several years, and had been active in mobilizing tradition-oriented women during the revolution. She was a small, slim woman in her mid-thirties, perhaps, carrying herself with simple dignity, and speaking with quiet assurance and clarity.

I was looking forward to finally getting an overall look at women's issues from an Islamic perspective, and, on her side, the opportunity to communicate to a group of concerned Americans was clearly an important one. She was aware that we might be skeptical and all-too polite, and started out with a direct request: "Please ask any questions. We will be glad to answer anything, and will be more offended if you hold back, and leave with questions still in your minds." She also had great expectations of us: "Go back with your hands full of the truth, and explain the problems and realities of Iran to the American people."

Her sense of trust in our delegation's willingness and ability to do that was new, but compelling. "Before, I had a feeling of hatred for the American people, until, during the time of oppression, we were forced to become close. Then I saw that you were bound in oligarchical oppression like we were; just the techniques of control are different. This strengthened our ties. We know you are striving like us for freedom and truth. You might be weak at first, but what you are after is so great that it will compensate for the weakness. We know that the ties are strong, and that you will succeed as we have."

As with nearly every issue that we came across in the new Iran, people's thinking about the role of women could not be separated out either from their own history or from Islamic ideology or from an over-all struggle against oppression. So she started out with a very brief overview of the suffering of the past and the factors that created a successful revolution. I was particularly aware that it was a woman telling this story, and thought about what it must have meant for other women.

"Here in Iran we have 70,000 martyrs, 100,000 injured and handicapped. Why did people give their lives? We lived under terrible oppression: despotism ruled; differences between classes were great; poverty was intense; workers were exploited; agriculture was destroyed; the culture was terribly debased; women were seen as sex objects; the prisons were full of our youth; our customs and beliefs were insulted; there were mass executions.

"Then Khomeini came and awakened the dead hearts of the people. Very fast, the Iranian people awakened and united to regain their rights. The Iranian revolution introduced a completely new type of revolution to the world: neither communist nor nationalist, but religious. Islam brought about the unity of the people and provided a revolutionary ideology. These two things allowed us to win (although we achieve total victory only when all our goals are obtained).

"The Imam offers charismatic and holy leadership, leadership that is tied to God. This is the most effective leadership. When human nature is aroused and awakened, it has great power. This is what the Imam did.

"Because of this, we were able to destroy all the corrupt institutions of the old regime. By ending the militaristic army system, for example, we were able to absorb the soldiers into the people. The goals of the revolution are in the direction of liberating people. They are based on Islamic ideals and principles, such as the principle of "tauhid", which is equality and unity. The revolution is for equality in race, religion, class and society. We are determined to destroy the dependent industries, to revive agriculture, and to revive a culture which is based on equality."

The style is strange to us—the intensity, the lack of qualifiers, the mixture of politics and religion. Only by understanding the depth of suffering, repression, and impotence people felt under the Shah can one begin to understand the fierce and passionate attachment that a person like Zahra Rahnavard has to the force that was actually able to mobilize the people to overthrow such a regime.

Having set the stage, and moving on to women's role in particular, Mrs. Rahnavard is vividly aware of how the western press has used the issue to distort and isolate the Iranian revolution: "As far as women are concerned, the West presents a picture of black-covered women in harems, under the control of the men, existing just to raise children and to be sexual objects for men. This stereotype has been carried to the West to be used against the Islamic revolution. As a vulnerable point, it has been used to take away the popular support that Islam had. Reporters could have asked about many other things, but they kept harping on this."

She goes on to discuss the limitations of role models that both traditional society and western culture have offered to women, and revolutionary Islam's response: "For 2500 years the system has been trying to make women into something that could serve it and be totally in its hands. In the previous regime, a woman could either be bound to the traditional role like her mother, being a good wife and mother and keeping the home, or she could choose to be a 'modern woman.' The main value to the modern woman was materialism; she presented herself to society with no true identity; she had only the western 'freedom' which even now the West does not offer freely.

"If we accept the sociological concept that people try to mold themselves in accordance with the values and criteria of society, then for the 'modern woman,' we had the models of Bridgit Bardot, Raquel Welch and Iranian singers. For the traditional woman, we had the model of the mother who stayed at home to cook and care for the family. Both are reactionary.

"But the Imam has changed the criteria and examples. He put Zainab up as an example. He compared the present revolution to that of Imam Husein (soon after Mohammed's time)—and Zainab, his sister, was there. Every time a martyr was given, she would die, then be there again. She was imprisoned, then when she got out, she travelled widely, urging the people to arise, throw off their oppressors, and re-establish Islamic values."

I have always been proud of, and thankful for, my relative freedom as a western woman—freedom of choice, action, and opportunity. I had assumed that the Shah's westernization program would simply spread such freedom more widely. While some of that has undoubtedly happened, it had not occurred to me that, when grafted onto an oppressive third world country's culture, the parts to blossom most vigorously would be freedom to abandon values, to welcome sexual exploitation, to lose identity. But then I realized that this was not just an isolated accident. It seems to be consistently true that the very worst parts of our traditions and institutions surface in all their rankness when transplanted to the third world.

I was impressed by the accuracy of this critique of western women's liberation, and hopeful for their potential of developing totally new role models from Iran's own tradition. If Iranian women are actually expected to embody the characteristics of those Islamic models, to be powerful fighters and leaders as well as nurturers of loved ones, then they are certainly on the right track.

Zahra Rahnavard continues with a discussion of how a new values system has opened up new possibilities for all Iranians: "There is another sociological concept: that people will always follow and adhere to the dominating values, whether they are wealth, money, power or beauty. All of these values were dominant in the old regime. But the Imam put all these values aside and introduced new values.

"One was the concept of martyrdom, which means moving and struggling in the direction of divine goals. A person who dies in that process gains eternal life, which is light, beauty, bounty. Our people were thirsty for this value. It helped people to give their lives graciously in this way."

"Our people were thirsty for this value." It made me think about our country. What are the values that Americans are thirsting for? What are the values that would really give meaning to our collective life? What would it be like to have our entire society revolving around a set of non-material values to which we were deeply committed? Again, she sets women in this larger context. True liberation for women can only be discussed in the context of liberation from those institutions and ways of thinking that keep the human spirit from soaring.

What did it mean for the women of Iran to be offered this whole new set of values? "Khomeini sent a message from France saying, "Any nation that has women like the Iranian women will surely be victorious." That made us proud. The women who died in the streets will be martyrs; this is the true picture of the Islamic women. Islam helped them to change their own values and achieve new ones, which in turn helped them to move toward the highest evolutionary goals.

"Let me close with some examples of women in Iran during the revolution:

—There are thousands of people in the streets. You can see the women: in one hand they hold up banners and flags; in the other, they carry children. Their belief in the ideology has brought them out.

—It is morning. People are going out to demonstrate. An old woman is sending her children out one by one—to go and become martyrs—because she cannot go herself.

—The masses in the streets are faced by soldiers and U.S. weapons. A blind woman is standing on the edge by a phone booth with a bowl of two rials (coins). They are for people to use if they need to make a phone call. People do all they can.

—It is Black Friday (September 8, 1978, when the regime's attack on demonstrators led to some of the heaviest casualties of the revolution). Soldiers are surrounding the people. Women in Islamic clothing say, 'If we surround you they will not kill us, and all will be saved.' Moments later the street is full of their bodies on the ground.

—A woman is lying on an iron bed, with a fire beneath her. She says only 'Allah O Akbar, God is Great.' She is tortured till she dies. This is the woman that Islam builds.''

Women in Islamic Society

Zahra Rahnavard has given us the essence of the very best that revolutionary Islam can offer to women, and it is very good. The role that women actually play in the society, and the role that is envisioned for the future, grows out of the interplay between the forward thrust of that ideology and the conservative pull that has kept women subordinate in Islamic culture (as it has done, in different forms, all over the world).

It is important to note from the beginning that Islam represented a significant step forward for women of the time (and was more progressive in many ways than either Judaism or Christianity). Mohammed modeled a new role for women. He spoke out against female infanticide. He did housework along with his wife. When a suitor asked his daughter's hand in marriage, he broke age-old custom and first went to ask her what she thought. In a symbolic gesture, he kissed the hands of two people—a woman and a worker—indicating who it was in society that deserved the greatest respect. But despite such modelling, it is certainly true that the vast majority of Iranian women have traditionally occupied a very limited and subordinate position in society.

The revolution offered the women of Iran a whole new way of seeing themselves. Zahra Rahnavard's answers to questions about women's role in the revolution illustrate both this change and the continuity (and clearly indicated the gap between women of the tiny modernized and educated sector and the millions of poor). ''In the previous regime there were underground ideological gatherings and organizations—but these were mostly for the intellectual woman. The mass of women took part in gatherings in the mosques and heard preachings there of the new role for women. Intellectual women took part in the underground armed struggle (1963-1977).

When it changed to a popular struggle, masses of both men and women took part. In the revolution women were chanting and marching in the streets. In the mosques they would rise and talk and say what they had to say. I have spoken in many mosques in South Tehran and all over the country.

"Maybe for cultural reasons the men tried to protect the women. They made rings around the women in the streets. When people opened their homes to the wounded, they usually took women and children first. This is because of the high value that is placed on women in the culture, and not an indication of their taking a lesser role."

The tension between tradition and change is perhaps the most striking in the symbol of the *chador*. As a garment that covers the woman's entire body (and has to be held in place by one hand), and is worn in public so that she will not excite men's lustful feelings, it is a stereotypical symbol of women's oppression. Who could help but applaud the Shah in his attempt to liberate women from the *chador*?

Yet the Iranian women students gave a different perspective: "The freedom that the Shah gave to women was freedom to be corrupt, but not social or political freedom. The Shah was afraid of awakening the Islamic revolutionary spirit. He was afraid of its symbols, such as the *chador*. So all women would come out in black *chadors*, united, from all classes. The Shah saw the *chador* as a symbol of reaction, but here were people shouting revolutionary slogans."

We were told of women from the educated classes, who had never worn a *chador* in their lives, going out to borrow one before participating in a street demonstration, so that it would be very clear that they were on the side of change. The *chador* now symbolized unity and revolution as well.

Though clearly a unifying symbol during the revolution, it is by no means the enforced universal garment, as we have been led to believe by the media. One of the things that first struck me in Tehran was the diversity of women's dress. In the poor southern part of the city the *chador* predominated, as it has for hundreds of years. But most of the women that we saw in the wealthier north, and many in the central business district, would be indistinguishable on the streets of a western city. Others wore western dress with a headscarf, evidently in symbolic acknowledgment of the religious tradition. And many members of the younger generation (including the students) have adopted a more liberating version of Islamic dress; we saw lots of young women in a big headscarf, long-sleeved tunic, and pants.

101

Even among the *chador*-wearers, the diversity took me by surprise. Colors ranged from blacks to other solids to bright prints, and styles from cheap cotton economy to lacy elegance to heavy embossed richness. Nor had I imagined the variety of foot and leg-wear: clumpy black shoes and lumpy black leggings, sneakers, blue-jeans and workboots, heels and stockings, pants, skirts of all lengths. Under the timeless uniformity of the *chador*, I was seeing expressions of hundreds of individual preferences and styles. Neither just a symbol of traditional oppression, nor just one of revolutionary unity, the *chador* has become a strange and complex combination of both.

The tension between tradition and change can also be seen in the new ideology's expectation that women assume a double role. They are called on to combine their newly-articulated political activity with the prime and highly-valued occupation of caring for the family and raising children. After discussing women's revolutionary activity, Zahra Rahnavard goes on to talk about the other half of the role: "Our goal is to orient women's power in the ideology. We don't want to debase the family and carry out the defeated experiences of the West. Maybe there will be some day-care centers, or grandmothers helping, or mothers organizing other ways of freeing up their time, but we don't want to separate women from their children."

In talking about men's and women's roles in the family, the students emphasized the belief in equality. The theory sounds exemplary. But underneath the words runs a current of ambiguity, an indication of the conceptual limitations that the culture still places on women: "The father is expected to share the family role with the mother, from feeding the babies to whatever else is needed. The role of the man is just like the role of the woman, really. But we know that the woman is kinder and softer than the man, which makes her especially important in the family.

"The wealth from work that a woman does (on a paid job) belongs to her just like a man's does. Everyone should be paid according to his or her work. From a social point of view, women and men are not separate. All are responsible for each other. It is just at home that our roles are separated. The man is expected to honor the woman and has a responsibility to bring about the comfort of the woman, like feeding the baby when the woman can't work. They are united in marriage to become one, to help each other move through life and move toward their goals. There is an Islamic saying that men are the clothing for women, and women are the clothing for men. Each completes the other."

The vocabulary is there, but the tone of paternalism—of "honor" and "help"—indicates the nature of the struggle that is still ahead in Iran (as it is, again, in most other places in the world).

A discussion of women's role in the mosque reveals the same tension, the overarching importance of an ideology that has equality at its core, with the culture of male domination in which it is imbedded. According to one of the students: "The issue of women in the mosque is a complicated one, and has to be seen in the context of the whole ideology. The separation of sexes at prayers is to keep from arousing sexual feelings. It also gives more beauty and order, and is more comfortable. There is the sense of unity of women and unity of men. But this separation is not a law.

"Women are active in the mosque, but, with the very strong oppression, especially under the Shah, most people haven't had the opportunity for that activity. Because of women's dual responsibility (in the home and in the larger society) they will never reach the level of Imam. But all else is available. There is no class in Islam called the clergy that is closer to God, or more religious than the rest; there are no intermediaries. There are just people who *know* more. Everybody—regardless of sex—has the potential to be close to God."

In education and training we heard mixed reports. In response to our question about public schools that had been coeducational under the Shah now being separated by sex, the students replied that only a few, mostly international, high schools had ever been coeducational. The move for separation could be seen more as a symbolic repudiation of western models than as a major shift in educational patterns; coeducational universities and kindergartens remained unaffected. The fact that, with a national illiteracy rate of 60%, a major literacy campaign is now under way all over the country would seem to be a more significant and solid indication of the direction in which women's education is moving.

While we heard that, as a measure to combat (male) unemployment, clear preference was being given to men for professional positions, we also saw that most of the women students were majoring in professional areas such as engineering, and assuming that their skills would be put to use for the benefit of the revolution. We were told that more women now were going into religious schools; we also heard the opposite. More basic than either is the Shi'ite expectation that every Moslem, regardless of sex, age, or level of education, will take responsibility at all times for studying and growing in their spiritual understanding.

Women in political life, women in the family, women in the

mosque, women in education—in each case, they are supported on the one hand by the revolutionary potential of the ideology, and challenged on the other with the conservativism of centuries of tradition.

Sexual Laws and Customs

Having heard much about the throwback to medievalism in sexual laws and customs, we had lots of questions for the students, and got a chance to hear a revolutionary Islamic perspective. Again, it is more complex and less hopeless than the media would lead us to believe.

In terms of family planning, Iranian women said that a high societal value is placed on the raising up of good Islamic children; the model role for a woman is that of mother. Within that context, contraceptives are acceptable as long as they are used to plan rather than totally prevent oneself from having children. Abortion, however, is excluded from acceptable birth control methods. To choose not to bring a child into the world is seen as justifiable only when the mother's or the child's life is in danger.

According to the students, it is customary, though not mandated, that a married woman who cannot have children will adopt. On the other hand, it is perfectly Islamic to be a single woman; there are lots of people to help and socially-useful things to do besides raising children. No force is used against a single woman who sleeps with men, but that is clearly *not* seen as Islamic.

The students' discussion of adultery illustrates that, much more important than a law itself, is the way in which laws are interpreted and enforced: "The Islamic law on adultery needs to be seen in the context of the society as a whole. In a just society, where everybody has work and minimum security and there is spiritual, mental, and cultural stability, adultery is completely prohibited. It is harder to condemn it in times of corruption and injustice, though it is still against Islamic law. For example, in the midst of the revolution, when the city was full of people, a group of people attacked a house of prostitution and drove the prostitutes out. The poor women had no place to go. At Friday prayers that week, Ayatollah Taleghani noted that the women were victims of corruption, not causes of it, and needed to be helped. The one or two women who were finally executed were those who had been doing it consciously, who had been selling little girls, and who had also been selling drugs. The son of Khomeini has said: 'When there is no chance for a woman to build her character, she shouldn't be punished for it.' " (This understanding that Islamic law can be enforced justly only in a society where there is economic equality and justice was also noted in the discussion on abortion.)

In terms of marriage and divorce, there is also more flexibility than meets the western eye. While the custom of arranged marriage persists, it is not Islamic law. Mohammed spoke out against it centuries ago, it is less and less common in the cities these days, and the Ayatollah who leads Friday prayers has encouraged children to decide for themselves. In place of arranged marriages, revolutionary Islam is holding up the model of marriage as a free choice, based on ideology rather than either good business or romance, and to be seen as a partnership in working toward common goals.

According to the students, it is also possible within Islamic law for a man and a woman to make a preliminary contract. Under such a contract, they agree to live together for a certain amount of time, then decide whether or not to make it eternal, and together make arrangements for the children if it doesn't work out. One of the students took particular pleasure in putting the Islamic stand on polygamy into context: "It is true that the Koran says that men are allowed to have more than one wife. But then it goes on to say [and a twinkle came into her eye] that the first wife must accept the others, and that the man must treat all his wives equally, and that since meeting those conditions is hardly ever possible, you probably shouldn't bother to try. But," she concluded, "these qualifications are hardly ever mentioned."

The ideal solution to marital difficulties is to use the Islamic *shora* (council) system within the family as an internal vehicle for solving problems. People are expected to try hard and be willing to compromise to keep the family together, especially if there are children. But when that is impossible, a couple may get divorced. During the revolution, the students said, Khomeini declared that women could divorce; if conditions that were set before marriage were not met, then dissolution of that marriage became legal. There is also a clear series of stages, for a period of three months after divorce, by which a couple can come back together. This interval allows a woman to discover if she's pregnant, in case that fact would change a decision about the future of their marriage. This information contradicts the things we have heard about the illegality of divorce. The student's information, of course, is not definitive, but it certainly points out the importance both of not accepting uncritically all that we hear in the media, and of realizing that the existence of a law does not necessarily indicate common practice or attitude. (One of the women offered a fascinating perspective on the nature of Islamic laws: "They are complete, and they solve all problems," she said, "but they are also very flexible and vary from region to region—though nothing can be done that goes against principle." She gave an example of the law that you must wash your hands before prayers: "If you don't have any water, then you use some clean dirt. If you can't do that, you do the best you can.")

The students' discussion of Islamic attitudes toward modesty and physical affection offers a stinging critique of the distortions of western culture and a vision of a society in which more is expected of people than the pursuit of personal pleasure. They also provide perhaps the clearest indication of the extent to which the best of revolutionary Islam still buys into assumptions about the role of women that western feminists would find oppressive.

"In most cases, the Koran speaks to both women and men. But for the woman, certain orders are given in accordance with her role and her biology. For example, we want society clean and pure from desires and lust. A woman exciting a man by her dress or her actions is deviating from our way. Sex is for the continuation of the human race. Although it happens to include enjoyment, that is not its object. We don't want our society to turn on the pivot of sex as it has done in the West. There are other problems in society that need to be solved. Modest dress also helps to keep a woman from being used by her appearance (the way capitalism uses a woman's body and face to create desires and sell products), so her personality comes out more fully. Bani-Sadr has said that we want the relation between men and women to be a relation first, between two minds; secondly, between two hearts; and only thirdly, between two bodies."

Iranian Women's Perspectives on the Revolution

We have been talking almost exclusively up to this point about women's issues from the perspective of articulate people in leadership (including the students holding the embassy) who are committed to Islam as a revolutionary ideology. Their position would be that all limitations that women presently face can be overcome by strict and complete application of the values and teachings at the core of Islam. Other sectors of the population—the tiny group of middle-class women who have internalized western values; the millions of poor, who lean on tradition and their religious leaders to guide their thinking and behavior; and educated leftists, who have their own, non-Islamic ideology—would come to the same issues with quite different perspectives.

I can only speculate about the attitudes of the first group, though, despite their small numbers, their views are probably the ones that have gained the widest coverage in western media. Those who were closely associated with the Shah's regime and fled the country would be among its members. Those who remain in north Tehran, holding on to professional jobs and continuing to wear western dress would be others. They likely find themselves in uneasy individual relation to society at large, caught between two cultures, understandably worried about losing the advances that westernization had offered them. These are the women in Iran for whom the revolution has not clearly been a step forward.

While poor women continue to look the most oppressed—uneducated, tied to family roles, hidden under the *chador*—they may well be the ones who have gained the most. Just the fact of participating in a revolution—marching in the streets, shouting, building barricades—did irreparable damage to the image of a model woman quietly staying at home and minding the family. Although they may not perceive of themselves as more powerful *women* as a result, they certainly see themselves as more powerful human beings.

We spoke with (mostly listened to, actually) a lot of poor women on the trip. On the streets, at their doorways, in the factories, at public prayers, they spoke out with confidence, with anger, with pride, with determination. The overall impression they conveyed was one of ownership. While their analysis is often simplistic and while they may still slip into apathy and complaints, they clearly see themselves as a vital part of the whole process. These are *their* values and this is *their* revolution. And somehow, when you are talking about power in that very basic sense, the question of women's rights seems a little tangential.

Leftist women are a bit more critical. From scattered conversations in Iran, left-oriented articles in the U.S. press and an understanding of Marxist ideology, we can sketch the broad outlines of their response. Leftist women in Iran would all probably share the overall perspective that the revolution has been a major step forward and has successfully united the people against imperialism, but that in the long term, Islam cannot provide the ideological framework within which a society can move to true equality. While noting the tremendous advances made by women in the process of actively participating in a revolution, and placing women's rights in the context of a larger struggle against all forms of oppression, they would see the Islamic attitude toward women as one of these long-term limitations.

Soussan Sarkhoch, a former political prisoner, a member of a Chinese-oriented leftist party, and an anthropology professor at the University of Tehran, articulates this general perspective. In a

March 1980 interview in the *Guardian*, she answers a question about women's rights in Iran as follows: "We can address this legally or socially. Legal reforms under the Shah (e.g., the right to divorce) were never used by the majority of women. Socially, women's massive participation in the revolutionary struggle has changed their position and power within the family. A woman in the struggle today, being armed, will not accept oppression from men— she is developing a personality and consciousness appropriate for resistance. We still have a very long road to go. We've learned every right has to be fought for to be won. The first step is that women in the course of struggle are achieving awakened consciousness and getting organized. The next step is to organize for our own rights as women, in our women's organizations."

When asked whether women can achieve emancipation within a strict Moslem outlook, she replies, "Only in a framework of socialism can women truly gain emancipation. Any other form of government is unable to emancipate women fully. For example, I don't think women in Europe or the U.S. are fully emancipated."

Beyond this overall perspective, however, leftist women differ on both the extent of the immediate threat to women's rights and the means by which women should continue the struggle. Some are sharply critical of what they perceive as a systematic attack on women's rights by the present government, especially in terms of employment discrimination, and would call for public protests. Others, although expressing some criticism, focus on the gains made during the revolution and are willing to participate in the government and give it time to prove itself. All would see the importance of educating, organizing and mobilizing women as a self-conscious political force in the on-going struggle to establish a new society. And all realize that they must come to terms with the tremendous power of Islam to shape the actions and attitudes of Iran's women.

Two Questions for the Future

The revolution has mobilized millions of women by interpreting their deeply held values as calls to stand up against oppression. It has offered them visions and models of active, powerful women leaders. The best of revolutionary Islamic ideology demands that women move constantly forward in taking mastery over their lives and larger environment. On the other hand, the conservative aspects of Islam exercise a constant backward drag. The present leadership of Iran seems to be contributing to both tendencies. Two questions are crucial for the future: On what side will Islam end up throwing its greatest weight, and how determinedly will women struggle as the new Iranian society is being built, not only for the benefit of all, but also for their own dignity, equality and freedom?

Just as women cannot achieve liberation without looking at the specific ways in which they are oppressed *as women*, neither can they succeed by focusing exclusively on their own particular demands. Zahra Rahnavard captures best for me the lesson that American women can learn from Iran, the context in which a struggle for women's rights must be seen if it is to move the whole of humankind forward: "You can't strive for the freedom of just one sex. The problem of women's subordination exists because of the larger oppression there. As long as oppression exists, equality has no meaning; you have to fight oppression as a whole for it to be a just struggle. Human nature strives to reach justice and freedom; this is innate in humankind. To all who have been oppressed, regardless of your race or sex, or the values in your culture: Respond to this thirst in your nature."

Impressions of South Tehran

John Mohawk

Iran is a desert country. January in Tehran is cold, sometimes it snows, often it rains. When it rains, everything that is not paved turns into thick, oppressive mud. Outside of a few trees which were planted for decorative purposes, there is practically no vegetation. The streets are lined by open sewers, the brick buildings are dull and weary-looking, and during daylight hours this city of three million seems somehow perpetually overcrowded. Those who have been to Tehran in winter would probably agree that the word that best describes its appearance is "bleak."

On our second morning in Iran, we journeyed to South Tehran. We rode a long time through traffic jams and past outdoor vendors plying wares from persian rugs to brassware. Finally, we turned down a street that passed a line of buildings and we were in the open. There was no vegetation as far as the eye could see, nothing but mud, power lines, and the city's skyline. Within a few minutes, we approached a shanty village. "This is where the poor of Tehran live," one of the students announced. "They are among the poorest people in any industrialized city in the world."

We were invited to inspect their conditions. There were perhaps twenty families occupying maybe three-fourths of an acre. They lived in hovels made from scraps which had been discarded. An average dwelling might be five feet high and eight or nine feet square with a dirt floor which, because of recent rains, was actually a mud floor. There was no water supply, or any other kind of supply either. The walls of some of the houses were made from steel barrels which had been split and hammered flat into a sheet. A board here, canvas there, a piece of tin, some plastic—of such were these shelters constructed. Next to these shelters were animal shelters made of the same stuff. It was often not possible to tell which was

This essay is excerpted by permission from "Iran: An Objective View," which appeared in *Akwesasne Notes: a Journal for Native and Natural Peoples*, Vol. II, No. 5, Early Spring, 1980.

the animal shelter, and which was the human shelter. A few chickens walked about, and there were a number of goats nearby.

I asked one of the men (through an interpreter) how long he had been living there. He said eleven years. Why did he come here? He said that he was originally a farmer in a village south of Tehran, but that he and his family had lost their land and they had nowhere else to go. He explained that during the Shah's regime, the soldiers would come occasionally and they would tell the people that they must leave. Then they brought the bulldozers and razed the little huts and they shot some people.

How were they able to live here, and how do they feed their livestock? The man replied that the goats live off the scraps that they find in the garbage dump, especially the orange peels, and that the chickens find what they can in the refuse and in the dirt. I wasn't certain until he mentioned it that we were standing on the edge of Tehran's garbage dump, but his words and the general air of the place confirmed it. The men work as manual laborers in the city whenever they can. He mentioned that in the winter, infant mortality is especially high in these camps. When asked about his hopes from the revolution, he mentioned that the government has promised new housing, and that he and his family are waiting.

An hour later, we were back in the city, still in South Tehran. Our guides, the students, took us down a street and through a door in a wall which opened into an alley. An open sewer ran through the center of the alley. We started downhill between two walls perhaps ten feet apart. Occassionally we could see through an open door in the walls that there were little courtyards ten feet square and small apartments off the courtyards. We continued to descend.

Within a few minutes, we turned up another alley. By now we had attracted quite a crowd of onlookers, some of them chanting "Death to Carter, Death to the Shah." We walked quickly, in single file, following the course of an open sewer, down this alley, up that one. Finally, the students opened a door in the wall and we went inside. There was a staircase, perhaps three feet wide, which descended in two stages to a courtyard perhaps thirty feet on a side.

I tried on a couple of occasions to ask one of the students to guess how old a building or a monument might have been, but I quickly found that it was no use. To the students, World War II was ancient history, and most history started since 1963 when Khomeini was exiled to Iraq. There was no point in asking them how old this part of the city is. What struck me was that I had never seen a photograph of this, and had never read an account of this section of the city. Of one thing I was certain; this had been here since the middle ages.

The buildings were built into the side of a hill, and layer upon layer of building had been amassed pueblo-style, except there were none of the things present which make Pueblo housing attractive. This was probably the most depressed housing that I have ever seen—at the end of a damp alley which was at the end of another damp alley, with practically no daylight, no water, no sewers, and from what we saw, no heat. There were, however, television antennas atop several buildings.

We went down into the courtyard. A woman who lived in one of the apartments told our interpreter that when the snows in the mountains thaw or when there is a lot of rain, water floods this place to a depth of four or more feet. She pointed to a water mark. She said that when this happens each year, many people who live here drown. A woman opened the door to her apartment so that we could see how she lived. The people here were all eager to show us their living conditions. This woman lived in what amounted to a cave in the wall. There were no windows. The room was dark and damp, and measured probably six feet by eight feet. Three people lived there. The other apartments were a bit bigger, and some had windows, which looked out into the courtyard. Twelve families, they told us, occupied that space.

We walked up the stairs and back into the alleyway. A crowd followed us. I stopped an interpreter and asked him to interpret a question to a woman who stood watching us pass. "What do you want people from the United States to do for you?" She answered, "Return the Shah."

We went into another little courtyard at the end of a little alley. The woman there told us that she pays $30 a month for her two-room apartment. We wanted to know why people such as herself had to live under such conditions. She said that the new government had put a public fountain in the alley nearby and that now they had a source of water. But in the Shah's time, they had to collect water as it ran off the steps. What did she want us to do? "Return the Shah."

Children surrounded us as we went up the alley. They were in a good mood, bouncing up the alley and running ahead to announce our approach. I stopped an interpreter and had him ask an old man who was leaning out of a doorway. "Return the Shah," he said. Occasionally the children would send up a chant: "Death to the Shah," it translated.

We walked quickly up the alley toward the street level. I wondered if any Western journalist had ever been down these alleyways, if any of the American tourists had ever ventured here. Along the walls of the alleys on both sides doors continued to open up into courtyards of startling similarity. From several points, we could see that this kind of housing extended for a considerable distance, and that thousands and thousands of people lived here. South Tehran—a medieval city in the modern world. The people who lived there rose from these near-caves during the revolution and went into the streets. Many of them were martyred. To a man, they seemed to blame the Shah for their living conditions. The Western press has spread propaganda to the effect that Ayatollah Khomeini and the religious leaders of the revolution were leading Iran back to the Dark Ages. But South Tehran stands as a monument, as living proof, that Iran was already living in the Dark Ages, brought there by the policies of the Shah and for the profits of the Shah—the Shah and his friends.

Since our arrival in Tehran, most of us were pretty sensitive to the fact that, as the guests of the Moslem Students Following the Line of Imam, people were going to argue that we had been "brainwashed" to their line of thinking. We were, after all, seeing the Iran that the students wanted us to see. There were some things, however, that a group of students just couldn't orchestrate. They could not create, for example, the poverty of South Tehran, and although they could have done some work preparing the people for our arrival and visit, they just couldn't have gotten the entire population of a whole section of the city to say exactly the words they wanted them to say. Our group as a whole asked questions of quite a number of people who were watching the process from the sidelines. One response was universally consistent—the people of South Tehran want the Shah returned to Iran. He has become a national symbol of evil in that country, the living symbol of all of the misery suffered by the masses of people.

Iran and the U.S. Press

Edward W. Said

Islam Rising

For more than a year, with increasing anxiety and passion, Americans have been acutely conscious of Iran. Few nations so distant and different from ours have so intensely engaged us. Never have we seemed so paralyzed, so powerless to stop one dramatic event after another from happening. And never, in all this, could we put Iran out of mind, since on so many levels the country impinged on our lives with a defiant obtrusiveness. Iran was a major oil supplier during a period of energy scarcity. Lying in a region of the world that is volatile and strategically vital, it was an important ally. It lost its imperial regime, its army, and its value in our global calculations during a year of tumultuous revolutionary upheaval, unprecedented on so huge a scale since October 1917. A new order, Islamic, popular, anti-imperialist, was struggling to be born. Ayatollah Ruhollah Khomeini's image and presence took over the media, which failed to make much of him except that he was obdurate, powerful, and deeply angry at the United States. Finally, as a result of the ex-shah's entry into this country in November, the United States Embassy in Tehran was occupied by a group of students; many hostages were taken. The crisis continues as this is written.

Even this rapid summary fails to convey anything of the seething passions Iran has aroused in Americans, passions aroused chiefly and justifiably by the deeply insulting and unlawful siege of the embassy and heightened, less justifiably, by the incredibly detailed highly focused media attention given to the event. It is one thing to know that members of our embassy's staff have been seized and that we seem powerless to free them; it is quite another to watch this story unfolding night after night on prime-time television. We have reached a point where we need to evaluate critically the meaning of the "Iran story," as it has been called, to understand its presence in our lives rationally and dispassionately. We must start to take stock

This article first appeared in *Columbia Journalism Review*, March/April, 1980, and is reprinted by permission. Copyright © 1980 by *Columbia Journalism Review*.

of what Iran has been to us, how it has looked, how it has been literally re-presented to us by the news media day after day.

Hovering like some immense yet scarcely visible monster over much of the most dramatic news of the past decade, including not only Iran but the Arab-Israeli conflict, oil, and Afghanistan, has been "Islam." Nowhere has this been more evident than in the long Iranian crisis, during which the American consumer of news has been provided a sustained diet of information about a religion no more than a poorly defined and badly misunderstood abstraction, really always, without exception, represented as militant, danger- ous, anti-American. Further back, in the public's subliminal cul- tural consciousness, there was a longstanding attitude of hostility to Islam, to the Arabs and the Orient in general, all of it part of a tradition from which is derived much of what is represented as Islamic/Iranian/Arab in the news media and in elite culture alike. Whether one looks in such recent highbrow fiction as V.S. Naipaul's *A Bend in the River* and John Updike's *The Coup*, or at grade-school textbooks, comic strips, television, or films, the iconography of Is- lam is uniformly the same: oil suppliers, terrorists, mobs. Con- versely, there is very little place either in the culture generally, or in discourse about non-Westerners in particular, to speak of, think about, much less to portray, Islam or anything Islamic sympatheti- cally. (Most people asked to name a modern Islamic writer would probably be able only to pick Kahlil Gibran—who wasn't Islamic.) Almost to a man or woman, the academic experts treat the religion and its various cultures within an ideological framework remarkably filled with passion, defensive prejudice, sometimes even revulsion. And to judge from the reporting of the Iranian revolution last spring, there was no inclination to accept the revolution itself as anything other than a defeat for the U.S. (which in a very specific sense, of course, it was), or as a victory of dark over light.

It was as if discriminations between religious passion, a strug- gle for a just cause, ordinary human weakness, political competi- tion, and the history of men, women, and societies seen *as* the history of men, women, and societies, could not be made when Islam was dealt with. "Islam" engulfed them all, reduced them all to a special malevolent essence. Instead of analysis and understand- ing, as a result, there could only be the crudest form of antagonism. Whatever Iranians or Moslems said about their sense of justice, their history of oppression, their vision of their own societies seemed irrelevant; what counted for us instead was what the "Is- lamic revolution" did right now, how many people were executed by the komitehs, how many bizarre outrages the ayatollah, in the name of Islam, ordered. Of course, no one equated the Jonestown massacre, or the destructive frenzy produced at the Who concert in Cincinnati, with Christianity; that sort of equation was reserved exclusively for Islam.

Why was it that political events seemed reducible in so Pavlovian a way to the peculiarities of Islam? Mainly because the news media, as well as governmental and academic experts, seemed to have agreed implicitly not to recognize political developments as political but to represent them as a cosmic drama pitting civilization as we like it against the uncivilized and the barbaric. In such a way history could be simplified, along with social processes, everyday reality, and the humanity of other people whose interests did not happen to coincide with ours. The result tells more about our society, its apparatus for producing and diffusing information, and its perception of things than it does about what was being reported. It also raises enormous political and moral questions about past, present, and future U.S. foreign policy, and about the role of the news media in contemporary Western society.

America at Bay

To sift through the immense amount of material generated by the embassy occupation in Tehran on November 4, 1979, is to be struck by a number of things. For one, it seemed that "we" were at bay, and, with "us," the normal, democratic, rational order of things. Out there, writhing in self-provoked frenzy, was "Islam," whose manifestation of the hour was a disturbingly neurotic Iran.

The press found plenty of evidence to substantiate this view. On November 7 the *St. Louis Post-Dispatch* printed the proceedings of a seminar held in St. Louis on Iran and the Persian Gulf. One participating expert was quoted as saying that "the loss of Iran to an Islamic form of government was the greatest setback the United States has had in recent years." Islamic self-governance, in other words, is by definition inimical to U.S. interests. *The Wall Street Journal* editorialized on November 20 that "civilization is receding" due to "the decline of the Western powers that spread these [civilized] ideals to begin with," as if not to be Western—which is the fate of most of the world's population, and Islam's to boot—is not to have had any civilized ideals. All the major TV commentators, Walter Cronkite and Frank Reynolds chief among them, spoke of "anti-Americanism" or more poetically of "the cresent of crisis, sweeping across the world of Islam like a cyclone hurtling across a prairie," as ABC's Reynolds put it on November 21; on December 7 he voiced over a picture of crowds chanting "God is great" with what he supposed was the crowd's true sentiment, "hatred of America."

If we were thus at bay, it became necessary to attack our antagonists, to deprecate their beliefs and belittle their customs. Later in the same December broadcast, ABC informed us that the prophet Mohammed was "a self-proclaimed prophet" (which prophet hasn't been?) and then reminded us that "Ayatollah" was "a self-styled twentieth-century title" meaning "reflection of God" (both, unfortunately, not completely accurate accounts.) The ABC short (three-minute) course on Islam was held in place with small titles to the right of the picture, and they told the same story of how resentment, suspicion, and contempt were proper for "Islam," which was reduced to a rush of images and symbols: Mecca, Purdah, Chador, Sunni, Shi'ite (accompanied by a picture of young mean beating themselves), Mullah, Ayatollah, Khomeini, Iran. Soon after this rapid-fire sequence, the program switched to Jamesville, Wisconsin, whose admirably wholesome schoolchildren—no purdah, self-flagellation, or mullahs here—were organizing a patriotic "Unity Day."

After more than a year's worth of journalistic enterprise on the subject—which included the December 11 publication of a symposium of scholars and experts—any lingering doubts about what we were to think about Islam were cleared up when, in the last four days in December, *The New York Times* published a series of long articles by Flora Lewis, all attempting a serious treatment of UPSURGE IN ISLAM, in the words of the running head. (*The New Republic* had already gone to the limit in the rhetoric of headlines, tying together two December 8 articles by Walter Laqueur and Michael Walzer with "The Holy Wars of Islam.") There are some excellent things in Lewis's pieces—for example, her success in delineating complexity and diversity—but there are serious weaknesses, too, most of them inherent in the way Islam is viewed nowadays. Not only did Lewis single out Islam from other religions in the Middle East (the upsurge in Judaism and Egyptian or Lebanese Christianity, for instance, was scarcely mentioned), but she went on to make statements, in particular in her third story, about the Arabic language (quoting expert opinion that its poetry is "rhetorical and declamatory, not intimate and personal") and the Islamic mind (an inability to employ "step-by-step thinking") that would be considered either racist or nonsensical if used to describe any other language, religion, or combination of ethnic groups. Too frequently her authorities were orientalists well known for their rancorous general views; one of them, Elie Kedourie, of the London School of

Economics, is quoted as saying that "the disorder of the east is deep and endemic"; Bernard Lewis, the Princeton orientalist, pronounces on "the end of free speculation and research" in the Islamic world, presumably as a result of Islam's "static" as well as its "determinist, occasionalist and authoritarian" theology. One could not be expected to get a coherent view of Islam after reading Flora Lewis—her scurrying about in sources and her unfamiliarity with the subject give her readers the sense of a scavenger hunt for a subject that wasn't one to begin with; after all, how could one get hold of the remarkably varied history, geography, social structure, and culture of forty Islamic nations and 800,000,000 people whose words "are an expression of wish rather than a description of fact"? The point about Islam was made, anyway, that even if "it" wasn't clear at all, one's attituted toward it were.

There were subtler ways to incriminate "Islam." One was to put an expert before the public and have him or her suggest that Khomeini was not really "representative of Islamic clergy" (this was L. Dean Brown, former U.S. ambassador to Jordan and special envoy to Lebanon and now president of the Middle East Institute, speaking on *The MacNeil/Lehrer Report,* November 16), that the "ironclad" mullah was a throwback to an earlier (obviously Islamic) age, and that the mobs in Tehran were reminiscent of Nuremberg, just as the street demonstrations were signs of the "circus as principal entertainment" habitually provided by dictators.

Another method was to suggest invisible lines connecting various other Middle Eastern things to Iranian Islam, then to damn them together, implicitly or explicitly, depending on the case. When former Senator James Abourezk went to Tehran, the announcement on ABC and CBS was made with a reminder that Abourezk was "of Lebanese origin." No reference was ever made to Representative George Hansen's Danish background, or to Ramsey Clark's WASP ancestry. Somehow it was considered important to disclose the vaguely Islamic taint in Abourezk's past, although he happens to be of Christian Lebanese stock.

Much of the most flamboyant use of suggestion originated in a small front-page item by Daniel B. Drooz in *The Atlanta Constitution* on November 8, in which it was alleged that the Palestine Liberation Organization was behind the embassy takeover. His sources were authorities in "diplomatic and European intelligence." (Coming in a close second was his November 22 discovery that "Where there are Shi'ites, there is trouble.") A month later George Ball stated gnomically in *The Washington Post* that "there is some basis to believe that the whole operation is being orchestrated by well-trained Marxists." Not to be outdone, CBS introduced its *Evening News* on December 12 with Marvin Kalb from the State Department quoting (equally unnamed) "diplomatic and intelligence experts" as affirming that Palestinian guerillas, Iranian extremists, and Islamic fundamentalists had cooperated at the embassy. The PLO men were the ones who had mined the compound, Kalb said; they were known to be inside, he went on sagely, by virtue of "the sounds of Arabic" being heard from the embassy. (A brief report of Kalb's "story" was carried the next day in the *Los Angeles Times*.) It remained for no less a personage than Hudson Institute expert Constantine Menges to argue exactly the same thesis first in *The New Republic* of December 15, then twice more on *The MacNeil/Lehrer Report*. No more evidence was given; it sufficed to conjure up the diabolism of communism in natural alliance with the devilish PLO and satanic Moslems.

Surprisingly, given the hundreds of hours of broadcast coverage and the millions of words in newspapers and magazines, one has the feeling of not having learned very much from all of this reporting. The media certainly provided abundant evidence of their power to be there, in Tehran, and of their knack for prodding events into assimilable, if rudimentary, shape. But there was no help to be had in analyzing the complicated politics of what was taking place. Returning to the U.S. after a grip abroad, Vermont Royster commented in *The Wall Street Journal* of December 19 that the accumulated pile of newspapers and TV programs he started going through testified to

> how little I learned about the Iranian crisis I didn't already know, despite the voluminous coverage given it. Once home I was startled to find myself inundated in a daily tidal wave of television, radio and newspaper stories about Iran. The papers carried long stories under huge headlines, while TV devoted most of the evening news to the topic and then ran late-evening specials almost every night.
>
> And from that arose another heretical thought, that the news media engaged in overkill.
>
> This may seem a strange reaction about a story of such obvious importance. . . . But the volume of words to tell a story doesn't necessarily equate with information imparted. The truth is that in much of that wordage there was no real news at all.

The news was the same; so was the narrow and quickly exhausted range of assumptions used to look for it. How long is it possible to rely on experts and reporters who are understandably concerned about the hostages, incensed at the impropriety of the thing, perhaps also angry at Islam, and still hope to get fresh information, news, analysis? If one were to read the *Chicago Tribune* on November 18—a piece by James Yuenger, citing experts who said that "this is not something that's up for rational discussion" or that Iranians have a "tendency to look for scapegoats" and "a sort of hunger for martyrdom"—and then either *Time* ("An Ideology of Martyrdom") or *Newsweek* ("Iran's Martyr Complex") the week after, and almost any paper of one's choice the week after that, one would continually keep coming up against the information that Iranians are Shi'ites who long for martyrdom, who are led by a non-rational Khomeini, who hate our country, are determined to destroy the satanic spies, are unwilling to compromise, and so forth.

Were there no events taking place in Iran *before* the embassy takeover that might illuminate things? Was there no Iranian history or society to write and speak about that *wasn't* translatable into the anthropomorphisms of a crazy Iran gratuitously taunting good-guy America? Above all, was the press simply interested in diffusing news seemingly in keeping with a U.S. government policy to keep America "united" behind the unconditional demand for the hostages' release, a demand shrewdly assessed by Roger Fisher of Harvard on the December 3 *Today* show as being itself subordinate to the real priority, which was not freeing the hostages but maintaining "the prestige and power of the United States"?

The Press Goes to War

Anyone saturated with superficial, loose-tongued reporting on Iran would be prone to turn for relief and genuine insight to the nightly *MacNeil/Lehrer Report*. But the programs—with their restrictive (and even conservative) format, choice of guests, and range of discussion—were unsatisfying at their best and mystifying at their worst.

Given an unconventional news story about as unfamiliar a part of the world as Iran, the viewer will immediately be made to feel an intense disparity between the Middle Eastern mobs and the program's carefully dressed, carefully selected cast of guests, whose uniform qualification was dispassionate experitise, not necessarily insight or understanding. The questions asked made it evident that *MacNeil/Lehrer* tended to be looking for support of the prevailing national mood—outrage at the Iranians—both by eliciting ahistorical analyses of what makes the Iranians tick and by guiding discussion to fit either Cold War or crisis-management molds. A telling indication of this appeared in the two programs (December 28 and January 4) on which the guests were the two sets of American clergymen recently returned from Tehran. On both programs the clergymen told of their obvious compassion for Iranians who had suffered under the ex-shah's despotic rule for twenty-five years. Lehrer was openly skeptical, not to say dubious, about what they were saying. When Foreign Minister Abolhassan Bani-Sadr and his successor Sadegh Ghotbzadeh appeared (November 23 and 29), the line of questioning stayed very close to what had emerged as the U.S. government position: when will the hostages be released, MacNeil and Lehrer wanted to know, and never mind talk of concessions or committees to investigate the ex-shah's misdemeanors and crimes.

The guest list was significant. Aside from the five appearances by Iranians, and two by supporters of Third-World and antiwar causes, most of the other panelists on the score of shows devoted to the crisis were newspapermen, government officials, academic Middle East experts, individuals connected to corporate or quasi-government institutions, and Middle Easterners known for their essentially antagonistic positions on the Iranian revolution. The discussions resulting from this lineup usually placed everything the Iranians said and did out of moral bounds, since few guests could truly communicate the essentially "foreign" language of distant, oppressed people who until now had silently endured decades of American impingement on their lives. Neither Lehrer nor MacNeil, moreover, tried to investigate what Bani-Sadr meant when evoking "the oppressed people of the world," he suggested that satisfaction of their claims did not demand the ex-shah's extradition, but required only a gesture of recognition from the U.S. that the oppressed had legitimate grievances.

Thus, in the very conduct of its investigation *The MacNeil/Lehrer Report* seemed to censor itself, prevent itself from straying into wider areas of human experience that antagonists or interlocutors thought were important. The questions invariably focused on how to deal with the crisis (not with trying to understand the new horizons being hewed out everywhere in the nonwhite, non-European world); the answers seemed to resort almost instinctively to received wisdom about sectarian unrest, Islamic revivalism, geopolitics, balance of power. These were the constraints within which MacNeil and Lehrer operated. And for better or for worse, they happen to be the very constraints within which the government itself operated.

In the context of such cautious and conformist journalism, we can now begin to appreciate the astonishing prescience of I.F. Stone's piece "A Shah Lobby Next?" which he wrote over a year ago and which was published in *The New York Review of Books* of February 22, 1979. He spoke there of how the ex-shah, who had just left Iran, could "rally formidable friends" from the Chase Manhattan Bank, the arms industry, the oil trust, the CIA, and "hungry academia" to get an American visa. Were he to be admitted to the U.S., Stone speculated, tempting possibilities might arise, even though "we should have learned by now, but haven't, to keep out of Iran's domestic politics, and we may get a parallel lesson in keeping Iran's politics out of ours." Why? Because, Stone's uncanny predictions continued:

> What if the new Iranian regime makes demands of its own . . . lays claim—as Khomeini has already indicated—to the foreign holdings and bank accounts of the Shah and the Pahlevi Foundation? What if it demands the Shah's return for trial on charges of plundering his country? . . . What if it accuses him, as absolute ruler, with absolute responsibility for untold tortures and deaths at the hands of SAVAK?

Stone not only happens to have been right; he is not, and has never pretended to be, an "expert" on Iran. Look through his article and you will find no reference to the Islamic mentality, or Shi'ite predilections for martyrdom, or any of the other nonsense parading as relevant "information" on Iran. He understands politics, he understands and makes no attempt to lie about what moves men and women to act in this society, as well as all others. Above all, he does not doubt that even though Iranians are not Europeans or Americans, they may have legitimate grievances, ambitions, and hopes of their own, which it would be folly for us to ignore.

With characteristic hardheadedness, syndicated columnist Joseph Kraft sketched *his* very different view of the matter in TIME FOR A SHOW OF POWER, which appeared in *The Washington Post* on November 11. It was what he wrote there, far more than all the standard reporting about diplomatic immunity and the sanctity of our embassy, that illuminated aspects of the underlying, perhaps even unconscious, rationale behind the news media's overall performance. The downfall of the shah, Kraft wrote, was "a calamity for American national interests." Not only did the shah make available regular supplies of oil; he imposed order on the Iranian plateau through "his imperial pretensions." This was good for America: it kept the oil flowing, of course; it kept the region, as well as "submerged nationalities," in line; it kept "us" appearing strong. Kraft went on to recommend, as part of the process of "rebuilding American policy toward Iran," that the U.S. find occasion "for an unmistakable, and preferably surprising, assertion of American power." How might this be done?

> [It] might take the form of supporting Iraq in its effort to stir up provincial resistance inside Iran. It might mean giving military assistance to Turkey . . . . The United States needs a capacity to do something besides sending Marines and bombing. It has to rebuild a capacity self-destructed only a few years ago—a capacity for covert intervention.

What is clear in Kraft's piece is his unwillingness to accept the Iranian revolution as ever having taken place; everything connected to it must be destroyed as the aberration he wanted his readers to believe it was. In other words, Kraft was projecting his personal version of reality onto a complex Iranian as well as American reality, thereby substituting his wishes for the facts. Kraft's version had the additional didactic merit of being entirely devoid of morality: it was about power, American power to have the world on our terms, as though twenty-five years of intervention in Iran had taught us nothing. If in the process Kraft found himself denying that other people have a right to produce a change in their own form of government, denying even that a change had definitively taken place, that did not much matter. He wanted America to know (and be known by) the world through its power, its needs, its vision. All else was an outrage.

Power, of course, is a complex, not always visible, very protean thing, unless one thinks only in military terms. Yet there are situations in which, as Kraft quite accurately observed, it cannot be employed directly (as it would be in a raid, CIA subversion, a punitive strike of some sort), but only indirectly (as when "America held hostage" is presented and represented by an information apparatus with seemingly limitless resources). It is not an exaggeration, in fact, to say that the feeling of "national impotence" of which Kraft also wrote resulted from the temporary eclipse of one kind of American power by another—the military's by the media's. After the occupation of the embassy, the military found itself stymied by a force which seemed outside the range of direct American power.

This same force, however, remained vulnerable to the limits placed on it by the rich symbolizing powers of the American media. For however much the Iranian had gained his or her freedom from the shah and the U.S., he or she still appeared on American TV screens as part of a large anonymous mob, deindividualized, dehumanized—and *ruled again* as a result.

Whether they did so consciously or not, the news media were in fact using their powers of representation to accomplish a purpose similar to that intended by our government in the past—the extension of an American presence, or, what to Iranians amounted to the same thing, negation of the Iranian revolution. This did not principally entail the presentation of news, for the analysis of or reflection upon an important new juncture in American foreign relations. With very few exceptions, the news media seemed to be waging a kind of war against Iran, even though, paradoxically, government and news media sometimes appeared to be antagonists.

Hence, for example, the flap caused by the government's attack on NBC for using the Gallegos interview. Or the frequent refrain coming from quarters either speaking for or like the government that, as George Ball put it during *The MacNeil/Lehrer Report* of December 12, "the greatest communications network in the world has been really at the service of the so-called government in Iran." Related to this theme, there was a constant effort to discredit testimonials, statements, or declarations broadcast, printed, or otherwise diffused by the media that might have served to undermine the government's version of events. Writing in the *Chicago Tribune* on November 22, James Coates reported that "hostages held in the United States Embassy in Tehran are undergoing psychological pressures similar to the brainwashing of American POWs during the Korean and Viet Nam wars, administration officials said Wednesday." Lois Timnick reported for the *Los Angeles Times* on November 26 that, according to one expert, "the world can expect to see and hear taped interviews with individual hostages in which they 'confess' to all sorts of misdeeds and make statements that are harmful both to themselves and to the United States." Although such accounts ran in the press, they were meant to preempt any doubts that the press itself might later encourage by reporting facts contradicting the government's version of events.

Overall, however, the press followed the government's lead. This is not to say that there was actual collusion between the media and the government, nor that *everything* reported about Iran was crippled by ideological hobbles. But it is to say that the world is much too complex now, and situations much too unconventional, for the press to join the government in treating all events as affronts to, or enhancements of, American power. We cannot continue believing, for example, that the most important thing about "Islam" is whether it is pro- or anti-American. The intellectual bias involved in so reductive a view of the world would guarantee a continued confrontation between the United States and the rest of an intransigent mankind and promote a policy of expanding the Cold War to include an unacceptably large portion of the globe. Such a policy could be considered active U.S. advocacy of the "Western way of life," but an equally good case could be made that the Western way of life doesn't necessarily involve provoking hostility and confrontation as a means for clarifying our own sense of our place in the world.

Reporting the Revolution

Joseph Kraft was not alone in trying to substitute his political theories for Iranian reality. The news media as a whole, in fact, seem never to have conceded that a popular revolution actually has taken place. For one, most journalists still refer to Mohammed Reza Pahlavi as "the shah," not "the ex-shah," which, of course, is what he is since the abolition of the monarchy in January 1979. More important, reporters and editors have clearly favored stories reporting atrocities, executions, and ethnic conflict over those on the country's extremely fluid, actually quite open, political struggle—which, although it does not conform to American norms, and may also have produced many disappointments, is certainly worth the effort necessary to comprehend it.

The hardest thing to understand about the news media is why, almost without exception, they regard the movement that overthrew the Pahlavi regime and brought in different, perhaps more popular groups, with such disdain and suspicion. A partial answer, no doubt, is that the movement employed a dramatically unfamiliar (to Western eyes) idiom of religious, as well as political, resistance to tyranny. Typical of efforts to understand this phenomenon is Ray Moseley's November 25 story in the *Chicago Tribune*, CONFORMITY, INTOLERANCE GRIP REVOLUTIONARY IRAN:

> People who consider dying to be an honor are, by definition, fanatics. Vengeful blood lust and a yearning for martyrdom seem especially pronounced among the Shia Moslems of Iran. This is what impelled thousands of citizens to stand unarmed and defiant against troops with automatic weapons during the revolution.

Each of these sentences contains highly debatable suppositions posing as truth, but they seem allowable simple because an Islamic revolution is in question: most Americans don't consider Patrick Henry a fanatic because he said "give me liberty or give me death." A desire to kill French citizens who had collaborated with the Nazis (thousands were killed in a matter of days after Liberation) does not mean that the French could be characterized in so general a way. And what about our own common admiration for people whose moral courage faces down armed troops?

125

With the Shah deposed, the necessarily long and difficult consolidation of the revolution became the story. "The New Barbarians are loose in Iran," wrote Hal Gulliver in *The Atlanta Constitution* on November 13; he spoke not just of the students holding the hostages, but of everyone in Iran. Or read a long, apparently expert piece in the October 14 *New York Times Magazine* by Youssef Ibrahim, who had reported from Iran during much of the revolution, until he was expelled, and you will be convinced that the revolution has already failed, that Iran is a smoldering lava bed of resentment, fear, and antirevolutionary passion. The evidence: basically some impressions, quotes from two government ministers, and for the most part discussions with a banker, a lawyer, and an advertising executive.

Such analyses of Iranian events were often supported by self-serving misinterpretations of Islam. Take, as an example, a CBS Evening News segment on Islam on November 21, during which Randy Daniels described Muharram, a month in the Islamic calendar during which Shi'ite Moslems commemorate the martyrdom of Hussein and Hassan, who, they believe, followed in the direct line of prophetic succession after Mohammed. In the words of Daniels, Muharram became a period when Shi'ites "celebrate Mohammed's challenge to world leaders"—a statement not only silly but needlessly provocative. In a similarly reckless vein, Moseley's attack on Iran in the *Tribune* was supported by a truly cosmic editorial in his paper the same day accusing Khomeini of nothing less than "a holy war on the world." The *jihad* (holy war) motif was also given an extraordinary run by the *Los Angeles Times* in an article by Edmund Bosworth on December 12. Leaving aside the fact that such authorities as the University of Chicago's Fazlur Rahman hold that "among the later Muslim legal schools . . . it is only the fanatic Kharijites who have declared *jihad* to be one of the 'pillars of the Faith.' " Bosworth goes on indiscriminately to adduce a great deal of historical "evidence" for the theory that *all* political activity, in an area that includes Turkey, Iran, Sudan, Ethiopia, Spain, India, for a period of about twelve hundred years, can be understood as emanating from the Moslem call for a *jihad*.

If aggressive hyperbole is one journalistic mode commonly used to describe Iran, the other is misapplied euphemism, usually stemming from ignorance, but often deriving from a barely concealed ideological hostility. Its most prevalent form is the device of displacing actuality with a plausible "explanation" of the reporter's own. Now the one subject the press has looked into only superficially is the previous Iranian regime: it is not popular to take seriously current Iranian grievances against both the deposed monarch and a longstanding U.S. policy to support him without reservation. Somehow, the violation of Iranian sovereignty that occurred in August 1953, when the CIA, in conjunction with the British Anglo-Iranian Oil Company, overthrew the government of Mohammed Mossadegh, merits little investigation—the assumption apparently being that we are a great power entitled to change governments and forgive tyranny when it is inflicted on illiterate non-Westerners at our discretion.

These views produced some remarkable euphemisms in late 1979, when everyone agreed the Iranians had committed an act of war against our embassy (and even Mansour Farhang, now the Iranian ambassador to the United Nations, had admitted that there was no way to condone the holding of hostages). Ernest Conine, editorializing for the *Los Angeles Times* on December 10, was typical:

> News accounts seem to bear out the contention by Middle Eastern scholars that what we are really seeing is a wide-spread revolt against the unsettling influences that have accompanied the Western-style modernization of recent years. The shah is hated not just because his police tortured people but also because he took away government subsidies from Muslim holy men, and presided over an industrial revolution that uprooted millions of Iranians from their traditional life styles in the countryside.
>
> "Satan America" is elected as the chief villain, not just in Iran but elsewhere, because for 25 years the United States has been the most visible power in the area, and is therefore a handy symbol of outside forces that have brought unwelcome changes.

Much in this arguement is weighted against the Iranians through unspoken assumptions, so it needs to be read carefully. Conine first of all implies that the "unsettling influences" of "Western-style modernization" are the result of trying in good faith to bring Iran and Islam out of the past into the present; in other words, Islam and Iran are backward, the West is advanced, and no wonder that backward people are going to have a hard time keeping up. These are eminently contestable value judgments. Moreover, Conine seems to be arguing, without any warrant except ethnocentric bias, that, unlike "us," Iranians were not moved to hatred by torture alone, but were reacting to insults to their "holy men," a phrase used to remind one of primitive people with their witch doctors. His final point develops the others by association, laying the blame on retrograde Iranians for not appreciating the well-intentioned efforts of

the U.S. and Pahlavi to get Iran going; thus not only are we exoner-
ated, but Iranians as a people are subtly indicted for not knowing the
value of our brand of modernity, which is why the ex-shah is a noble
figure after all.

Throughout reports of the Iranian events, little mention was
made of the fact, which is neither esoteric nor hard to come by, that
not only the shah but U.S. corporations reaped vast profits in the
area (it should not have been difficult to connect the wealth of the
Pahlavi family and oil company profits) and that most Iranians, like
those Saudis who do not happen to members of the royal family, see
American-connected wealth as a burden. If it was bruited about that
the shah occasionally resorted to torture to maintain his new order,
well, said *The Washington Post* on December 16, ''it can be argued
that he was entirely in the tradition of Iranian history.'' In other
words, it is enough for Iranians to know that ''we'' know that they
have always been tortured; any attempt to change this foreordained
fate of theirs is a betrayal of their own history, to say nothing of their
own nature.

This unbreakable double bind turned up in a Don A. Schanche
story for the *Los Angeles Times* on December 5, where Schanche
argued that because the new constitution was ''one of the most
bizarre political documents of modern times,'' and because it didn't
happen to resemble closely the U.S. Constitution (no checks and
balances!), Khomeini's ascendancy was at least as bad as the ex-
shah's. That there would be ''provisions for popular elections of
president and parliament and an organized judicial system'' was
dismissed as ''the trappings of democracy.'' Schanche simply omit-
ted to mention what Eric Rouleau analyzed in detail in *Le Monde* on
December 2 and 3—the very busy, competitive debate about the
constitution, as well as the disagreements as to Khomeini's exact
role.

With the noteworthy exception of Andrew Young, no high public figure in this country had anything to say about what—to observers like the two groups of clergymen who were in Tehran in late
December—the previous regime meant to the Iranians as they took
action against the U.S. And, collaborating in this silence, the press
treated the ex-shah exclusively as a charity case for at least twenty
days after he was admitted to this country. Stripped of his political
past, he appeared to be somehow unconnected to what then happened at the embassy in Iran. A few journalists, Don Oberdorfer of
The Washington Post chief among them, tried to reconstruct the
devious steps by which David Rockefeller, Henry Kissinger, and
John McCloy had pressured the government into bringing the ex-

shah here. But these facts, as well as information on the longstanding association between him and the Chase Manhattan Bank—
which would have helped to explain Iranian animosities—never got
the play they deserved nationwide. Instead we were given numerous stories euphemistically explaining the hostage crisis as the result of Khomeini's manipulation, his need for distracting the popu-
lace, economic difficulties at home, and the like.

More generally, one would have thought it a worthwhile effort
to report in detail what it means for a country's national existence,
after decades of severe oppression, to have a dozen political parties
vying for influence and power, in a political environment relatively
free of the oppression that characterized the previous regime. What
does it mean for a nation to have a leader who, although stubborn
and in many ways unattractive, has only an unclearly defined official position, who is not too interested in central government, who is
clearly venerated, and who speaks with such conviction of *al-
mostazifin* (the weakened and oppressed)? Few Americans can
have understood from the press that the government in Iran was
provisional, pending the setting up of a new state, or that debate
about the new constitution raged for months, or that there are
numerous parties operating freely (religious and secular, right-
wing and left-wing), or that 230 newspapers appear regularly, or
that there are actual political issues (not by any means all reducible
to sectarian or ethnic or religious factionalism) exercising large
numbers of Iranians, or that the conflict between the ayatollahs
(Khomeini and Shariat-Madari) concerns political as well as religious interpretations of Islamic principles, or that the future of Iran
need not naturally fall into patterns viewed as desirable or undesirable by middle-class reporters for American newspapers.

Another Country

Another way of formulating these points is to check the overall
American version of the Iran story against a European version, Eric
Rouleau's series of daily articles in *Le Monde,* which ran from the
first week of the crisis through the end of December. Of course it is
important that Rouleau is not an American, that no French hostages
were held, that Iran has never been in a French sphere of influence.
Rouleau, who has been covering the region for twenty-five years,
also did not have to overcome many of the obstacles facing American correspondents, who usually did not know Farsi, had no background in Iranian affairs, and were usually rotated out after a short
tour of duty. (On the other hand, his resources were certainly more
limited than the Americans'; *The Australian* estimated in Decem-

ber that between them the networks were spending a million dollars a day in Tehran.)

It is also important to acknowledge that the prodigious quantity of American coverage meant that a certain number of extremely valuable, generally (but not always) anti-consensus reports did appear. Op-ed pieces by Phil Freshman in the *Los Angeles Times* and by Fred Halliday in *The Boston Globe,* articles on alternatives to force and on Iranian realities (Richard Falk in the December 9 *Atlanta Journal and Constitution,* Roger Fisher in the January 14 *Newsweek*), excellent background reporting on the ex-shah's admission to this country, occasionally good political analysis and news stories (Doyle McManus in the *Los Angeles Times,* John Kifner in *The New York Times*); these are some of the high spots occasionally accessible to readers looking for something beyond the narrowly patriotic line hewed to most of the time. One should also mention two powerful articles on the new jingoism of Americans wearing "Iran Sucks" and "Nuke Iran" buttons that appeared in the December 24 and January 7 issues of *Inquiry* magazine.

But all in all, TV, the daily press, and the weekly news magazines reported Iran with nowhere near the insight and understanding that Rouleau displayed in his sequence for *Le Monde.* To put matters very strongly, it would have to be said that what he wrote made Iran seem like a different country from the one represented in the American media. Rouleau never lost sight of the fact that Iran was a country still undergoing massive revolutionary change, and that, being without a government, it is consequently in the process of creating a completely new set of political institutions, processes, and realities. The U.S. Embassy occupation had to be viewed within that process, not isolated from it, it became clear.

Rouleau never used "Islam" to explain events or personalities, because he veiwed his reporter's mandate as comprising the analysis of politics, societies, and history—complex enough as they are— without resorting to ideological generalizations and mystifying rhetoric. No American reporter spent the kind of time Rouleau did reporting the extended debate in Iran over the constitutional referendum; nor did others match his analyses of the various parties, tactics of struggle, personalities, ideas, and institutions vying for power and attention. Even crucial events (such as Bani-Sadr's visit to the students in the embassy on December 5) were largely ignored by his American counterparts, and none of them so much as mentioned the important role played in the embassy by Hajitolislam Khoeiny, who also happens to have been a candidate for Iran's presidency.

What is more important is that Rouleau seemed able to grant that personalities or currents of ideas at work in the crisis might have a potentially serious role, and he therefore seemed able to avoid jumping to conclusions encouraged by officials. For example, Representative Hansen's visit emerged as a much more successful undertaking in what Rouleau told us about it than one would have suspected from American accounts. There was even substantial evidence given by Rouleau on November 28 that Hansen's success with the Iranians was deliberately allowed to shrivel up by the White House (and of course the U.S. new media), just as a possible congressional investigation into U.S.-Iranian banking procedures (sought by the Iranians, possibly as an exchange for the hostages' release) was snuffed out by the White House.

In Rouleau's hands, Iranian politics quite simply took on new meaning. He was able to adduce the real reason for Prime Minister Mehdi Bazargan's fall (certainly not because he was a liberal democrat, as the U.S. news media liked to argue, or because he had shaken hands with Brzezinski in Algiers, but because he was inefficient and incompetent in fulfilling his government's stated policies). He chronicled the struggle between Bani-Sadr and Ghotbzadeh (the former a determined socialist and anti-imperialist, the latter a conservative on political and economic issues). He sketched in detail the apparently paradoxical positions they took on the hostage crisis (Bani-Sadr for defusing it, Ghotbzadeh for escalating). What we can surmise through Rouleau's work is that the U.S. preferred dealing with Ghotbzadeh, and seemed to encourage Bani-Sadr's removal (by not taking him seriously, by actively derogating his suggestions, by actually calling him a ''kook''), which is important information for understanding future U.S. policy toward Iran, given Bani-Sadr's victory in the presidential election. Rouleau also shows how the U.S. conducted a sustained economic war against Iran well before the embassy takeover in November; a sinister aspect of this is that the Chase Manhattan Bank has continued to play a leading part.

In sum, Rouleau's reporting on Iran for *Le Monde* was political in the best sense of the word. The U.S. news media's simply was not; or, one could say, it was political in the bad sense. What seemed unfamiliar or strange to U.S. reporters was branded ''Islamic'' and treated with commensurate hostility or derision. Iran as a contemporary society going through extraordinary important change had no impact on the press; certainly Iranian history was never allowed to appear with any integrity. Clichés, caricatures, ignorance, unqualified ethnocentrism, and inaccuracy were inordinately evident, as was an almost total subservience to the government thesis that the only thing that mattered was "not giving in to blackmail." Along with this went a shocking assumption that if the U.S. had forgiven the ex-shah and declared him a charity case, it did not matter what Iranians (or Iranian history itself) had to say.

So poorly and with so much incitement did the press report Iran that it is not wrong to suspect that a number of opportunities to resolve the crisis were lost, and perhaps this is why the Iranian government has suggested that fewer reporters in Iran might quieten the tension and produce a peaceful resolution. What is most serious about the media's failure, and what does not augur well for the future, is that so far as international issues are concerned, the news media do not see themselves as performing an independent, truly informational task. There seems to be no awareness that the new era we are entering cannot with impunity be represented in confrontational dichotomies (us versus them, the U.S. versus the Soviet Union, the West versus Islam), unless, of course, it is going to be our policy with the Soviet Union to destroy the world.

It is alarming that the U.S. press seems generally incapable of learning much about the world, that its reports one day seem not to have incorporated very much learned the day before, that it seems generally unwilling to refine its perceptions by looking in new places. It would have been helpful, for example, if, after many hundreds of pictures and actualities of Iran mobs, reporters and editors had read Ervand Abrahamian's classic December 1968 *Past and Present* article, "The Crowd in Iranian Politics, 1905-1953," which explains the remarkable meaning of the crowd as a major factor in Iranian history, something that has very little to do with mere disorganized mob behavior. Why did no reporter seem to avail himself of the crucial material contained in the Summer 1979 issue of *Race and Class*—for example, the material on Ali Shariati, an Iranian friend of Algerian revolutionary Frantz Fanon, who with Khomeini was the major influence on the revolution?

For a journalist, blindly serving his government is as perilous as assuming that his audience is incapable of learning. Neither course is acceptable for a society like ours, and no amount of going on about free competition, openness, and democracy ought to obscure the issues. Bad journalism is bad journalism, but for the U.S. it is worse. True patriotism is wanting to know as much of the truth as possible, not just the part that encourages us in the feeling we are right.

Tehran Diary

William Worthy

Editor's note: William Worthy of The Baltimore Afro-American *was one of three journalists to accompany the Committee on an American-Iranian Crisis Resolution's delegation to Iran in February, 1980. The notes here are taken from his diary:*

February 5

Wire services, networks, New York dailies all at Kennedy. Cameras and tape recorders turned off while Norman Forer read carefully drafted 15-minute statements. Then barrage of questions—quite a few hostile—about delegation's prospects for seeing hostages, bringing them back home, State Department clearance for the trip, legitimacy of delegation.

Don't recall a single press question to delegation about their possibly delving into 26 years of Iranian grievances, CIA's training SAVAK agents in torture techniques, US's returning Shah's wealth, high-level payoffs to Americans by the Shah's Pahlavi Foundation (650 Fifth Avenue), and the involvement of every US president since Truman in the bill of particulars against the Shah. (In a not-so-subtle threat, Pahlavi has said publicly that if he deserves to be tried, then seven presidents should also be tried.)

Rhetorical question: how much longer must the hostages be held before our press impresses on everyone that the Iranians, too, have been through a holocaust and are reacting accordingly?

February 7

Awoke to sight of nearby mountain range and of an ancient city where considerable building is going on. Got reports that some Shah-era luxury construction was halted before completion, with cranes and scaffolding left in place to symbolize break with the past, and that other buildings intended for the wealthy were converted to

This excerpt first appeared in *The Boston Phoenix*, March 4, 1980, and is reprinted by permission. Copyright © 1980 by *The Boston Phoenix*, Boston, MA.

housing for those living in the giant South Tehran slum.

It's also a city of five million caught up in a night-marish traffic snarl, one reminiscent of the *New Yorker* cartoon of a driver arriving at the Jersey entrance to the Holland Tunnel only to find a barrier and a sign: "Sorry. New York's all filled up."

Iranians damn the insanity of the previously unplanned society's setting the car as the status symbol, neglecting public transportation, to the point that traffic often can't move and traffic control is so poor as to create a real hazard for pedestrians. The popular belief is that Imam Khomeini, as he is called here, should ban private cars and make everyone ride buses. But even if there were enough buses, would Khomeini have sufficient moral authority to make such an edict stick?

Also learned that the "modern, progressive" regime of the Shah left the capital with no sewage system. The human waste goes straight down into the earth beneath the buildings in which it's produced.

A late breakfast, then off to the Cemetery of the Martyrs—the place to which Khomeini first came in January of 1979, when he returned from his 16-year exile. First an Islamic memorial service conducted in Persian by the chanting students (our first exposure to their devoutness), in what we'd call a small chapel. Gruesome pictures on walls of torture and murder victims of SAVAK. ("Do you know what the head of the Iranian army told one of our people?" said Hubert Humphrey in 1960. "He said the army was in good shape, thanks to US aid, and it was now capable of coping with the civilian population.")

Then out to the cemetery itself, where quite a few relatives, old and young, were weeping. A state TV crew filmed the visit, aired it on the evening news, and apparently made it available abroad. Some of the grieving Iranians told us family stories of both indiscriminate and premeditated terror.

Late this evening, by telephone, fed National Public Radio in Washington a half-hour taped interview with Hossein Sheik-holislam, who's not on the students' Central Committee but who nonetheless shoulders important responsibilities (such as negotiating at the airport and serving frequently as our interpreter). Phone circuits back to States often weak (some say because so many US intelligence agencies tap into telecommunications into and out of Iran!).

February 9

Am beginning to feel that even by Western standards, post-revolution Iran allows a large measure of personal freedom. None of the feel of a police state. Have been in enough post-revolution settings not to equate repression and terrorization of the population with the sight of armed civilians or revolutionary guards or a people's militia.

Also from experience, I am able to put all the governmental "confusion" in perspective. I remember sailing into Djakarta from Singapore in 1953 and seeing droves of Dutch professionals and technicians, with families, leaving Indonesia to return to Netherlands—in many cases because of psychological inability to adjust to "brown power" in a post-colonial milieu.

Since the Dutch East Indies government had allowed only a few hundred Indonesians (out of some 70 million) to get a university education in the years just before the Japanese occupation, during WW II, and since the years 1945 through '49 were taken up with popular resistance to two Dutch "police actions" after Sukarno's proclamation of an independent Indonesia, administrative and political "confusion" throughout the country's 3000 populated islands had been colonially programmed.

Ditto Cuba after the overthrow of Batista. Often deliberately enticed by the CIA, US-educated Cubans with urgently needed skills were leaving for Miami on every ship and plane out.

So also today with many Westernized (often US-trained) Iranians who may not have liked the Shah's *modus operandi,* but whose hearts nevertheless are with his kind of privileged, sparkling-on-the-surface, rotten-at-the-core society. Every post-revolution government preoccupied with delivering on revolutionary promises has to decide whether to deny exit permits at the risk of constant sabotage by a sullen middle-class labor force or to say "good riddance" and ride out the "confusion" painfully and slowly. From the number of departures, it seems Iran is apparently resigned to a brain drain.

Late last night, in hotel dining room, Randy Goodman and I had chance encounter with Hossein Sheikholislam, and intimate conversation for two hours. He startled us by revealing that the students' original plan was to seize and hold the embassy for three days at most. They expected to find a maximum of 15 embassy personnel and were amazed to find many more. The overwhelmingly favorable popular reaction in Iran, including Khomeini's, had come as a pleasant surprise. Rest is history.

Feeding 50 hostages day after day, with necessary security precautions against any poisoning of the food supply, is an onerous responsibility. The students themselves fast at least two days a week, following (as are many other Iranians) Khomeini, who started fasting after Carter's military threats in late November. Up on seventh floor of hotel, students ate much simpler food than what was served in dining room.

Other points in the conversation with Hossein:

—During Kurt Waldheim's January visit to Iran on the hostage issue, it was the embassy students who released photos of him kissing the hand of the Shah's sister during a visit he made several years ago. The students also reminded the world that during this earlier visit, Waldheim had refused to receive an Iranian delegation that wished to present him with a complaint about the Shah's atrocities ("The worst in the world," an Amnesty International report stated).

—The students will obey an order by Khomeini to release the hostages, because of his political position over the years.

—Khomeini is usually ahead of public opinion. He will never go against Iranian public opinion. And Iranian public opinion wants the Shah back in exchange for the hostages.

—Because of the USSR's anti-religious and materialistic tendencies, Iranians are as much opposed to it as they are to the U.S. But the US government is the main enemy at this time.

—Russia's commercial arms sales to the Shah and China's official welcome for his sister during his reign didn't endear either country to Iranians.

—The right is eternal. The wrong will be destroyed eventually. You must be on one side or the other. If you're on neither side, you're nowhere.

—Hamilton Jordan's hasty secret journey to Panama set the stage for Shah to leave Texas. Iranians believe Carter was creating an opportunity for the eventual extradition of the Shah, which may become more and more likely the closer election day comes, if Carter is desperate and has lost public support.

After just three days, a major topic of conversation among the Americans: the vast discrepancies between students'—and many others'—non-negotiable demand for Shah's return, and totally misleading US press garbage about "imminent" release of hostages. For some delegates, it's their first, direct experience of the American press playing footsie with the government in stringing public (and hostages' families) along week after week.

In ironic contrast, have been amazed to discover how *au courant* the students are about El Salvador, South Africa (Iran stopped selling oil to Pretoria right after the revolution), China, the Soviet Union, and, indeed, much of the rest of the world. Puzzle: with daily guard duty at embassy, political-strategy sessions, and strenuous efforts to keep up with their individual class work, when do they find time to stay abreast of foreign news?

February 10

Beginning to get a feel for ingredients of Khomeini's revered leadership. When he was arrested and exiled, in 1963, there were uprisings in which 15,000 protesters were killed by the Shah's army. A prelude to the mass killings in the last pre-revolution years, such as that on Black Friday—September 8, 1978, when 3,000 to 5,000 were killed.

From a modest cottage in a French village—unheated after he decided to show solidarity with the poor back in Iran—Khomeini, with no armed force, no opposition party, no mass organization, relentlessly directed revolution strategy against the Shah.

With an estimated one SAVAK agent or informer for every 400 Iranians, the revolution of necessity had to be decentralized. Only small, intimate cells could be safe from infiltration. Khomeini's sole weapon was the cartridge tape. He would record his remarks. With alligator clips leading from the tape recorder to the two poles inside every telephone mouthpiece, the message would be fed into an overseas-telephone circuit, recorded on the Iran end by one of a larger number of secret contacts, and then reproduced for underground distribution. Hossein told us that trusted state telephone workers helped facilitate these highly dangerous calls from France and made it technically almost impossible for SAVAK to trace the recipient numbers.

William A. Dorman and Mansour Farhang, writing in the May/June, 1979, issue of *Politics Today,* noted that everyone underestimated the strength of the revolution and quoted CIA director Stansfield Turner as saying, "It was like a series of volcanoes bubbling up. But it certainly appeared that no one of them would bubble up so much that the government couldn't control it. What we didn't forecast was that . . . a 78-year-old cleric who had been in exile for 14 years would be the catalyst . . . and that we would have one huge volcano—a truly national revolution."

There's nothing new about the press's, the CIA's, the scholars' off-the-wall assessments of "bubbling" revolutionary situations. Lest we forget, on January 1, 1959, an AP bulletin from Havana "reported" that the guerrilla columns of Che Guevara and Raul and Fidel Castro had been wiped out by Batista's US-trained army, and that the revolution had been aborted—just as Batista was fleeing Cuba and the guerrillas were entering Havana. Shortly before his death, in 1964, after nearly 45 years on the *Globe,* Lucien Price of

"Uncle Dudley" fame remarked to me, "From my box seat, I know that most of the US press has lied about every major revolution of the 20th century."

For the most part, they're still lying.

Two months ago, Kurt Waldheim was badly shaken when introduced in Tehran to five-year-old Abolfazi Safayi, who, at the age of three, had been tortured by SAVAK in the presence of his father, to make the father reveal who had given him a tape recording of a Khomeini speech. Both the boy's arms were cut off. The father still wouldn't talk. Two of Abolfazi's brothers, one six months old, were then tortured to death in the father's presence. He still refused to talk.

On January 9, 1979, the *New York Times* reported: "Jesse J. Leaf . . . had been the chief CIA analyst on Iran before resigning from the agency in 1973 . . . Mr. Leaf said a senior CIA official was involved in instructing officials in SAVAK on torture techniques . . . The CIA torture seminars, Mr. Leaf said, 'were based on German torture techniques from World War II . . . . I know that the torture rooms were toured (by Americans) and it was all paid for by the USA.' "

Today, a working day in Iran, is a big day for the delegation. A four-hour meeting with 120 of the students inside the "former US embassy—nest of spies," mainly to exchange views on the widest range of subjects. It was still daylight when the two buses pulled up at the sprawling 27-acre compound. The normally relaxed, often jocular student leaders—Mariam (Mary), Amir, Hossein, two-Muhammads, and others—became extraordinarily uptight during the several minutes it took to get everyone off the buses and into one of the buildings.

Security was even tighter during our departure, after dark. "Mr. Worthy," said Amir, a med student at the University of Tehran, "you must hurry along. It's *very* dangerous." Not difficult to understand this anxiety. From page one of today's *Tehran Times,* this trial balloon:

FORCE TO FREE HOSTAGES?

"London (AP)—Iranian Foreign Minister Sadegh Gotbzadeh said in an interview broadcast here Friday that Iranian authorities would use force 'if necessary' to free the US hostages being held in Tehran."

It's certain that the students all along have had contingency plans for any US-oriented commando raid on the embassy: It's a political given that all the hostages in Iran would die in any attack on the embassy, whether instigated by Americans or Iranians. The popular support the students enjoy is such that one hears the phrase "civil war" in connection with the idea of an Iranian raid.

No picture-taking in the embassy courtyard. Before the meeting got under way, three different signals on taking pictures inside the building: first yes, then a reversal, and finally yes once more. Again, the session was filmed by a state TV crew, and excerpts were aired on the news this evening. Seems clear the students have staunch supporters in the media, and they get coverage whenever they seek it, even if Americans choose to believe their own propaganda about the students' "isolation."

February 14

On bus to Evin Prison, in northern Tehran, delegates query one of students about his "Free Puerto Rico" button. Most important prisoner to be interviewed: Hassan Sana, social and political adviser to head of SAVAK, General Nasser Moghaddam. Ninety percent of persons arrested had some sign of physical abuse on their bodies. Practically no difference in the torturing of men and women. We were referred to 1977 International Red Cross report for independent corroboration.

Profile of a SAVAK type, Hassan Sana: age 45, bachelor's degree in philosophy from University of Tehran. In charge of security there for eight years. SAVAK was started 22 years ago, at start of his service with government. Says, "It was started to fight Communism." ("You can imagine where that came from!" interjects Sadegh of Ministry of National Guidance.)

Sana: "There were American, British, and Israeli advisers. As government operations expanded, so did SAVAK. There were problems with university students, clergy, etc. Whatever jeopardized the regime became the concern of SAVAK. In every class of 40 students, there were two or three informers. Also informers at higher levels of universities, including professors.

"In the last two years of his regime, at annual conference of Shah, Cabinet members and professors, Shah said in a rage that if there were any campus riots in the following year, 'I'll smash student heads myself.' Nine student activists were taken in middle of night to hill behind this prison and were executed.

"Shah ordered shoot to kill, whether students were armed or not. Students were arrested on various specious grounds: having the Koran in hand or anything else the regime felt hostile to, or saying a slogan, or passing out leaflets. Gatherings of more than two students were forbidden.

"SAVAK's first aim after an arrest was to terrorize the person, not to get information. Beatings on soles of feet up to 500 times. Victim would pass out after 60 blows, would be revived, made to walk on feet. Some would die. Some would have to have their legs amputated. SAVAK knew that if released, they'd tell friends and create fear."

"Any SAVAK activities the Shah didn't know about?"

"No. He was in on everything that was going on."

"How many people worked for SAVAK?"

"Five thousand official personnel. Sixty thousand employed as sources of information."

"Any SAVAK connection with the International Police Academy in Washington, and any training there?"

"I know of 35 SAVAK agents who went to US for further training. Twenty-four went to Israel. Sixteen to 20 went to England. Torture was part of the training."

February 15

Random notes from tonight's final session with students:

"It looks like we'll be staying in the embassy forever, so you can contact us there," said one. "The telephone number is 8200091 to -98. All eight lines go through the State Department switchboard in Washington, and they don't always let calls from the US go through."

Shahpour Sobhi (the student with the best sense of humor, a merry smile perpetually on his face): "If you phone me at the embassy, ask for me on the national desk." Earlier, when Shahpour asked me to send him some newspapers from the US, I asked to what address. He wrote:

US Embassy (nest of spies)
Taleghani Avenue
Tehran, Iran

I and everyone else standing around cracked up when he handed me back the piece of paper.

Under the leadership of several progressive religious figures and educators in Aliabad, most of the population had supported Mossadegh and travelled into Shiraz to demonstrate in his favor (much as they participated in pro-Khomeini demonstrations in late 1978 and early 1979). In this early period Seyyid Yakub, his relatives, and other allies took the part of the Shah, for they profited from their connections with his government. After the coup, Seyyid Yakkub's henchmen attacked the homes of the pro-Mossadegh leaders in the middle of the night and beat them severely. At least one of the leaders was then exiled from the village for a number of years; others were punished as well.

A second set of events that contributed to the reservoir of popular anger grew out of a peasant sharecroppers' strike in the late 1950s. This was significant because of its effect on the distribution of land following the 1962 land reform. The peasant sharecroppers declared their share of the crop to be insufficient. Seyyid Yakub Askari, then representative of the former landlord, was forced to hire labor to farm the land himself. At the end of this year, neither the former landlord nor many of the peasants were yet willing to relent. Seyyid Yakub announced that all previous sharecropping agreements were null and void and rights to agricultural land were available to any and all for asking. Some peasant sharecroppers had by then found jobs elsewhere, and others, too stubborn and resentful of the former landlord and his representative, abandoned their traditional agricultural rights. In the end, Seyyid Yakub and many of his relatives and supporters took over full rights to the agricultural land in dispute. Several traders, absent for long periods of time due to their work and who thus often maintained a neutral position in village affairs, also took advantage of this opportunity. Because land reform stipulated that land should go to those presently possessing agricultural rights, those former sharecroppers who had forfeited their rights after the strike lost out and did not receive any land; while many men who had been traders or landless shortly before land reform, took possession of land.

The process of land reform, more than any other aspect of peasant-landlord relations, aroused the greatest outrage and deepest resentment. First, because many families had abandoned their traditional farming rights during the strike or because their agricultural activities were not economically viable, received no land whatsoever or such a small area of land that they considered it useless and refused to accept it. Secondly, as the former landlord was an in-law of the Shah, he had received advance warning of the impending land reform. He quickly sold half of the village to friends there, although apparently this did not become public knowledge until later. Seyyid Ibn Ali Askari bought two-thirds of the land for sale and one-third was purchased by Seyyid Yakub and some 20 others. As a result, only half of the village land was distributed among the persons holding agricultural rights; they felt it was their right to receive all of the land. Thirdly, the best land—flat, irrigatable, and close to the village—went to the new small landowners. Only the dry, hilly land further from the village was left for those with agricultural rights. Fourthly, many of those peasants who had kept their agricultural rights after the strike feared that the land reform official seeking the dimensions of their land was doing so for the purpose of taking it from them. They reported an acreage less than what they were actually farming, and then received less land than was their right. Other people owning rights to land but working in other jobs or trading outside of the village were absent during the few days allowed for registering for land reform and did not receive land.

Directing all of their fury about these discrepancies in land distribution at Seyyid Ibn Ali and his family, the villagers refused to sign the required papers and violence broke out between the two factions. The villagers succeeded in routing the landlord faction from the village. But Seyyid Ibn Ali used his period of absence from the village to rally support from among his contacts with government officials. He even succeeded in obtaining a letter from the Shah, according to some reports.

After some months he triumphantly re-entered the village, accompanied by several truck loads of armed gendarmes. Three days of virtual marshall law followed. Men and boys hid in terror. Women didn't dare go outside of their homes. All those seized were tortured and beaten, held a few days within the village or the gendarmarie station several kilometers away, and then taken to prison in Shiraz. Young boys were hung upside down and beaten on the bare soles of their feet for a day or more, until they revealed the whereabouts of older brothers and fathers. Four or five persons, reportedly, died as a result of beatings and torture received. At least 27 men were imprisoned for about six months. Following their release they moved, as others had already done, to other villages to avoid further retribution from Seyyid Ibn Ali and his family. The wrath of the villagers was reduced to a smoldering resentment.

Seyyid Ibn Ali's advantageous connections with government officials and those in authority were inherited from the former landlord, who was from a national prominent family. In addition, through his heavy involvement in opium trading and processing, he had contacts with heads of government offices in Shiraz, many of whom used opium. With others he had ties based on bribery that related to his smuggling activities. He also discovered another method of widening his connections in political circles—using the land he had bought before land reform. He sold a large area of land, which actually had been appropriated to holders of agricultural rights under land reform, and used the money to bribe personnel in the court system. He sold sections of land for a moderate price to the chief of police in Shiraz, to the head of the court system, and to several other influential persons. He continued to encroach for his own use on areas of land and water resources reserved for the peasants. He antagonized the other small landowners by doing likewise with their land, until he controlled an estimate two-thirds of the village land, instead of the one-third which he had "legally" purchased.

After land reform, agriculture in Aliabad declined drastically. Relatively little land or water was left to the agriculturalists after Seyyid Ibn Ali confiscated these resources, often selling them to Shirazis for villas or factories. The villagers blamed this decline, and the fact that subsequently most men were forced to either move into Shiraz to work or to commute to jobs in the city on Seyyid Ibn Ali and his supporters. But there was no recourse open to them, and they experienced years of helpless fury.

Political Expectations

Given this suppressed hatred of the people of Aliabad, it is rather remarkable that, after the fall of the Shah's regime which propped up Seyyid Ibn Ali as a village dictator, they did not immediately challenge the supremacy of the Askaris. Their failure to do so is related to perceptions about the impact which the revolution and the new government would have on political structure and process within the village.

During the course of the revolution, Seyyid Yakub and his allies were outspoken in their opposition to Imam Khomeini and in their support of the Shah. Seyyid Ibn Ali, on the other hand, was politically astute. He correctly sensed the probable outcome of the struggle at an early date and professed his devotion to Imam Khomeini. The sons of both Seyyid Yakub and Seyyid Ibn Ali as well as of their allies were active in the revolution. Indeed, Seyyid Muslim, the 27-year-old son of Seyyid Yakub, was a main organizer of revolutionary activities. A highly successful entrepreneur dealing in the lucrative real estate business of leasing gardens, and also in trade, he was not tied to an employer and was free to organize the village youth and bus them into Shiraz for daily demonstrations. In addition, he was an experienced administrator. The villagers were quite accustomed, however grudgingly, to looking to him as a leader. Finally, as both his father and he were on excellent terms with the gendarmes, he did not fear punishment for his revolutionary activities. Although Seyyid Yakub was responsible for giving the names of those active in the revolution to the gendarmerie head, he would hardly have given them the name of his own son.

Upon the success of the revolution on February 11, 1979, all expected the new authorities to reward those who had helped bring about their victory. Should the Khomeini forces prevail, as they eventually did, Seyyid Muslim and the other young Askari men were expected to be able to protect their elders from summary revolutionary justice. Similarly, should the Pahlavi regime retain power, the older Askaris were prepared to shield their sons from any official retribution. In either case, assumed the villagers, the Askaris had situated themselves to maintain their local power and influence, and few anticipated any practical change in the political structure even in the event of a Khomeini victory.

Reflecting the common assumption that Imam Khomeini's political role and performance would be similar to those of the Shah, one peasant proudly told me that he was old enough to remember five shahs—including the present one. Many people expected a secret service organization, similar to the Shah's SAVAK, in any Khomeini regime, and that the same type of political organization, of exchanging favors, would be operative. All power and authority would continue to emanate from the central government and the central figure of Imam Khomeini. They assumed that this power would come down to the local level, available for the Askaris to run the village. Seyyid Ibn Ali Askari would no longer be the power intermediary with Seyyid Yakub Askari serving as administrator; now the visiting *mullah* from Qom would delegate authority to Seyyid Muslim Askari for local administration.

Political activity was based on these assumptions for several months after the revolution. Thus, although no one paid the customary and required visit of congratulations to Seyyid Yakub on New Year's Day (March 21, 1979), many people did call on the visiting *mullah*. Even persons from other villages came to the *mullah* with their problems and disputes, as previously people had gone to Seyyid Yakub for assistance. By taking gifts to the *mullah*, villagers hoped to get on his good side and thus be granted special consideration in future times of trouble, just as in the past they had taken trouble to be on Seyyid Yakub's good side. The *mullah* worked closely with Seyyid Muslim, as the most influential local political figure, and was a frequent guest at his home. Seyyid Muslim was in charge of organizing the village men to guard the village every night. When the *mullah* was provided with rations from the Shiraz authorities to give the night sentries, he handed them over to Seyyid Muslim for distribution.

Seyyid Yakub and his allies, to gain the good graces of the new authorities, visited the mosque and were verbally chastised by a religious figure from Shiraz for failing to support the Imam Khomeini. They expected all would be forgiven with an apology, as had been customary when joining forces with the victorious contender in a political struggle.

Gradually, however, both the *mullah* and the people realized the situation had changed drastically. The *mullah* did not have the backing to enforce his decisions, nor to help people with problems and resolve conflicts. Dissatisfied with the lack of obedience to his rulings, the *mullah* eventually left. The gendarmes, fearing revenge for their past brutal treatment of the villagers, either left the area or stayed at their post but refused to involve themselves in village affairs. The *pasdaran* (Revolutionary Guards) from Shiraz were unorganized, inexperienced, unwilling to jeopardize their popularity, and too few in numbers to have an effect on security in the region. Unsure of what the new policies would be, personnel in the government offices were reluctant to take action of any kind. Religious leaders were fearful of taking initiatives which might lead to further dissension and strife and certainly were unprepared to champion such an unpopular family as the Askaris, even if some members *had* participated in the revolution. Minor attacks against Askari property went unpunished. In May, a young man actually assaulted Seyyid Muslim. The gendarmes failed to make an immediate appearance and arrest the young man; the Askaris, for their part, speedily and cheerfully patched up the quarrel!

The villagers noticed this reluctance on the part of the authorities to back the Askaris and became aware that more local initiative and activity were permissible under the new conditions. They began to organize, gradually overcoming their fear and gaining new confidence in their cause and devotion to it, much as had happened among the Iranian population as a whole during the course of the national revolution. During this local process, the symbols, political categories, and activities developed during the course of the revolution were used by activists to legitimize their actions for themselves, for potential supporters and for government authorities.

Symbolic Weapons

Shortly after the revolution the educators and religious figures who had been enemies of the Askaris since the time of Mossadegh resumed their efforts to regain peasants' land confiscated by Seyyid Ibn Ali. They filed complaints with the many government offices in Shiraz and even traveled to Tehran to confer with officials of the land reform offices, but with no results. The changed perceptions and attitudes, though, gained momentum over the summer months of 1979.

The reformist and revolutionary emphases in Shi'a Islam took on local meaning. This vocation to struggle against injustice and oppression could apply to situations other than ridding the country of the Shah. Villagers began discussing the past exploits and characteristics of the notorious Seyyid Ibn Ali in the vocabulary of the victorious revolutionaries: *zolm* (oppression), *zur* (force), *taqouti* (decadent, idolatrous), *zede enqelab* (anti-revolutionary), *estabadad* (tyranny), *savaki* (SAVAK agent), *mofsed* (corruptor), and *roushveh* (bribe).

Just as mosques had been centers in national revolutionary acitvity, the Aliabad mosque became a form used by the activists to arouse sentiment against Seyyid Ibn Ali. During July of 1979, every Friday the mosque was the scene of inflamatory speeches by visitors from Shiraz and local leaders denouncing Seyyid Ibn Ali. Although in the past mosque activities had been completely regulated and financed by the Askaris, the former rulers were all too aware of the change in their position, and did not even attempt to enter the mosque during these months.

The villagers were not content to emphasize the Shi'a injunction to struggle against unjust leaders: They also expounded on its socialistic aspects. Men and women would comment positively on the simple life led by Imam Ali, and then mutter that it wasn't Islamic that some people should have hundreds of acres of land while others had none whatsoever, that some people should own whole apartment buildings in Shiraz (as did Seyyid Ibn Ali), while others had not even a home to their name. Through discussion and education, the anti-Seyyid Ibn Ali alliance increased in numbers over the summer. Then, on October 2, 1979, Seyyid Ibn Ali made a move calculated to win him the sympathy of Shiraz's religious hierarchy; but it backfired, further unifying the opposition to him and mobilizing it into action.

Accompanied by a group of four Revolutionary Guards and engineers, Seyyid Ibn Ali arrived in Aliabad prepared to divide some 40,000 meters of his land among 40 *mostazefin* (poor and oppressed). Upon learning that the landlord planned to give away land actually belonging to the peasants to so-called *mostazefin* (who were in fact his own relatives and a few influential persons whom he hoped to buy off), the peasants and landless protested. The *pasdaran* and engineers, innocent of contention for the land, stopped their work and asked the protestors to explain their case to the court the following Saturday. Early Saturday morning, October 6, several hundred irate men left in buses, pick-ups, taxis and private cars to chant in front of the governor's office and the court and to swear out more than a hundred complaints against Seyyid Ibn Ali, including four accusations of murder. Seyyid Ibn Ali was arrested the same day. For several days in a row the men of Aliabad commuted into Shiraz to shout slogans and chants in front of government offices and homes of religious figures and to add to the file against Seyyid Ibn Ali. Seyyid Muslim organized the Askaris for a competitive show of force, but they were badly outnumbered and outshouted.

In hopes that Seyyid Ibn Ali would be able to reach a compromise with the peasants, the authorities let him out of jail on October 10. Accompanied by his relatives and other supporters in a noisy caravan of cars, Seyyid Ibn Ali came to Aliabad with the aim of pacifying his enemies. But the population reacted with outrage, crowding into the village square and even shouting in anger at a jeepful of normally revered Revolutionary Guardsmen sent to preserve the peace: "You think we're still back in the Shah's time so that you should stick up for tyranny?"

At six the next morning the mosque loudspeaker broadcast the message to gather for another trip to Shiraz: "Don't be afraid! Fight for your rights!" Several hundred men repeated their trek to Shiraz to shout chants in front of the governor's office. The leaders spoke with the governor's representative, explaining why the people of Aliabad wanted Seyyid Ibn Ali put back in prison. The landlord was again seized, this time in the process of arranging to leave the country!

With this second imprisonment, more people in Aliabad, who at first had been reluctant to defy Seyyid Ibn Ali openly, allowed themselves to be persuaded of their Islamic duty and joined forces with the opposition. The Shiraz Court eventually acquiesced to continuous pressure and granted the activists explicit, written permission to farm those areas of Seyyid Ibn Ali's land which he himself had failed to plant. (Allowing peasants to sow land not currently farmed was a general policy designed to encourage agricultural productivity.) Armed with this document and optimistic about the final outcome of the dispute over land, the leaders announced that on November 1 and 2, all married natives of Aliabad who wished to receive land should register at the mosque. With those natives who were currently living in Shiraz also eligible, the signatories totaled some 800 men. On Friday morning, November 2, crowds of men gathered at the mosque and marched out to a section of land previously controlled by Seyyid Ibn Ali. In the forefront was the green flag of Islam. Two groups chanted the alternate phrases of a revolutionary couplet, as was customary in the large national marches and demonstrations against the Shah. At the site, the green flag of Islam was planted in the ground and men took turns sowing by hand, while the elated onlookers shouted *"Allah-o-akbar"* and other inspiring slogans.

Since it was late into the winter wheat season, the activists decided that rather than waste precious time dividing the land up at this point, they would farm the land jointly this year. Ten men were hired to be responsible for agricultural work, and each new shareholder was taxed 400 *tumans* to defray expenses. All shareholders were expected to participate in the necessary communal activities, such as cleaning out the irrigation ditch.

Another incident two weeks later aroused the Aliabad population again and further undermined the position of the Askaris. Gendarmes and revolutionary guardsmen caught the Askaris in the act of firing rifles and throwing rocks from the roof of Seyyid Yakub's home upon unarmed crowds below. Seyyid Yakub, his sons, Seyyid Ibn Ali's sons, and other allies were arrested. They were subsequently released, but warned by authorities in Shiraz not to return to the village. Virtually exiled and fearful for their safety, they remained in hiding. Other supporters did not dare return to the village and stayed with friends or relatives in Shiraz

Taasua and *Ashura*, the eve and the day of the anniversary of Imam Hussein's martyrdom, had in 1978 been the turning point of the Iranian Revolution. Proclaiming that it is more important to follow Imam Hussein's example by being prepared to die in the struggle against injustice and repression than it is to weep for his demise, Imam Khomeini urged Iranians to defy the orders of the Shah's government and take to the streets. He instructed them not to weep and beat their chests and to lash their backs with chains, a traditional manifestation of grief for the death of Imam Hussein, but to exhalt in his spirit of courage and altruism, to follow in his path and to be prepared to die for their faith and for the freedom of succeeding generations. For the first time, all over the country, thousands upon thousands braved the military to scream in terrible anger, "Down with the Shah." This marked the beginning of the struggle-to-the-death with the Pahlavi regime.

Revolutionary Meaning of Shi'a Islam

For the People of Aliabad, commemoration of *Taasua* and *Ashura* in 1979 was a celebration of the fact that the newly understood revolutionary meaning of Shi'a Islam was alive in their own village. By planning and organizing the commemorations themselves, the activists effectively demonstrated that Imam Hussein and his martyrdom belong to those who fight for justice. It is not the property of the wealthy and powerful to legitimize their supremacy, as had been the case in the past. Then, the Askaris had organized, regulated, and financed *Ashura* activities, as befitted their *seyyid* status. This year the Askaris did not even dare make an appearance.

Seyyid Ibn Ali had managed to bribe his way out of prison the day before *Taasua*. This provided the activists with an opportunity to put into immediate practice their contention that the sturggle against injustice is more important than mourning the death of Imam Hussein. Upon learning of Seyyid Ibn Ali's escape, men and women abruptly halted the mourning rituals and went to the nearby gendarmerie office to complain. When they were informed that the matter was out of the jurisdiction of this branch office, the men continued on to Shiraz to demonstrate in front of the homes of religious leaders and influential persons. They did not return until they were assured that the landlord would again be imprisoned. By this time, 10 o'clock at night, it was too late for the customary afternoon and evening ritual of *Taasua*. But people assured one another that it did not matter; the more important obligation was to go after Seyyid Ibn Ali and bring him to justice.

By the time of my departure from Aliabad in December 1979, the landlord still had not been apprehended. The pressure on government officials to continue the search for him went on, but several more thoughtful persons confided that it would be better if he fled the country. People would begin to forget, and his relatives and supporters, if not personally guilty of unjust acts, could be assimilated into the community again. If there are no drastic reversals of the new situation in Aliabad, the gratification of the villagers at freeing themselves from the power of the village tyrant and his cohorts should mean consideragle loyalty in the future to Imam Khomeini and the Islamic Republic.

*   *   *

This article is reprinted from the second of three special issues of *MERIP Reports* on post-revolutionary Iran. #86, *The Left Forces,* features Ervand Abrahamian's history of Iran's guerrilla movement and Fred Halliday's interviews with spokesmen of the major left organizations. #87, *The Rural Dimension,* examines the extensive participation of young Iranians of village origin in the revolution, and the fusion of social and economic demands with the nationalist and religious ideology that mobilized Iran's masses. #88, *The First Year,* evaluates the revolution's accomplishments and limitations so far, with a particular focus on the workers' councils that have become a feature of Iranian factory life. This issue contains a full translation of The Ayatollah Khomeini's New Year's speech of March 1980. A special double issue, *Iran in Revolution* (#75/76) included eyewitness accounts and a photoessay of the last days of the Shah, interviews with oil workers, documents from the political movements, and a survey of the opposition forces. *Reports* #69 and #71 analyzed in depth the economic contradictions and political challenges that produced the popular upheaval. Earlier issues look at Iran's strategic role in the Middle East and critique U.S. policy there: #43, *Land Reform and Agribusiness in Iran;* #40, *America's Shah, Shahanshah's Iran;* and #37, *Iranian Nationalism and the Great Powers.* All issues are available for $2 each, except #75/76 which is $2.50 plus 75 cents postage. Subscriptions to *MERIP Reports* are $14 per year. Write MERIP, Dept. B, PO Box 1247, New York, NY 10025.

We Could Just Ask Them To Forgive Us

Jim Wallis

As this month's *Sojourners* goes to press, we face the threat of war with Iran.

Fifty United States citizens have been held hostage in the U.S. embassy in Tehran for more than six weeks. The frustration of the American public is intensifying. Angry feelings of revenge and racism against the Iranians boil just beneath the surface, sometimes breaking out in ugly demonstrations. The political climate is increasingly self-righteous, demanding "toughness from an insecure president facing a difficult re-election campaign."

Most Americans seem genuinely astonished at the depth of the Iranian people's anger toward the United States. Confused and defensive, they appear quite unable to understand why their country has been singled out for attack and wonder aloud, "Who do these people think they are?" This may be the most significant thing to recognize in the present crisis, for it demonstrates that the American people have not come to terms with the role of their government in the world.

In August of 1953, the nationalist prime minister of Iran, Mohammed Mossedegh, was overthrown. The coup was organized by Kermit Roosevelt of the Central Intelligence Agency, a grandson of another Roosevelt who was also quite experienced in intervening in the affairs of other countries. Having been restored to power, a grateful Shah Reza Pahlavi told Mr. Roosevelt, "I owe my throne to God, my people, my army—and you."

From that day until he was forced to flee his country by a popular uprising last February, the Shah's principal backer was the United States—politically, militarily, and economically. In exchange, the Shah supported American political and military interests in the area while pursuing Western-style capitalist development. Every Iranian knows this.

The chief beneficiaries of the arrangement were the Shah's family and the multinational corporations which did business in

This article first appeared in *Sojourners*, Vol. 9, No. 1, January, 1980, and is reprinted by permission. Copyright © 1980, People's Christian Coalition.

Iran. Corruption became a way of life in Iran as the royal family amassed a fortune estimated in the billions of dollars, while the majority of the people remained poor. Traditional cultural and religious values were trampled to make way for "modernization."

The Shah's regime was brutal and dictatorial. It has been said that every family in Iran was touched by the Shah's tyranny. Dissent from the policies of the government was not tolerated, and all opposition was crushed or exiled. Shah Reza Pahlavi personally ordered the torture and execution of many thousands of his own people. The evidence documenting his atrocities is incontrovertible.

A quarter century of this corruption and political abuse is the root cause of the crisis we now face.

To hold 50 American hostages responsible for the crimes others have committed is unfair and cruel. These unfortunate persons and their families have become the victims and pawns of much larger emotional and political forces. Their safety and release must remain a central priority.

But to isolate the taking of hostages as the only real issue involved insults the Iranian people and puts the hostages in greater jeopardy.

The Carter administration has repeatedly said that now is not the time to discuss the demerits of the Shah's regime.

Yet now is *precisely* the time to talk about the Shah's crimes against the people of Iran and American complicity in them. Only such an honest recognition of the truth of the past could be the basis for beginning real negotiations with the Iranians.

Yet the administration has been silent about the Shah's regime and about the United States' role in Iran. It has simply reiterated the demand that the hostages be released, while retaliating against the Iranians economically, diplomatically, and with military threats.

Admitting the Shah to this country for medical treatment and then granting him protective haven on an Air Force base in Texas is to the Iranians what a U.S. decision to harbor Nazi war criminals would have been to the Jews.

The Iranians have no reason to interpret this behavior as anything other than continued U.S. support for the Shah and his regime.

The biblical virtues of confession and repentance have an obvious political relevance in this crisis. Nothing could more potentially ease the conflict and redeem the situation than a genuine acceptance of our responsibility in the great suffering caused by the Shah and a commitment to make restitution to the people of Iran.

What if we asked the Iranian people to forgive us for installing and maintaining the Shah, for interfering in their country, for profiting from their poverty, for corrupting their traditional values, for equipping and training the police that tortured and killed them?

The United States pressed for an international legal process at Nuremburg to try Nazi leaders for their crimes. Will the U.S. now support an international tribunal in which the Iranian government could make its case to the world against the acts of the Shah and the role of his U.S. supporters?

Public indications from Iranian officials suggest that convening such a forum might begin to break the impasse and even hold out hope for the release of the hostages.

Apparently, Americans still don't want to face the fact that our government has become a consistent supporter of dictatorship around the world. We still don't want to recognize what it means for the United States' best friends to be men like the Shah, or Somoza of Nicaragua, Park of South Korea, Marcos of the Philippines, Pinochet of Chile, and a host of others.

We should be learning from the Iranian crisis that to support dictators who oppress their people is to insure that our nation becomes a target of these people's hatred. That hate may take decades to develop into social revolutions, but ultimately revolutions will come. To ignore that historical inevitability or to point only to the excesses of the revolution is both a moral and political failure.

U.S. support for dictatorships around the world is sowing the seeds of violence that will grow to turn back on us. In the Iranian crisis, we can see our future. Already, the United States has become feared and hated in the poorer countries of the world because of our support for tyranny. It is no longer possible to say that anti-American feelings are motivated by communism. For example, the Iranian Moslems are fiercely anti-communist. Their anger is motivated by the role the United States has played in their country.

The Bible says if we sow the wind, we will reap the whirlwind. If we don't change our course, the Iranian crisis will be repeated in different forms and circumstances around the world. If we could face the truth now being so painfully revealed in Iran, it could be a turning point in U.S. foreign relations.

However, the U.S. political climate is not very congenial to the spirit of reflection and repentance. Instead the cry is to get tough and show the world that we can't be pushed around. The volatile responses of an insecure superpower sensing its loss of control in the world hold great potential for violence.

If our national pride and arrogance prevail over our reason and compassion, we will indeed reap the whirlwind.

Reflections on Religion and

Revolution in Iran

Leslie Withers

In the name of God, the compassionate, the merciful.

Visiting Iran, we heard that opening phrase over and over: from the students holding hostages at the U.S. embassy, from government and religious leaders, college professors, textile workers, victims of SAVAK's torture.

"Our revolution introduced a totally new thing to the world—not Marxist, not nationalistic, but religious," said Mrs. Zahra Rahnavard, a noted Iranian scholar and revolutionary leader. "We could do nothing without Islam. I was not always religious, but now I see it's the only way we can make the changes. I say this as a scientist and as a sociologist."

Why was there a religious revolution in Iran? Who led it, and what made it work? What does Islam say to Moslems who continue to struggle for liberation? And what does it mean for people of other faiths? For us as Americans?

Iranians will tell you that their revolution succeeded, when previous attempts to overthrow the Pahlavi dynasty had failed, because of two essential ingredients: ideology and leadership. Both were Islamic.

The Koran

The ideology—the theological understandings which undergird the Islamic revolution—are based on the Koran as taught by a generation of religious leaders in Iran who, particularly within the last 15 years, have breathed new life into an ancient religion by blowing the dust off the old words and re-interpreting them in the light of current realities. A revitalized Islam provided both the consciousness and the courage necessary for the revolution to succeed.

The language of the Koran is highly symbolic, as is the language of the Bible. And just as every Jew must learn again what it means to refer to God as a shepherd and every Christian has to struggle to understand what Jesus meant in referring to a Samaritan as a neighbor, so does the imagery of the Koran need to be translated anew for each generation of Moslems.

Dr. Ali Shariati, sociologist and devoted Moslem, was a key figure in helping Iranians find and understand their self-identity in the Koran and find prescriptions for change in his explanations in popular, vivid contemporary language. Shariati never talked revolution—SAVAK agents poured in vain over his writings looking for anything treasonous he could be convicted for. He never said the Shah or the SAVAK were evil: he didn't need to. His writing was basically what we call consciousness-raising. He believed, correctly, that when people understood Islam they would know what they had to do.

What was it that Islam had to say to people that made it such a source of strength?

Islam is based on the "Five Pillars," or basic practices, through which Moslems confirm and practice their religion. The five are confession, pilgrimage, alms giving, prayer, and fasting. Confession, in particular, became a revolutionary act under the Shah. Now confession does not, at first glance, seem to be a revolutionary act. But as Jim Wallis points out in the preceding article, for Americans to confess out collective guilt in supporting the Shah, to repent of that support, and to pledge not to support repressive governments in the future would certainly be a radical act.

What Moslems confess is *Allah o Akbar*—God is the highest, the greatest. And that confession is meant to be not simply saying words but living lives that in fact put nothing higher than God—not even the life of the individual who confesses. Striving personally and as a society to come as close as possible to God's ideal is the only important goal: everything else is secondary.

Martyrs

Islam reserves special places for martyrs—those who give their lives in service to Allah. The martyr does not die, but lives forever in paradise. Sixty thousand people died in Iran in 1978— shot down by the Shah's army with American-made automatic rifles or tortured to death by SAVAK. Among the dead are women and men, old people and babies, workers, students, the poor of the slums and rural countryside. In Behesht Zahara, the cemetery of the martyrs in Tehran, I watched a man with a pocket knife patiently carve his son's name into the anonymous gray flagstone marking his grave. On all sides of him rows of similar blank stones extend to the horizon. Iranians have no shortage of martyrs to commemorate.

"The martyr is the heart of the revolution," they told us at Behesht, "who brings new life to the struggle. In the dawn of liberty, we miss the martyrs. The martyrs cannot testify, so we bring the testimony here, and the very dirt will speak for them."

Religious Leaders

Religious leaders in Iran were not only theoreticians. They also played key roles in the revolution itself, as they continue to do today in building an Islamic society. They planned the strategies, called the general strikes and mass demonstrations, trained and educated people, were the communications network, and took both the credit and the risks of being up front in a revolution against one of the most cruel and repressive governments the world has ever seen.

"We believe that in a holy war the place of the religious leader is in front—where he will be the first to go," we were told. And those in front paid a heavy price. Dr. Shariati was exiled and then assassinated; Ayatollah Montazeri, who will probably eventually succeed Khomeini as Imam, was imprisoned under torture for ten years; Imam Khomeini himself lost a son and was forced into exile.

A highly developed and subtle system of leadership made it possible for the *mullahs* (religious leaders) to lead the faithful into struggle and even martyrdom. According to Ayatollah Montazeri, Islamic religious leaders must "pursue justice, defend the rights of the people, and live like the oppressed. If you want to eat good food, have good clothes, and live in luxury while others go hungry, that is not right," he told our delegation. "If you are full while your neighbor is empty, that is not just. Such people should not be rulers."

The houses of the two ayatollahs we visited demonstrate that humility and simplicity are essential qualities of an Islamic leader. In dramatic contrast to the opulence surrounding secular rulers under the Shah (or American presidents, or, for that matter, many bishops) their houses were simple and austere. Ayatollah Khomeini's house in Qom looks the same today as twenty or forty years ago, and no material privilege surrounds him or the other religious leaders.

How religious leaders live is important not only as a personal expression of a just life, but also because Islamic leaders deeply feel a responsibility to stay in touch with the people they lead, by feeling what they are feeling and being closely in tune with their needs and wishes. A person becomes a religious leader in Islam because people follow them, and not because they are selected by a church hierarchy. A complex interaction between the leader and the led ensures that an Imam can be followed into danger or even death because he has the absolute trust of the people: trust built up through a lifetime of careful listening as well as a demonstrated righteous and godly life.

Religion in Daily Life

The Islamic values that made revolutionaries out of Iranians continue to undergird the attempts to build a just society in Iran today. Pilgrimage and prayer, two of the five pillars mentioned earlier, unify Moslems across divisions of social class or even nationality. In Iran, all the faithful gather together for Friday prayers. Once a week the businesses close down at noon as the *muezzin* call the faithful to prayer. The whole village or city gathers together: in Tehran, between half a million and a million assemble on the grounds of the University of Tehran each Friday. There they celebrate, pray, visit with each other, and listen as religious leaders instruct them both in personal piety and in the building of an Islamic society.

There the "Friday Imam," or leader of the prayer service, has the power to call the faithful to *jihad*, or holy crusade. *Jihad* has been called twice in Iran since the revolution. In June, Imam Khomeini called a *"jihad* for reconstruction"* to rebuild the ravaged country. He called on the faithful to leave jobs or school and pitch in to build housing, roads, schools; to dig new irrigation ditches to carry precious water to the rural villages; to plant food. And Iranians from all walks of life joined together in a massive volunteer campaign that continues today.

The second *jihad* was for literacy, in a country where more than half of the population is still illiterate. Khomeini said that every literate person had a sacred obligation to find someone who could not read and teach them. Every illiterate person had a holy obligation also: to find someone who could read and get instruction.

In addition to providing needed services, *jihad* has united people across the boundaries of city and countryside, wealth and poverty, privilege and ignorance by bringing people together in the common tasks of reconstruction. Such a *jihad* contrasts strongly with the images most of us have as Westerners of bloodthirsty hoards sweeping across Europe in the Dark Ages.

Nevertheless, the concept of an Islamic state—even if it wars against poverty and ignorance instead of against Christians, leaves most Americans uneasy. Even if Americans had not been taken hostage by Iranians, we would worry about a state founded on religion. We grew up with a doctrine of separation of church and state, policy formed out of the direct experience of early settlers who had fled to this country because of religious persecution in their home-lands.

Hojatoleslam Shabestary, editor of a Moslem newspaper in Tehran, told our delegation that he often found Christians puzzled as to how religion can form the basis of a revolution, especially when that revolution involves violence. Revolution becomes a religious necessity, he told us, when people and institutions become so corrupt that true worship of God is no longer possible. True religion can only happen when people are free to mold their lives—only then can a relation between God and humanity have meaning. Therefore, when conditions of repression make true worship of God impossible, religious people have a sacred obligation to work for the overthrow of the oppressor.

Iranians, for their part, are puzzled and frustrated at the repeated failure of the faithful in this country—particularly Christians—to put their religion into practice. "How can the followers of Jesus Christ," they asked us over and over, "accept what the United States government has done in Iran? How can you be a Christian and not be on the side of the oppressed?" For them the essential conflict is not between Islam and Christianity (or Judaism) but between spiritualism and materialism. Ayatollah Montazeri said to us, "We have no conflict with the American people, especially Christians. True followers of Christ can't be oppressors." And Hojatoleslam Shabestary said, "Moslems share with radical Christians the concept that spiritual values are more important than material goals."

What then can people of faith struggling toward the Kingdom of God in the United States learn from Moslems striving to build an Islamic society in Iran?

Iranians see the two superpowers on either side of them—the Soviet Union and the U.S.—as centers of the demonic forces loose in the world today. The U.S. to them is the greater of the two threats, because they have suffered greatly under a U.S.-imposed dictatorship. Their message to concerned peope living "in the belly of the beast" is simple:

Open your hearts and minds to the suffering of the Iranian people. "We are speaking in the hope of the power of the martyrs who have died," a victim of SAVAK's torture told us—"the power to move those who hear." See and understand the role that your government has played in Iran.

Repent of the things that were done here in your name and with your tax dollars.

Cleanse your hearts and minds and purify your lives. Reject the empty pursuit of money and power and align your life with God's will.

Resist evil—in yourselves, in your society, in your government's policies. Work actively for justice, against oppression.

Or, in the words of the prophet Micah: "God has shown thee, oh people, what is good. And what does God require of thee but to do justice, to love mercy, and to walk humbly with thy God?"

In the name of God, the merciful, the compassionate.

Mirror of Iran: A Photographic Essa

Randy
Goodma

Two Faces of Tehran

Above—The modernized North for the minority who "benfited" under the Shah's regime.

Below—The impoverished shantytowns of South Tehran

Woman and child in front of their home in South Tehran

The bejeweled bedroom of one of the twelve palaces of the Shah's sister, Ashraf

168   Note given to visiting Americans from workers in a textile factory

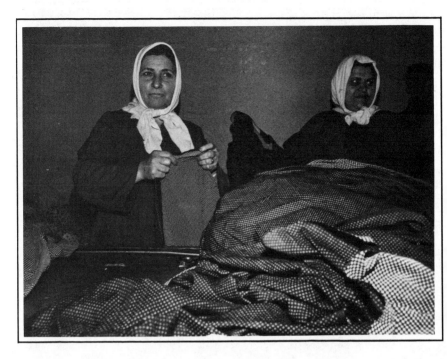

Factory workers

170   Moslem women wearing chador gathered in prayer at the University of Tehran

Cemetery of the Martyrs

174 Moslem woman praying at the grave of her six sons, all tortured and killed by SAVAK.

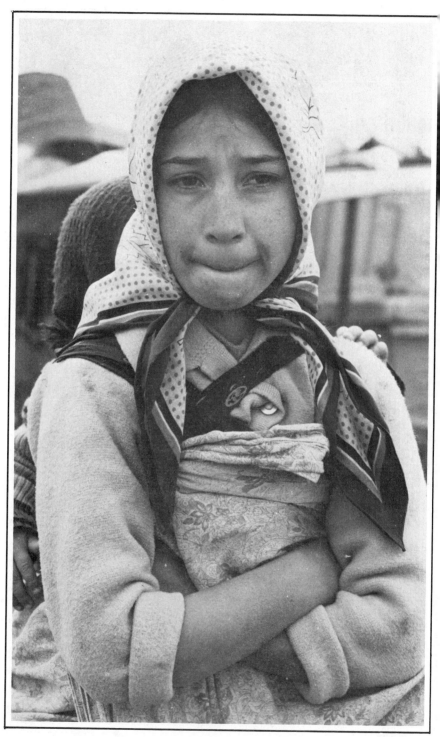

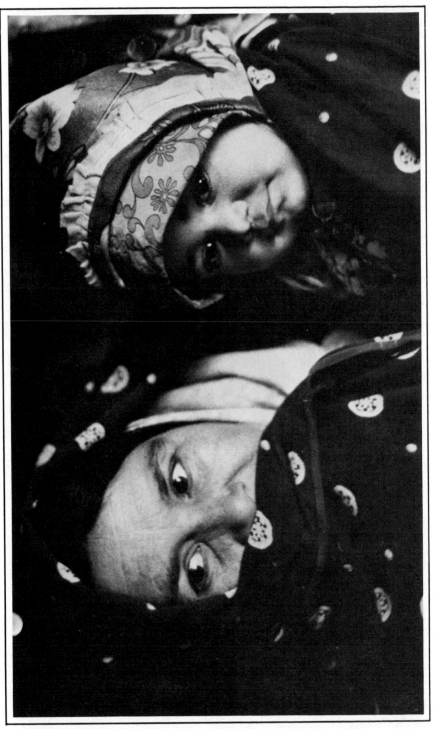

Voices of the Revolution

"If one sees that a government has made oppression its calling, makes encroachments upon the limits of the divine laws, breaks the covenants and pacts of God, cultivates opposition to the methods and manner of the Prophet of God, and acts sinfully and unjustly among the bondspeople of God—under such conditions, anyone who does not by actions and speech restrain such injustice and insolence should know that it is God's prerogative to take this one to the dwelling place of that oppressive ruler and put them both to torment."

—Hazrat Ali

Dr. Ali Shariati

Our Children Understand

When a person becomes poor, the good things that he does are looked down upon, while someone who has power and wealth can force his defects on others as art, his nonsense as good conversation, his rude belches as philosophy, science and religion. His bad jokes and tasteless humor bring riots of hollow laughter.

What is true of people is also true for nations.

When we Moslems had wealth and power, when Spanish and Italian professors, philosophers and scholars got up to lecture in their universities, they put on our Islamic robes. They made-themselves look like Avicenna, Razi and Ghazali.

(Now today, when our professors put on the academic robe, they think they are doing what Europeans do! They think they are imitating Kant and Descartes when they make themselves look like the professors of Spain, Italy, France and England!)

Christian craftsmen in Europe, in order to imitate us, would stamp their goods with the mark, *Allah,* on their crosses.

When the Crusades took place, they came to fight us; we fought back. Eventually Christian colonialists and Zionists got together and Moslems became divided. Sunnis fought with Shi'ites, Shi'ites with Sunnis, Turks with Iranians, Iranians with Arabs, Arabs with Berbers. Whereas Islam taught Oneness, Moslems themselves fell into different groups and ways of thinking.

Spread a map of the world in front of you. Draw a line from the Persian Gulf across to Spain. Then draw another line up from Spain to China, and another back down to the Persian Gulf. This triangle was the Islamic nation: one country, one faith, one book.

But now?

Moslems professing one faith, with one spiritual tongue, in one area, inside one mosque, insisted on performing the congregational prayer in several different ways.

If brother disagreed with brother, each clan, each people, each ethnic group, each country fell away from Islam, pulled towards dead palaces, ancient ruins, dried up bones. They removed God from their memory and replaced Him with dust.

Foreigners have become the instrument by which we have been destroyed. They have seduced us into playing in sand boxes, playing with blood, forming sects, competing with hardware, distracting our minds with irrelevant thoughts, trapping us in fascination with bread and circuses. We have become numb and useless.

The Mongols came and burned and killed and plundered. The Europeans came and stayed.

But we were either too busy preventing each other from seeing or not wanting to see or else we could not see because we were tied up with fighting each other. Or had we simply gone back to prehistoric times, looking for graves, so that our heads weren't up to see what was going on?

The Westerners woke up and we fell asleep. Christians, colonialists and Zionists united, whereas we Moslems separated into a hundred groups. They became wealthy and we became poverty-stricken and weak.

And what are we up to now?

Some of us are still so busy disputing about the past that we haven't a clue of what today's world is about.

Some of us have gotten smart and gotten to know what the world is all about. We sit down and like monkeys in the zoo, watch people. And whatever people do, we monkeys imitate them.

In the eyes of these intelligent ones, only foreigners are people. They are the people to reckon with because foreigners have money and power.

The rest of us have become poverty-stricken. The good in us is looked down upon, while those who have become wealthy, force others to see their defects as art.

They want us all to become monkeys: our professors, our poets, our leaders, our artists, our philosophers, our women, our men, our lives, our cities, our families and . . . even our children. They are afraid of only one thing and that is that we will no longer imitate them. When will it be possible for us to no longer imitate them? Only when we can perceive things for ourselves.

They are only afraid of our perceiving. However strong your body may become does not frighten them. You will never be bigger than a cow and they milk cows. You will never be stronger than a donkey and they load donkeys down. You will never be faster than a horse and they ride horses.

What they are afraid of is your thoughts.

Our decision makers must make decisions about useless

things. You children must be brought up to learn how to do everything but think for yourselves. You must be clean, fat, happy and . . .

They flash fancy audio-visual devices at you, teaching that only your eyes should work or only your ears, independently of your brain and your feelings. Why? So that you do not see the things they do behind your back, so that you will not hear the things that they do softly and silently around you.

Whatever they bring and whatever they take, they do it on tip toes. But you children can see a sneaky black cat who climbs up on a wall and slips in through your window. You can hear its soft, padded footsteps.

You children perceive. What about the keen intelligence in the eyes of our barefooted children who live along the edge of the desert?

Yes, our children perceive all things.

They perceive the universe and all the things in it, the movement of all things, whether they be empty, full of meaning, part of this world, of the other world. They perceive for themselves, for humanity, for God, with the eye of the martyr, the eye of

Unity
   One
      Followed by
         An Eternity of
            Zeros

Approaches to the Understanding of Islam

The duty of today's intellectual is to recognize and know Islam as a school of thought that gives life to man, individual and society, and that is entrusted with the mission of the future guidance of mankind. He should regard this duty as an individual and personal one, and whatever be his field of study, he should cast a fresh glance at the religion of Islam and its great personages from the viewpoint of whatever may be his field of study. For Islam has so many different dimensions and varying aspects that everyone can discover a fresh and exact vantage point for viewing it within his field of study.

This essay is excerpted from the translation from the Farsi by Hamid Algar and is reprinted by permission from *On the Sociology of Islam* (Berkeley, California: Mizan Press, 1979). Copyright © 1979 by Mizan Press.

Since my field of study is the sociology of religion and the project is connected with my work, I have tried to codify a kind of sociology of religion based on Islam and drawing on the terminology of the Qur'an and Islamic literature. In the course of my work and research, I came to realize that there are many totally untouched topics that we have not even imagined existed. One of the facts I encountered in my study of Islam and the Qur'an was the existence of scientific theories of history and sociology peculiar to the custom and method of work of the Prophet. What is implied here is something different from taking the Qur'an, certain verses of the Qur'an, the philosophy and certain methods used by the Prophet, or the political, social, psychological and ethical system of life of the Prophet, and then analyzing them by means of contemporary science. We might, for example, try to understand the cosmological verses of the Qur'an with the help of physics, or to deduce the meaning of the historical and sociological verses of the Qur'an in the light of sociology. What I mean is something quite different; namely, that I extracted from the Qur'an a whole series of new topics and themes relating to history, sociology and the human sciences. The Qur'an itself, or Islam itself, was the source of the ideas. A philosophical theory and scheme of sociology and history opened themselves up before me, and when I later checked them against history and sociology, I found them to be fully correct.

There are several important topics in the human sciences that I discovered with the aid of the Qur'an that have not yet been discussed by these sciences. One is the topic of migration. In the book *Muhammad, Seal of the Prophets,* published by the Husayniya-yi Irshad, the topic is discussed only in its historical dimension; i.e., the movement of peoples from one point to another. From the tone in which the Qur'an discussed emigration and migrants, from the life of the Prophet, and, in general, from the concept of migration held in early Islam, I came to realize that migration, despite what Muslims imagine, is not merely a historical event.

The understanding that Muslims have of the hijra is that a number of the Companions migrated from Mecca to Abyssinia and Medina on the orders of the Prophet. They imagine that migration has the general sense in history of the movement of a primitive or semi-civilized people from one place to another, as a result of geographical or political factors, and that for Muslims, migrations represents simply an event that took place in the life of the Muslims and the Prophet of Islam. But from the tone in which migration is discussed in the Qur'an, I came to perceive that migration is a profound philosophical and social principle. Then, turning my attention to history, I realized that migration is an infinitely glorious principle, and that it constitutes a totally fresh topic, one by no means as simple as history and historians have made it out to be. Even the philosophers of history have not paid attention to the question of migration as it truly deserves, for migration has been the primary factor in the rise of civilization throughout history.

All the twenty-seven civilizations we know of in history have been born of a migration that preceded them; there is not even a single exception to this rule. The converse is also true, that there is no case on record in which a primitive tribe has become civilized and created an advanced culture without first moving from its homeland and migrating.

I deduced this topic, which is of great relevance to both history and sociology, from Islam and the tone in which the Qur'an discusses migration and commands permanent and general migration.

All the civilizations in the world—from the most recent, the civilization of America, to the most ancient that we know of, the civilization of Sumer—came into being on the heels of a migration. In each case, a primitive people remained primitive as long as it stayed in its own land, and attained civilization after undertaking a migration and establishing itself in a new land. All civilizations are, then, born of the migrations of primitive peoples.

There are numerous subjects and topics that I came to understand in this way. Islam and the Qur'an, in proportion to my own degree of knowledge of them, helped me to understand questions of history and sociology in a better, fresher and more precise fashion. I thus came to realize that through applying the special terms of the Qur'an, it is possible to discover numerous topics even in the most modern of sciences, the human sciences.

The subject I now wish to discuss, with respect to the sociology of Islam, is the greatest dilemma of both sociology and history: the search for the basic factor in the change and development of societies. What is the basic factor that causes a society suddenly to change and develop, or suddenly to decay and decline; the factor that sometimes causes a society to make a positive leap forward; to change totally its character, its spirit, its aim and its form, in the course of one or two centuries; and to change completely the individual and social relationships obtaining in it?

The Motor of History

Attempts to find an answer to this question have been continuing for centuries, and particularly during the last 110 years, all the different schools of sociology and history have constantly lavished clear and exact attention on the search for an answer. The question constantly raised is this: what is the motor of history, the basic factor in human society's development and change?

The various schools of sociology part company at this point, each one devoting attention to a particular factor.

Certain schools do not believe at all in history, but regard it as nothing more than a worthless collection of narrations from the past. They also refuse to accept that sociology should have any fixed laws, principles or criteria.

A certain kind of scientific anarchism exists in the world. It is pessimistic with regard to the philosophy of sociology and the human sciences, and considers accident to be the basic factor. It says that the changes, advancements, declines, and revolutions that take place in nations all come into existence as the result of accident. For example, suddenly the Arabs attacked Iran; by chance, Iran was defeated and later the Iranians became Muslim. By chance, Ghengiz Khan attacked Iran; it so happened that Iran's government was weak at that time, so that it was defeated. The Mongols entered Iran, so that the Mongol culture and way of life became intermingled with the Irano-Islamic way of life, and a certain change took place. Similarly, the First and Second World Wars also broke out by accident; it was possible that they should not have taken place. In short, this school regards everything as the outcome of chance.

Another group is composed of the materialists and those who believe in historical determinism. They believe that history and society, from the very beginning down to the present, are like a tree, devoid of any volition. In its origin it was a seed. Then it emerged from the seed, appeared above the ground, put forth roots, stems, branches and leaves and grew into a great tree, compelled to yield fruit, to wither in winter, to blossom again in spring, to attain perfection and finally to decay. This group believes that human societies traverse a long life throughout history in accordance with determining factors and laws that play in human society exactly the same role as the laws of nature in the natural realm.

. According to this belief, individuals can have no effect on the fate of their societies, and society is a natural phenomenon that develops according to natural factors and laws.

The third group consists of those who worship heroes and personalities. It includes the fascists and Nazis, as well as great scholars like Carlyle, who also wrote a biography of the Prophet of Islam, and Ermrson, and the like. This group believes that laws are no more than a tool in the hands of powerful individuals and have of themselves no effect on society. Average and sub-average persons, equally, have no share in the changing of society; they too are like tools for others to use. The only fundamental factor in the reform or advancement of society, or the cause of its downfall, is the powerful personality.

Emerson says: "Give me the names of ten powerful personalities, and I will tell you the whole of human history, without ever studying it. Tell me about the Prophet of Islam, and I will tell you about the whole history of Islam. Present me with Napoleon, and I will expound for you the whole history of modern Europe."

In the view of this group, the destiny of society and mankind is in the hands of powerful personalities, who act as the guides for all societies. The happiness or wretchedness of societies does not, then, depend on the masses of the people, nor is it caused by inevitable laws of environment and society, nor is it the result of mere accident; it depends solely on great personalities who every now and then appear in societies in order to change the destiny of their own societies, and sometimes that of mankind.

In his biography of the Prophet of Islam, Carlyle writes as follows: "When the Prophet of Islam first directed his preaching to his own relatives, they all rejected him. It was only Ali, at that time a ten year-old boy, who arose in response to the call of the Prophet and gave him his allegiance." Carlyle then concludes, in the light of his own way of thought: "That small hand was joined to the large hand, and changed the course of history."

The opinion also exists that the people, the generality of society, do play a role in determining their destiny; but no school of thought, not even democracy in its ancient or modern forms, claims that the masses are the fundamental factor in social development and change. Democratic schools of thought believe that the best form of government is that in which the people participate; but from the time of Athenian democracy down to the present, none of these schools has believed that the broad masses of the people are the decisive factor in social change and development. The most democratic of sociologists, then, even while believing that the best form of government and of admininstrative and social organization is that in which the people participate by casting their votes and electing the government, do not regard the "people" as the basic factor of social change and development. Instead, they regard determinism, great personalities, the elite, mere chance or divine will as the decisive factor.

The worshippers of personality can be divided into two groups. The first group consists of those who believe that a great personality like the Buddha, Moses or Jesus appears and changes human society. They are the pure hero-worshippers.

The other group consists of those who believe that initially a personality appears and then he is joined by a group of the elite, the outstanding geniuses of his people, so that a team comes into being. It is this elite team which directs society on a path and to a goal of its own choosing. This group might more correctly be called "elite-worshippers."

In Islam and the Qur'an, none of the foregoing theories is to be found. Now from the point of view of Islam, the prophet is the greatest of all personalities; and if Islam were to believe in the role of the prophet as the fundamental factor in social change and development, it would have to recognize all the prophets, and especially the Prophet Muhammad, as constituting that fundamental factor. We see, however, that this is not the case. The mission and the characteristics of the Prophet are clearly set forth in the Qur'an, and they consist of the conveying of a message. He is responsible for conveying a message; he is a warner and a bearer of glad tidings. And when the Prophet is disturbed by the fact that the people do not respond and he cannot guide them as he would wish, God repeatedly explains to him that his mission consists only of conveying the message, of inspiring fear in men and giving them glad tidings, of showing them the path; he is not in any way responsible for their decline or advancement, for it is the people themselves who are responsible.

In the Qur'an, the Prophet is not recognized as the active cause of fundamental change and development in human history. He is depicted rather as the bearer of a message whose duty it is to show men the school and path of the truth. His mission is then completed, and men are free either to choose the truth or to reject it, either to be guided or to be misguided.

"Accident" also has no decisive role to play in Islam, for all things are in the hand of God, so that accident, in the sense of an event coming into being without any cause or ultimate purpose, is inconceivable, whether in nature or in human society.

If personalities are mentioned in the Qur'an, other than the prophets, their mention is frequently joined with a sense of condemnation or distaste. Even if they are mentioned for their righteousness and purity, the Qur'an never considers them as an effective factor in their societies.

The conclusion we deduce from the text of the Qur'an is, then, that Islam does not consider the fundamental factor in social change and development to be personality, or accident, or overwhelming and immutable laws.

In general, those addressed by every school of thought, every religion, every prophet, also constitute the fundamental and effective factor of social change within that school. It is for this reason that we see throughout the Qur'an address being made to *al-nas,* i.e., the people. The Prophet is sent to *al-nas;* he addresses himself to *al-nas;* it is *al-nas* who are accountable for their deeds; *al-nas* are the basic factor in decline—in short, the whole responsibility for society and history is borne by *al-nas.*

The word *al-nas* is an extremely valuable one, for which there exist a number of equivalents and synonyms. But the only word that resembles it, structurally and phonetically, is the word "mass."

In sociology, the masses comprise the whole people taken together as an entity without concern for class distinctions that exist among them or distinguishing properties that set one group apart from another. "Mass" means, therefore, the people as such, without any particular class or social form.

Al-nas has exactly the same meaning, i.e., the masses of the people; it has no additional meaning. The words *insan* and *bashar* also refer to man, but they refer to ethical and animal properties respectively.

From this we deduce the following conclusion: Islam is the first school of social thought that recognizes the masses as the basis, the fundamental and conscious factor in determining history and society—not the elect as Nietzsche thought, not the aristocracy and nobility as Plato claimed, not great personalities as Carlyle and Emerson believed, not those of pure blood as Alexis Carrel imagined, not the priests or the intellectuals, but the masses.

We can fully realize the value of this point of Islamic doctrine only when we compare it with other schools of thought.

To whom do the various other schools of thought address themselves? Some of them address themselves to the educated and intellectual class; others, to a certain selected group within society. One addresses itself to a superior race, another to supermen, while yet another focuses its attention on a certain class of society, such as the proletariat or the bourgeoisie.

None of the privileges and distinctions assumed by these schools exist in Islam. The only fundamental factor in social change and development is the people, without any particular form of racial or class privilege, or any other distinguishing characteristics.

Islam and Humankind

How was humankind created in the view of Islam? Can we understand the status and nature of humanity from the manner in which the creation is described in the Koran, the Word of God, or in the words of the Prophet of Islam? This is what we shall attempt to deduce.

God addressed the angels, saying, "Behold I will create a viceregent for Myself on earth." Take note of the high reverence accorded humankind by Islam. Even post-Renaissance humanism has not delegated such a high position for humankind. At this moment, the mission of humanity begins, to be the representative of God on earth.

The angels respond by crying out, "Do you wish to create someone who will again engage in murder, crime, hatred, and vengeance?" (It seems that before Adam there were people who were guilty of such conduct. The angels wished to remind God that if granted this second opportunity, humankind would repeat its wrongdoings.) God responds, "I know something you are unaware of," and sets about His creation.

It is at this point that one may view the symbols under which the deep aspects of human ecology are hidden. In His creation, God should have chosen the purest and most valuable matter on earth, but on the contrary chooses the opposite. The Koran refers to the material of human creation as "potter's clay", "black putrid earth", and finally, as "simple mud". Then God breathed His own Spirit into clay and the creation of humankind was completed.

In contemporary rhetoric, the basest symbol of wretchedness is "mud". In the same terms, the highest and most sacred is God, while of the purest of every being is its spirit. So Adam, God's representative, is created from both the lowest and highest things imaginable. Human nature is dualistic, unlike that of all other beings. One dimension is that of meanness and lowliness, stagnation and immobility, inclining toward the sediment like the precipitate left behind by flood waters. But the other dimension of humankind, the divine spirit, aspires to ascend and reach the *summa*—to God and God's Spirit.

Human nature is thus involved in a constant struggle of the will—downwards into the mud or upwards toward the Almighty.

(This essay is excerpted from a lecture given at the Petroleum College of Abadan.)

This struggle of the inner being continues, until the individual chooses one of the directions as the determination of destiny.

The "Names"

According to the Koran, God taught Adam "The Names", but what is meant here is not altogether clear, and is a matter of interpretation. But there is no doubt that the "Names" refers to teaching and instruction. The angels complained to God when He taught humankind the Names, "We are created from smokeless fire while humans are created from mud; why do You endow humankind with these higher qualities?" God replied, "I know something you do not know. You must prostrate yourselves before humankind."

This is true humanism. See the glory and stature accorded humanity that, despite the inherent superiority of the angels in being created from light rather than mud, they are commanded to bow. Adam knows the names unknown to angels. The prostration of angels before Adam confirms humanity's nobility and dignity, based not on race or origin but upon knowledge.

It is contended that Eve was created from Adam's rib. However, the translation "rib" is incorrect as the real meaning of both the Hebrew and the Arabic is "nature or disposition". Eve—that is woman—was created out of the same nature of disposition as man. The Koran does not view man as superior to woman—they share the same origin, as is said, "O Humankind! We created you from a single pair of male and female."

Trusteeship

God summoned all the creations of the earth, animate and inanimate, and told them, "I have something to present to all of you—the earth, sky, mountains, seas and animals—to hold in trust." All refused the offer but humankind. So it is evident that humankind has another virtue, originating in the courageous acceptance of the role of being not only God's representative, but also trustee for the entire world.

Humankind administers this trust through free-will, which is its distinctive quality as compared with all other creatures. Humans are the only beings capable of acting against their own instinctive demands and nature. It is only humankind which can resist or defy spiritual or physiological needs, who can act in accordance with intelligence or against it, who can pursue the path of good or the path of evil. Humankind is free to descend into the mud or ascend toward God.

God, the Almighty, the possessor of Absolute Will, has given the power of will to humankind. Humans can act like God, but only to a certain extent; they can act against the laws of their bodily natures, but only to the extent made possible by their similarity to God.

The following conclusions can be drawn regarding the philosophy of the creation of humankind in Islam:

1. All people are not only equal, but are siblings. There is a difference between "equality" and "brotherhood". Equality is a legal concept, while brotherhood acknowledges the single nature of all people; all races of humankind originate from the same source.

2. Men and woman are equal. They are created out of the same substance at the same time by the came Creator; they have the same inheritance, and are brothers and sisters to each other.

3. Human nature is superior to that of angels on account of knowledge. Despite their superiority of lineage, angels must prostrate themselves to humans who are in possession of the "Names".

4. Human nature is mixed of the lowly mud and the Spirit of God, and, possessing will, is responsible for choosing between them. From an Islamic point of view, human beings are not only responsible for their own fate; they are responsible for the fulfillment of God's mission in this world and are the bearer of God's Trust in the world and in nature. Humankind has learned the "Names" and can comprehend the scientific truths inherent in the world; it therefore has a responsibility to do so. Humanity must fashion its destiny by itself, as it says in the Koran, "The fate of the old civilization is what they brought on themselves; your destiny depends upon what you yourselves acquire."

The Ideal Society—The Umma

The ideal society of Islam is called the *umma*. Taking the place of all the similar concepts which in different languages and cultures designate a human agglomeration or society, such as "society," "nation," "race," "people," "tribe," "clan," etc., is the single word *umma*, a word imbued with progressive spirit and implying a dynamic, committed and ideological social vision.

The word *umma* derives from the root *amm*, which has the sense of path and intention. The *umma* is, therefore, a society in which a number of individuals, possessing a common faith and goal, come together in harmony with the intention of advancing and moving toward their common goal.

While other expressions denoting human agglomerations have taken unity of blood or soil and the sharing of material benefit as the criterion of society, Islam, by choosing the word *umma*, has made intellectual responsibility and shared movement toward a common goal the basis of its social philosophy.

The infrastructure of the *umma* is the economy, because "Whoever has no worldy life has no spiritual life." Its social system is based on equity and justice and ownership by the people, on the revival of the "system of Abel," the society of human equality and thus also of brotherhood—the classless society. This is a fundamental principle, but it is not the aim, as in Western socialism, which has retained the world-view of the Western bourgeoisie. The political philosophy and the form of regime of the *umma* is not the democracy of heads, not irresponsible and directionless liberalism which is a plaything of contesting social forces, not putrid aristocracy, not anti-popular dictatorship, not a self-imposing oligarchy. It consists rather of "purity of leadership" (not the leader, for that would be fascism), committed and revolutionary leadership, responsible for the movement and growth of society on the basis of its world-view and ideology, and for the realization of the divine destiny of man in the plan of creation. This is the true meaning of Imamate!*

*The region or country ruled over by an Islamic spiritual leader.

This essay is translated from Farsi by Hamid Algar and is reprinted by permission from *On the Sociology of Islam* (Berkeley, California: Mizan Press, 1979). Copyright © 1979 by Mizan Press.

Islamic Economics: Ownership and Tauhid

Abolhassan Bani-Sadr

Editor's note: Tauhid, *as described in the introduction, is the Islamic worldview in which the universe is regarded as a unity, with a single form, possessing will, intelligence, and purpose that is God. Its opposite is* shirk, *the worldview which regards the universe as discordant, possessing conflicting tendencies and contradictions.*

It is obviously impossible to discuss the Islamic concept of ownership without considering its legal, political, economic, sociological, and philosophical ramifications. The "legal" conceptions of ownership take on meaning only within the framework of social, political, and economic relations. In this context, we will evaluate the Islamic concept of ownership and its relation to the principle of *tauhid.*

Ownership—The Relationship Between the Individual and His/Her Work

Any relation between an individual and his/her earnings which is incompatible with the principle of *tauhid* is an unIslamic relationship. Therefore the *reality* of absolute ownership is not acceptable in Islam because it would imply acceptance of the *concept* of absolute ownership which would be a denial of *tauhid.*

Absolute ownership is God's alone; to reflect the principle of *tauhid,* human ownership must be relative only. Everyone's work in reality belongs to God; only to the extent that the individual can be God's viceregent upon earth can s/he have ownership.

In order for relative ownership of the individual over his/her work and its fruits to be continuously realized, there must be a relation between the individual, society, and God which is at once the cause and embodiment of this principle, and which reveals the possibility of ownership at all. It is this relation which must now be explored.

This essay is excerpted from the author's *Tauhidi Economics* and has been translated and edited by A. Dabirian and David H. Albert.

The Relationship Between the Individual, Society, and God

In all vital affairs, the relations between the individual and God is established only through the relationship between the society as a whole and God. Thus, ownership by the community as the primary viceregent of God always takes precedence to that of the individual and the viceregency by the community is retained for all affairs in which community ownership is the condition for the individual's ownership of his/her own labor and its fruits. The origin of all relations is thus:

God ⟶ society ⟶ individual

Based on this relation, individual ownership is rejected for some things and community ownership is rejected for others. The community can determine the extent of individual ownership but is not allowed to prohibit an individual from working or owning the fruits of that work.

It also follows that no one is permitted to own another's labor or its results. This limitation on ownership must be continued from generation to generation, ensuring that every able-bodied person is able to exercise his or her abilities without any restriction.

Having declared this principle, we are confronted with three questions:

1. Whether individual ownership of labor and its fruits is transferable?
2. If so, what is the direction of this transfer?
3. Is ownership continuous or not?

According to the principle of *tauhid*, the movement and activity of all things is from relativity to absoluteness—that is, toward God. Transfer of ownership is a case of this movement from relative to the absolute, and thus the common direction of transfer must be from the personal to the social. When conditions for the transfer from the personal to the social realm exist, it should be accomplished. But because the role of the individual as the viceregent of God is a continuous phenomenon, the individual's ownership of his/her work must also have a constant and stable character.

Until the time when the possibilities of centralization and accumulation of wealth have been removed, until firm borders are established so that the centralization of productive surpluses of the society within one or a few centers becomes impossible, until these centers of accumulation can no longer be transformed by representatives of the society into centers of power, the social relations of dominant/dominated will continue. Past history and the current human situation is evidence of this fact. Therefore, just because the society makes its facilities accessible to the individual for use, it does not follow that it has the right to take away the people's reserves and put them in the hands of the government. Until the society is released from domination relationships, and there are ways to prevent the centralization of wealth and power, the taking away of the people's reserves will merely concentrate all the produced wealth into the hands of the bureaucrat. Rulers will thus be transformed into tyrants over the people's fate, for which there are already too many examples. But because Islam wants, by solving this "accumulation complex", to reach a *tauhidi* society, it tries to establish alternative kinds of relations for the distribution of the fruits of labor and residual of the individual's activity within the community and within a "natural" territory. This distribution must follow the path of the relation between God, society, and individual and thus move from individual ownership to social ownership.

The stability of ownership in the hands of workers from generation to generation marks the continuity of the community's relation as viceregent. The reserves built up only from the fruits of labor will not trigger a complex of capital accumulation. But the method of distribution from the Islámic point of view must also be a method of reaching toward community ownership. Thus the distribution of inherited wealth according to Islamic principles is a system for eliminating the accumulation complex, not for promoting it or for placing a boundary between individual and community ownership.

Indeed, if the picture which we draw from the society of the Twelfth Imam (ed. note: in Shi'ite Islam, it is believed that the Twelfth Imam will appear someday to usher in the ideal society) is realizable, it must be that a truly Islamic policy could lead toward it. It would not be reasonable to assume that a system would be presented to the people and its objectives be defined but that legal foundations be set up which would make it impossible for the society to move toward those objectives.

Even if the picture of the ideal society (that of the Twelfth Imam) had not been presented, the *tauhid* principle itself would be enough for a healthy mind not to countenance the accumulation and centralization of power as the basis for an Islamic society. It is simply not reasonable to be striving toward the objective of a *tauhidi* society, but like capitalist societies or those which have different productive systems but possessing centralized centers of political and economic power, to make it possible for the labor of all the people to be placed in the pockets of the few.

Therefore, until the time that an economically prosperous society is set up within which scarcity and the possibility of accumulation and centralization is removed, Islam prefers the transfer of the fruits of labor after the deduction of "God's share" to be distributed according to Koranic principles. The result of each person's work, tools, and land should thus be placed in the hands of descendants. Principal is returned to the society which is the place of *tauhid*.

To sum up, both the society and individual can own, according to the viceregency principle, and to the extent that this ownership of labor and its fruits help remove accumulation of capital and centralization of power forever. And with regard to the tools of labor, ownership must ultimately belong to the society, and the direction of transfer of ownership should make the fulfillment of this principle possible.

Islamic Theory and the Fraudulent Attitudes
Engendered by the Powerful

Under a system of private ownership, absolute ownership is assumed. Someone puts a barbed wire fence around a piece of property and then claims ownership. What happens then? What happens if the owners let no one inside to work on it? The masses of people will be obliged to put themselves in the hands of the owners and thus, in a position of submissiveness, say, "Whatever you say, boss." Or they will be obliged to go to the factories and be ground up in the gears of the machinery or to the construction sites where they will work until they fall. This occurs because it is in the interest of these owners for it to occur. Are not these masses "obliged" to obey the orders of the absolute owners, who have forgotten God, because the owners have "saved" them from death by starvation?

These relations, which are the dominant relations of the *shirk* (atheistic and discordant) world, are not Islamic relations and must be rejected by Islam. The common supposition that the above situation is normal or even Islamic has no relation to the truly Islamic view. The basis of this system is force, is based on the *shirk* economy, and is incompatible with the Islamic point of view based on *tauhid*, in which common ownership is the kind of ownership which allows all the people to own their own labor. It is obvious that this is not realizable under a system which legalizes the grabbing of land, resources, and tools from the people.

A society which is true to its own nature as a society has its members do common work together in protecting them from dangers, providing for the needs of each, and ensuring that nobody robs someone else's fruits of labor through cheating or force. A society will reach its objectives of ensuring the needs of all and equalizing opportunities for everyone to the extent that everyone owns his/her own labor; no one uses his/her own labor for destructive activities; individuals do not engage in activity without relation to the total activity of the community or against the interest of the community; and people work as members of the society as a whole. This is *tauhid*, and possesses the components for unity.

Tauhid and Stability of Ownership Over Time

Over time, generations after generations have relative ownership of land and resources and the fruits of labor. When it is said that "You are the owner of the land you are working," it means that you and the human community and future generations and past generations are partners in this ownership. The maintenance of *tauhid* through time is one of the most important elements in the legislating of Islamic law. All rules must be established in accordance with *tauhid*. This is true even with respect to the individual's own person. The *tauhid* principle requires a prohibition on suicide because an individual does not have absolute ownership even over him/herself, but belongs to God and through the viceregent principle belongs to the society, to future and past generations which have labored and are still working and will work for him/her and for which the individual has a responsibility to work.

Governments are not forever and cannot make decisions which lead to the deprivation of future generations. For example, it cannot choose to exhaust the oil and leave the well dry during the lifetime of a single generation, or dry the land and empty the mines for future generations. To make the present time absolute is a kind of domination relation and represents an exploitative point of view. It leads to the forgetting of the principle that every individual and every society is part of the totality of being. Neither individuals nor governments have the right to exploit for the sake of their own wants. Islam does not have a class perspective—it doesn't look from the top to the bottom, or from the point of view of the oppressed upward. The Islamic view is based on *tauhid*. God exists and all are equal in God's sight. Preference is given according to virtue. There is not a single sub-role or class which is not included in the Islamic view. And it cannot be otherwise, and couldn't be.

The meaning of this is that Islam is a system in which every rule and law and condition reflects the guiding principles. If it were not so, Islam would not be a system. And the reason that Islam has gotten into the present situation is that rules and conditions have become bankrupt of these guiding principles.

Furthermore, in Islamic theory the origin of ownership and its results and the validity of its extensions must be established in such a way so that the objective face of human society reflects the guiding principles. That means ownership is limited to constructive purposes; destructive ends are prohibited. Constructive purposes are those which add to the store of human opportunities in such a way that does not tend to the future destruction of opportunities. If labor is not constructive and creative, how could the Koranic verse, "The ascension of things is toward God," acquire its meaning? If the individual does not add to the store of human opportunities and does not consciously seek evolution, how can s/he ascend to God? By working with nature and with the community, the individual can forget him/herself and ascend through evolution. If people do not use their labor for the extension and growth of the human dimension, they cannot reach toward a *tauhidi* society or ascend towards God.

Conclusions

In the Islamic theory of ownership, absolute ownership is reserved for God alone. As human relativity and activity is not realized except in relation to God's absoluteness, individual ownership over labor cannot be realized except in relation to God's absolute ownership. Otherwise, force would be the basis of all relations; both dominating and dominated would lose their own freedom and their authority and become estranged from themselves. To the extent that the human race upholds the principle of viceregency, and maintains the right of labor and the right of innovation for all people without exception and without discrimination in all times and places, and as long as ownership is maintained relatively, humans are the heirs of God. This relation between the community and the individual is to be organized by the Imam.

Accordingly, ownership is one aspect of the God-human relationship. The relation has two directions: that of origin—God ⟹ society ⟹ individual, and that of ultimate end—individual ⟹ society ⟹ God. Absolute ownership is that of God and the nearest ownership to absoluteness over the earth and resources is that of the community. Next is that of the individual who, however, maintains relative ownership over his/her own labor. Therefore in transfer with respect to destination, ownership should move from individual to the community, from the community to the society-at-large, and then to the Imam, God's active representative. Until then, all tools of labor should be placed in the hands of those who can make constructive use of them, according to capacity. Work opportunities are to be increased. And the differences between individual abilities should be reduced through the just distribution of opportunities.

Alas that the problem has not been faced this way among the religious community of Islam. The Islamic religious community has always adjusted itself to the economic relations of the time. The truly Islamic view which holds the possibilities for the final freedom of humankind, the view which has been made known in the Koran and described in the religious traditions and sayings, has been forgotten when the political power of tyrants has been established.

The reason for these details and even repetition is that the commonly held ideology based on *shirk*—atheistic contradictions—must be rejected. Once we have done so, we can ask, according to this paradigm of ownership based on the principle of *tauhid*, how such ownership can be realized and how Islam can organize itself in this vital realm. And in answering these questions, we must study the adjustments of ownership for consistency with the way Islam must fight accumulation of capital and the centralization of power.

Objectives of the
Islamic Revolution

Ayatollah Morteza Motahheri

What is the objective pursued by the Islamic movement and what does it want? Does it aim at democracy? Does it strive to liquidate colonialism from our country? Does it rise to defend what is called in modern terminology "human rights"? Does it attempt to do away with discrimination, inequality? Does it want to uproot oppression? Does it labor to undo materialism and so forth and so on?

In view of the nature of the movement and its roots and also in view of the statements and pronouncements given out by the leaders of the movement, what one may gather as an answer to these questions is "Yes" as well as "No".

"Yes" because all the objectives mentioned above form the very crux of it. And "No" because the movement is not limited to only these or any one of these objectives. An Islamic movement cannot, from the point of its objective, remain a restricted affair, because Islam, in its very nature, is "an indivisible whole," and with the realization of any of the objectives set before it, its role does not cease to be.

However, it does not mean that, from a tactical point of view a particular set of objectives does not enjoy priority over another set and that the stages of realization of these objectives are not needed to be taken into consideration. Did not Islam pass through a tactical revolution? Today the movement is passing through the stage of rejection and disregard of the ruling authority and of striking hard at despotism and colonialism. Having emerged victorious out of this struggle, it shall address itself to stability and reconstruction, and other objectives shall then demand its attention.

The core of the philosophy of the Islamic reformation can be summed up in four dictates from Imam Husain, son of Ali:

This essay is excerpted from Motahheri's *Islamic Movements in Twentieth Century*, translated by Maktab-E-Quran-India (Kashmir, India: 1979).

1. "The effaced signs on the path leading to God be reinstated." It refers to the original principles of Islam and return to these very principles. Innovations done away with and their place be filled by true and original customs. In other words it means reform in the very thought, the very conscience and the very spirit of Islam.

2. Fundamental, actual and far-reaching reforms which would invite the attention of every observer and would be carrying in them seeds of welfare for the people at large, in urban and in rural areas and the society as a whole be brought about. It means the most radical reforms in the living conditions of the masses of the people.

3. God's humanity under victimization be given security against the oppressor. The tyranny of the oppressor be eliminated. It means reform in the social relations of human beings.

4. God's commands hitherto suspended and the Islamic laws hitherto ignored by revived so as to establish their supremacy in the social life of the people.

Any reformer who succeeds in activating the above mentioned four fundamentals; who is able to direct the attention of the minds toward the true Islam; who is able to banish corrupt practices and superficialities from the lives of the people; who can satisfactorily bring order in the civic life by providing, among other things, the basic necessities of food, shelter, medical aid and education; who can help establish human relationships on the basis of equality, fraternity and sense of good neighborliness; and, finally, who can give the society a truly Islamic cadre of administrators to lay down rules and regulations for the conduct of puritanic administration shall have, in fact, achieved the maximum success as a reformer.

The current Iranian movement is not restricted to any particular class or trade union. It is not only a labor, an agrarian, a student, an intellectual or a bourgeois movement. Within its orbit fall one and all in Iran, the rich and the poor, the man and the woman, the school boy and the scholar, the warehouse man and the factory laborer, the artisan and the peasant, the clergy and the teacher, the literate and the illiterate, one and all. An announcement made by the preceptor of the highest station guiding the movement is received in the length and breadth of the country with equal enthusiasm by all classes of the people. The call reverberates with as much din in villages as in the cities. It has as much impact on the masses in remote parts of Khorasan and Azerbaijan as on the Iranian students in the distant cities of Europe and the United

States. It has galvanized into as much action the oppressed and the victimized as the unaffected one. The unexploited has developed as much hatred against exploitation as the exploited under its spell.

Movement Disproves Dialectical Materialism

The movement is one of the glaring historical proofs which falsifies the concept of materialistic interpretation of history and that of the dialectics of materialism according to which economics is recognized as the cornerstone of social structure and a social movement is considered a reflection of class struggle. The materialists' belief that all roads end with the fundamental requirement, i.e. food, does not hold water in the present context. Furthermore, the Shia divinity has, in practice, rejected the thesis of Karl Marx that there has been a triangle of religion, government and capital throughout the course of history, interactive and the factors have been in collusion with one another; that they shaped a class against the masses and that the three factors mentioned above are the result of self-estrangement of the people.

The present movement is like the movements which the prophets have led in the course of human history and which have issued forth from a "divine self-realization" or "realizing of God." The roots of divine self-realization are embedded in the depths of human nature. It emanates from the subconscious. When an oracle is delivered which awakens the instinctive consciousness in people regarding their origin and roots, regarding the city and the country where they come from so that they feel a strange and mysterious self-attachment; this attachment as a matter of course results ultimately in drawing a person nearer to God. Attachment to God, the most valuable of attachments, carries with it virtues like beauty, equitable justice, equality, forgiveness, sacrifice, dedication and the urge for the good of others.

The sentiment of seeking and worshipping God remains hidden in every human heart. The prophets awaken this sentiment in human beings so that they should aspire for the lofty and discard the lowly in all forms and figures. It gives people an idea that they should be supporters of truth and right and not because their benefit lies in it. Notwithstanding the loss or gain involved, virtues like justice, equality, truth and righteousness emerge involuntarily as the object and the aim because these are divinely values and not merely instruments to achieve success in life's conflicts.
achieve success in life's conflicts.

Once people achieve divine awakening and higher human values become their objective, they cease to be a friend or a foe for the mere fact of it. They become the upholder of justice, not of injustice. They become the enemy of oppression and not the oppressor. Their protagonism and antagonism to justice and oppression respectively does not emanate from their psychological and personal constraints but from a principle and an ideology.

Search and Find the East

Ayatollah Rouhollah Khomeini

*In the Name of God
the Merciful, the Compassionate*

*And indeed sent We Moses with Our signs saying:
"Lead thou out thy people from the darkness into the light
and remind them of the days of God;
verily in this are signs for the patient, the grateful"*

Koran, 14:5

*God is the Guardian of those who believe
He taketh them out of darkness into light
and those who disbelieve, tyrants are their guardians and
they take them out from the light into darkness
They are the companions of the fire, therein shall they abide.*

Koran, 2:257

These are two subjects which oppose each other—"the taking out of darkness into light" and "the taking out of light into darkness"—the doing away with darkness and the taking of people to the light and opposing this, doing away with light and taking people to darkness. This latter is the profession of the tyrants. All disharmony is darkness, all backwardness is darkness, all "westoxication" is darkness, those who turn their attention to the West and foreigners, have taken the West to be their direction of prayer. They have moved into darkness and their saints are idols.

Eastern societies which, by means of internal and external propaganda and by the orders of internal and external agents, have turned to the West and, having the direction of their prayers, the

Edited from an address given by Iman Khomeini at the Faiziyeh School in Qom, September 8, 1979, to mark the anniversary of the massacre of the 17th of Shahrivar (Black Friday, September 8, 1978).

204

West have lost themselves. They do not know themselves. They have lost their gloriousness and honor and in place have put a Western mind. Their saints are idols. They have entered darkness from the light.

All of the problems of Easterners and, among them, our problems and miseries, are caused by our losing ourselves. In Iran, until something has a Western name, it is not accepted. Even a drug store must have a Western name. The material woven in our factories must have something in the latin script in its selvedges and a Western name is put on it.

Our streets must have Western names. Everything must have a Western color to it. Some of these writers and intellectuals either put a Western name on the books they write or, when they express an idea, they do so on behalf of a Westerner. The defect is that they are also "westoxicated" and so are we. If our books did not have these titles, or our material did not contain that script and if our drug stores did not have that name, we would pay less attention to it. When we turn to a book, a great deal of attention is paid to finding foreign words. We forget our own phrases and the word itself.

Easterners have completely forgotten their honor. They have buried it. In place of it, they have put others. These are all darknesses which a tyrant transforms us to from light. It is these very tyrants—of the past and present—who have reached out towards "westoxication". They take all their subjects and sources from the West and have given them to us. Our universities were at that time Western universities. Our economy, our culture were Western. We completely forgot ourselves.

I recall that a member of the family of the deposed, accursed Mohammad Reza got tonsillitis and they brought a surgeon from Europe, while for the doctors here it is a simple operation. You know what damage this does to Iranian medicine. This is traitorous to the people of Iran that they are introduced to the belief that in all of its country, there is no doctor to operate on someone's tonsils. How much this helps colonialism and the West! How much self-respect of our country is lost with this way of thinking!

When I was young, I remember my eyes weakened—they are still weak—and at that time, Amin ol-Molk, God's Mercy be upon him, was an eye doctor. I went to Tehran to have him treat my eyes. A person who knew him and me suggested I go to see Dr. Amin ol-Molk. He said, "One of the Daulahs [of the court] had become near-sighted. He had gone to Europe to see a doctor. That doctor asked him, "Where are you from?" In answer, he said, "I am from Iran." The doctor had asked, "Isn't Amin ol-Molk there?" He had answered, "He may be, but I do not know him." That professor had then said, "Amin ol-Molk is better than we are."

We have good doctors but our minds have become Westernized. We and they have both lost our self-respect and our sense of nationality. If this nation does not come out of this "westoxication", it will never find independence.

The attention of some of our women is turned to the idea that such and such a mode must come from the West and such and such an ornamentation must come from there, here, so that whenever something is found there, it is imitated here. As long as you do not put aside these imitations, you cannot be a human being and independent. If you want to be independent and have them recognize you as a nation, you must desist from imitating the West.

As long as we are in this state of imitating, we do not wish for independence. As long as all of the words of our writers are Western, we do not hope to have our nation be independent. As long as these names appear on our streets and our drug stores and our books, and our parks and in all our things, we will not become independent. It is only the mosques which do not have Western names and that is because the clergymen, until now, have not succumbed.

"And those who disbelieve," disbelieve in God's blessings and realities are dark and covered in darkness. Their saints are idols. "They take them from light into darkness"—from absolute light, from guidance, from independence, from nationalism, from Islam—they take these out and put them into darkness. We have now lost ourselves. Until the lost be not found, we will not become independent. Search and find it. Search for and find the East.

As long as we are as we are, as long as our writers are as they are, as long as our intellectuals think that way, as long as our freedom-seekers seek that kind of Western freedom, it will remain as it is. They cry out that there is suffocation, there is no freedom. What has happened that there is no freedom?

They say, "these clergymen do not allow men and women to turn somersaults together in the water. These clergymen do not let our young people go to bars or gambling houses and seek out prostitutes. They do not allow our radio and television to show naked women and that type of ugly lewdness. They do not allow our children and young people to be entertained." This is an imported kind of a freedom which has come from the West. It is a colonialistic freedom, that is, colonialist countries dictate to those who are traitors to their own countries so that they can promote these freedoms. They are free to take heroin. They are free to smoke hashish. They are free to go to gambling houses. They are free to go to houses of entertainment and, as a result, our young people, who must be active in relation to the fate and destiny of their country, become indifferent.

An indifferent person cannot think for a country. Those who are and have been deceived from abroad are foreign agents and they promote prostitution. The promotion of these actions pulls our young people towards corruption. As a result, thoughts about what goes on in this country is put out of their heads. In place of serious minds, silly minds appear. As a result, the person who should be a human being, who thinks about his own destiny, this thought is taken away from him. This is a type of freedom which we have to call colonialist freedom. This is other than the freedom which must be amidst a people. This is a type of freedom which has come from abroad.

A young person who forms a habit with these kinds of things no longer thinks about who takes our oil, our steel, our gas. He says, "What's it to me! Leave me alone to my pleasures. Do I have time to waste, putting efforts into those things?" This is how they brought us up.

If these writers do not save our young people from these kinds of thoughts and do not promote a healthy kind of freedom and do not prevent their steps and their pens from writing about these corrupt freedoms, there is no hope that we will have an independent and free country. This hope must be taken to the grave.

Moses was appointed to take his tribe from darkness to light. The assignment of all of the prophets was that they take people away from darkness and from these things which oppose the way of humanity and enter them into the light.

An enlightened heart cannot stand by silently and watch while traditions and honor are trampled upon. An enlightened heart cannot see its people being drawn towards baseness of spirit or watch in silence while individuals around Tehran live in slums. Yet the West wants to bring you up in such a way that you remain indifferent in all of your affairs. They do not ask why these poverty-stricken people have remained in poverty and why others take our oil. It never appears in your mind that we have such problems. Look at how your hearts were fifteen, twenty years ago when there was no perseverance.

The second command which God gave to Moses was to "remind people of the Days of God." All days belong to God but some days have a particularity and because of that particularity are called the Days of God. The day that the great Prophet of Islam migrated to

Medina is one of the days that is called the Day of God. The day that he conquered Mecca is one of the days called the Day of God. It is the day that God showed His strength as when an orphan who everyone rejected and who could not live in his home, after a short time, conquered Mecca. He brought the tyrants, the wealthy and the powerful under his influence and he said to them, "You are free." Thus such a day is one of the Days of God. The day of Khawareh is a day when Hazrat Ali unsheathed his sword and did away with these corrupt and cancerous tumors. This was also one of the Days of God.

These are all Days of God and they are things which relate to God. One of the Days of God is the 15th of Khordad (June 5, 1963) when a people stood against a force and they did something which caused almost five months of martial law. But because the people had no power, they were not consolidated, they were not awake, they were defeated. Of course, they were defeated on the surface, but actually, that was a point of victory for the people. The 17th of Shahrivar (September 8, 1978) was another one of the Days of God when a people, men, women, young people and older people, all stood up and, in order to get their rights, were martyred.

You must recall these Days of God as you have and you must not forget them. It is these days which build human beings. It is on these days that our young people leave their places of entertainment and enter the battlefield. These are the Divine Days. These Days awoke our people. God commands that you enter the Days of God into the minds of people.

Do not forget this great Day which passed for our people and were Days of God like the 15th of Khordad, the 17th of Shahrivar and the Day that that wicked man left. A nation which had nothing, broke a force in such a way that nothing remained of it. Not only was that power opposing you, but all of the powers of the world, as well. I was aware that the whole world had supported him. America was holding him up with both hands. When he fled, they held up Bakhtiar with both hands. They sent people to us saying, "This is from us. This belongs to us." They were servants. Do not be surprised that they kept someone for 10, 15, 20 years in the false form of a nationalist for the day when it will serve their purposes. It is possible that a person pray in a mosque for 20 years and worship God and then one day work for them. It is possible that a person claim honesty and claim to be a nationalist and swear at foreigners, write articles against them so that they influence the hearts of the people for the day when they want to come to power.

One of the great Days of God, the Most High and Exalted, was the night when they had planned a coup d'etat when we were in Tehran. They announced a 24-hour martial law so that even in the daytime people should not come out. Later they informed us that they had intended that night to kill the leaders of Qom and whoever opposed them, finish them off and end the job. God did not want it to be so. That was an enlightened insurrection of a responsible nation which took place and we were victorious. This was one of the Days of God which you, the enlightened and noble people of Iran, with your hearts filled with faith, should not fear. Even though they had announced martial law that day, you went into the streets and did away with that which they had wanted. They had wanted the streets to be empty so that they could bring in tanks and place them everywhere and at night be busy with their crime. God, the Most High and Exalted, answered the cries of this nation. That day is one of the great Days of God.

Do not forget that we had a 15th of Khordad and this is the beginning of the Islamic movement of Iran. Do not forget that we had a 17th of Shahrivar and we must not forget that on that day, we gave so many martyrs and so much blood and the nation arose against foreigners and their agents. Blood was spilt, but it was victorious and also all the other innumerable days.

Recall days that they attacked us with complete cruelty and you, with complete courage, your men and women, stood against them. Someone told me, "I saw, with my own eyes, that a child of 10 or 12 was riding a motorcycle and went towards the tanks. The tank ran over and killed him." A spirit was born which prompted a child to do such an act. Empty handed, a monarchial empire of 2500 years, 2500 years of criminals was done away with.

Do not forget your honor. Our intellectuals and writers and all of our groups of scholars should turn their attention to their own honor and glory. They should not prostrate themselves so much towards the West and writers of books. You yourselves have things to say. What difference does it make to you what so and so from the West said? Why do you quote from a foreigner so that the spirit of our young people becomes melancholy? You people must protest and not buy anything from a drug store with a foreign name until they change its name. These beloved university students of ours should pay attention to the fact that when a writer quotes from a foreigner, do not buy that book and do not read it. If you do this and buyers pull back, they will stop doing it. They want customers. When a commodity has no customers, it is discontinued.

Push away and turn your backs on things which pull you to the West and trample upon your honor and in place of it put Western things. I pray for you. May God continue His Mercy upon this nation